TODAY'S MOMENT OF TRUTH

*Devotions to Deepen Your
Faith in Christ*

LEE STROBEL
MARK MITTELBERG

ZONDERVAN®

To our dear friends Karl and Barbara Singer, who are tenaciously committed to sharing the love and truth of Christ.

CONTENTS

INTRODUCTION

"OF ALL THE COMMANDMENTS, WHICH IS THE MOST IMPORTANT?" asked a teacher who had been listening to Jesus.

"The most important one," answered Jesus, "is this: 'Hear, O Israel: The Lord our God, the Lord is one. Love the Lord your God with all your heart and with all your soul and with all your mind and with all your strength'" (Mark 12:28–30).

Many Christians are good at loving God in two of these ways— with all their *heart* and with all their *soul*. That may be due, in part, to the fact that most devotional literature tends to cover those two areas.

What seems to be lacking is devotional material that addresses the third and fourth areas Jesus mentioned: loving God with all our *mind* and with all our *strength*. And because many Christians are less equipped in these areas, they often react to our increasingly secular culture with spiritual confusion, defensiveness, or compromise.

As a result, far too many believers end up being, as the apostle Paul put it, "tossed back and forth by the waves, and blown here and there by every wind of teaching and by the cunning and craftiness of people in their deceitful scheming" (Ephesians 4:14).

It doesn't have to be that way. Instead, Paul went on to explain, we need to be people who speak "the truth in love," so "we will grow to become in every respect the mature body of him who is the head, that is, Christ" (v. 15).

It was with this vision—to communicate the truth in love and in ways that would help us better love God with all our mind and strength—that my longtime ministry partner, Mark Mittelberg, and I set out to write *Today's Moment of Truth*.

We're convinced that one of the best ways to strengthen Christians in their life with Christ is to provide daily infusions of truth to help them better understand *who* God is, *what* they should know about him, and *why* he can be trusted.

Beyond that, we wanted to compose these daily devotionals in a way that will not only reinforce the faith of Christians, but also make the evidence for the Christian faith accessible to spiritually curious readers—including students—who are interested in better assessing the case for biblical faith.

These entries draw from the facts of Scripture as well as science, history, philosophy, archaeology, experience, and other areas of learning. Ultimately we want to point you back each day to the One who said, "I *am* . . . the truth" (Jesus, in John 14:6, emphasis mine).

As you will see, we start each reading with a short passage from the Bible that is relevant to the topic we will explore that day. Then we address the subject, often beginning by quoting a thinker who challenges the Christian position, followed by logic and evidence that show what is true and why we can believe it. Then we end each reading with a succinct summary, under the heading "Truth for Today."

There are 180 readings. You can go through these alone or with a friend or family member. You might also want to encourage your small group or church class—or your entire congregation—to read these on the same schedule, so you can discuss and encourage one another on the topics you are all learning about.

Some of what you learn will be immediately applicable in your life. Other truths will naturally be stored away and come back to you later when you need them. And still more will provide information that will help you in conversations with others, enabling you to present the truth of the Christian faith confidently to people who need to know Christ.

That happened to me once when Mark and I were preparing for an open-mic question-and-answer session with hundreds of believers and their nonbelieving friends at a church in Atlanta. During our time of preparation, I sensed God was prompting me to be ready to respond to a question about the influences that mythical religions supposedly had on Christianity (challenges we discuss in the devotionals; see "A Copycat Religion?" and "Myths About Mithras").

I gave extra focus to that issue as I prepared—in fact, it's almost all I thought about that afternoon—and when the event started, I was ready. Then, during the two hours of questions and answers that evening, *nobody* asked about this topic! I went back to my hotel room that night scratching my head. I had been so confident that God had led me on this.

But then, about two weeks later, Mark and I were back in what was our home church in Chicago, where we did a similar Q&A event. After another two hours of responding to a variety of issues that the audience brought up, Mark told the group that we had time for just one more question.

You guessed it—the final question that night was from a man sitting in the front row, who was troubled by the matter of whether or not mythical religions had influenced the stories of the New Testament. After the man explained his concerns, Mark replied, "That's a really good question. I think I'll let *Lee* reply to this one," as he glanced at me with a smile.

Finally! I thought, and I proceeded to give him one of the best-prepared answers I've ever given on any topic. And, get this: after I finished, the man said as he sat down, "Thank you. That was very helpful. In fact, it was the final issue keeping me from becoming a Christian."

That very night he gave his life to Christ!

So remember this as you go through these readings each day: some moments of truth are for you that very day, some are for you for the future, and some are for the people God wants to reach through you.

May God bless you as you read—and as you share—*Today's Moment of Truth.*

—LEE STROBEL

"Then you will know the truth, and the truth will set you free."

JESUS, IN JOHN 8:32

SCIENCE MEETS SCRIPTURE

In the beginning God created the heavens and the earth.

GENESIS 1:1

MUCH HAS BEEN WRITTEN ABOUT THE ORIGIN OF THE universe. Has it always been here, or did it have a beginning? If it did have a beginning, what caused it to come into existence?

In the early twentieth century an understanding emerged that gradually formed the prevailing theory among cosmologists. "In the beginning there was an explosion," explained Nobel Prize–winning physicist Steven Weinberg. "Not an explosion like those familiar on earth, starting from a definite center and spreading out to engulf more and more of the circumambient air, but an explosion which occurred simultaneously everywhere, filling all space from the beginning, with every particle of matter rushing apart from every other particle."[1]

Within the tiniest split second, the temperature hit a hundred thousand million degrees Centigrade. "This is much hotter than in the center of even the hottest star," he wrote.[2]

The matter rushing apart, he explained, consisted of such elementary particles as negatively charged electrons, positively charged positrons, and neutrinos, which lack both electrical charge and mass. Interestingly, there were also photons: "The universe," he said, "was filled with light."[3]

"The matter of the Universe," wrote Robert Jastrow, astronomer and founding director of NASA's Goddard Institute for Space Studies, "[was] packed together into one dense mass under enormous pressure, and with temperatures ranging up to trillions of degrees. The dazzling brilliance of the radiation in this dense, hot

Universe must have been beyond description. The picture suggests the explosion of a cosmic hydrogen bomb. The instant in which the cosmic bomb exploded marked the beginning of the Universe. . . . In a purely physical sense, it was the moment of creation."[4]

From an infinitesimal point—which scientists call a *singularity*—the entire universe and time itself exploded into being. And science can't account for it.

Yet the very first verse in the Bible explains: "In the beginning God created the heavens and the earth" (Genesis 1:1). As theologians have classically put it, "God created everything *ex nihilo*"—meaning "out of nothing."

Science is catching up with Scripture. Jastrow, who was not a Christian, famously remarked, "For the scientist who has lived by his faith in the power of reason, the story ends like a bad dream. He has scaled the mountains of ignorance; he is about to conquer the highest peak; as he pulls himself over the final rock, he is greeted by a band of theologians who have been sitting there for centuries."[5]

Truth for Today

As Christians we should be lovers of truth. So seize opportunities to learn from both theology and science—while worshiping the God of all truth.

A DELICATE BALANCE

*God made two great lights the greater light to govern the
day and the lesser light to govern the night. He also made
the stars. God set them in the vault of the sky to give light on
the earth, to govern the day and the night, and to separate
light from darkness. And God saw that it was good.*

GENESIS 1:16–18

MANY PEOPLE THINK THE EXISTENCE OF LIFE IS JUST A HAPPY
accident. All the right elements came together by chance and—
poof!—here we are.

Consider, for instance, how our sun and moon are essential
for life on earth. Without the sun, water would remain frozen, and
neither plants nor animals could live. And the moon plays a vital
role as well. But isn't our sun an ordinary star, and isn't our moon
just like countless others in the solar system? Are the factors that
contribute to life on our planet really so unusual?

As astronomers have discovered, our sun and moon are much
more exceptional than once thought. Our sun is far from ordinary;
it has exactly the right mass and composition and is the ideal distance from the earth to enable life on our planet. If it were much
smaller, its luminosity wouldn't allow the high-efficiency photo-
synthesis necessary in plants; if it were much closer, the water
would boil away from the planet's surface. Similarly, our moon is
just far enough away and just the right size to stabilize the earth's
tilt. Without the moon's stabilizing presence, the earth would experience wild temperature swings, with devastating consequences
for life.

The factors that allow for life on our planet are unusually ideal.

The sun and moon are only two among innumerable variables that have been aligned perfectly since the beginning of the universe to set the stage for human life.

So, as God admonishes us in Isaiah 40:26, "Lift up your eyes and look to the heavens: Who created all these? He who brings out the starry host one by one and calls forth each of them by name. Because of his great power and mighty strength, not one of them is missing."

The Creator lovingly designed and balanced the starry host to provide everything we need for life. And that was no accident!

Truth for Today

Look up into the sky again—maybe after dark tonight—and remind yourself of who created everything you see. Then praise him for putting everything in place so we could thrive and, ultimately, know and worship him!

THE ORIGINS OF LIFE

God said, "Let the water teem with living creatures,
and let birds fly above the earth across the vault of the sky."

GENESIS 1:20

"DARWIN . . . WOULD NOT BE DRAWN OUT ON THE QUESTION of how life got going in the first place," said physicist Paul Davies in an op-ed piece in the *New York Times*. "In spite of intensive research, scientists are still very much in the dark about the mechanism that transformed a nonliving chemical soup into a living cell."[1]

I asked origin-of-life expert Walter Bradley, coauthor of the landmark book *The Mystery of Life's Origin*, about the various theories scientists give for how the first living cell could have been naturalistically generated—including random chance, chemical affinity, self-ordering tendencies, seeding from space, deep-sea ocean vents, and using clay to encourage pre-biotic chemicals to assemble. He demonstrated that not one of them can withstand scientific scrutiny.[2]

Many other scientists have reached that same conclusion. "Science doesn't have the slightest idea how life began," journalist Gregg Easterbrook wrote about the origin-of-life field. "No generally accepted theory exists, and the steps leading from a barren primordial world to the fragile chemistry of life seem imponderable."[3]

Bradley not only shares that view, but he said that the mind-boggling difficulties of bridging the yawning gap between non-life and life mean that there may very well be no potential of finding a theory for how life could have arisen spontaneously. That's why he's convinced that the "absolutely overwhelming evidence" points toward an intelligence behind life's creation.

In fact, he said, "I think people who believe that life emerged naturalistically need to have a great deal more faith than people who reasonably infer that there's an Intelligent Designer."[4]

Biochemist and spiritual skeptic Francis Crick, who shared the Nobel Prize for discovering the molecular structure of DNA, acknowledged, "An honest man, armed with all the knowledge available to us now, could only state that in some sense, the origin of life appears at the moment to be almost a miracle, so many are the conditions which would have had to have been satisfied to get it going."[5]

"If there isn't a natural explanation and there doesn't seem to be the potential of finding one, then I believe it's appropriate to look at a supernatural explanation," said Bradley. "I think that's the most reasonable inference based on the evidence."[6]

I think the author of the book of Genesis would agree.

Truth for Today

People go to great lengths to find answers other than the ones given in the Bible. But increasingly Jesus is proven right when he says to the Father in John 17:17, "Your word is truth."

MADE IN GOD'S IMAGE

God created mankind in his own image, in the image of
God he created them; male and female he created them.

GENESIS 1:27

THE FACT THAT HUMANS ARE MADE IN THE IMAGE OF GOD IS one of the most important biblical revelations for Christians—and it is also one that those outside the faith have viciously attacked.

It's true that the endless murders, rapes, assaults, genocides, and other forms of violence and cruelty in our world tend to taunt us: How can humans be created in the image of God when we commit such evil acts? How do we explain wars and abuse if we share some of the characteristics of God himself? Some people even claim that while we may be more sophisticated and advanced than the rest of the animal kingdom, our ultimate value is no greater than that of any other creature since, these people believe, we've all evolved naturally and without any divine imprint.

Imago Dei means "the image of God." Ultimately, this phrase refers to two things: the characteristics of the human spirit and our ability to know the difference between right and wrong, good and evil.

Our human spirit provides evidence that God's traits—his love, justice, and freedom—are alive in us. Human nature is utterly without peer on earth. Even evolutionist scholar Ian Tattersall concedes, "*Homo sapiens* is not simply an improved version of its ancestors—it's a new concept."[1] At the most basic level of this nature is our self-realization, which is grounded in our self-consciousness, our ability to reason, and our emotions, such as anger and love. Our consciousness enables us to see that we have inherent value apart from our utility or function.

Another quality we share with God is the moral ability to recognize good and evil, which God showed through Adam and Eve. We can therefore act freely in a morally good or evil way. We can choose either to reflect the moral image of God or to reject it, but either way, the ability to make the choice reveals our underlying similarity to our Creator.

It cannot be overstated just how different humans are from the rest of creation. The vast chasms separating self-realization from consciousness and morality from amorality speak to the strong evidence that we are indeed made in the image of God.

Truth for Today

Among all of creation we are uniquely made in God's image. This reminds us that we were created with great value and for noble purposes—and that we have great potential. What worthy goal does God want you to pursue today?

JESUS IN GENESIS?

The Lord God said to the serpent, "Because you have done this, . . . I will put enmity between you and the woman, and between your offspring and hers; he will crush your head, and you will strike his heel."

IN THE OPENING MOMENTS OF THE MOVIE *THE PASSION OF the Christ*, there was a scene that probably puzzled some viewers. It was when a snake slithered out from under Satan, who was standing near Jesus and taunting him. The snake slid up in front of Jesus as he lay on the ground praying to the Father.

It was a frightening scene for those watching the film. But Jesus barely seemed to notice the snake. That is, until he stood up and—without warning—stomped on its head!

What did this mean? It was an illustration of the prediction in the opening pages of the Bible, in Genesis 3:14–15. There God warned the serpent, soon after it had tempted Eve to disobey him, that he would "put enmity between you and the woman, and between your offspring and hers; he will crush your head, and you will strike his heel."

This is the first prophecy in the Bible about the coming Messiah. After Adam and Eve's rebellion, God doled out punishments to those involved: first to the serpent, then to Eve, and finally to Adam. When God told the serpent that he would "put enmity" between the serpent and Eve, he was referring not only to their particular story but also to the story of all of humankind—a story plagued by Satan, the evil one.

Then the verse makes a subtle shift. It moves from discussing "her offspring" generally to a very specific "he"—the One who would crush Satan's head. This points to Christ himself, who would one day overcome and defeat Satan.

When the time was right, Jesus came into the world (John 1:14; Galatians 4:4–5). Yes, Satan succeeded in "striking Jesus' heel" when he was crucified. But it was only a heel wound because it was soon overcome by Jesus' resurrection. Jesus, on the other hand, came to destroy the work of Satan and ultimately Satan himself—thus "crushing his head" in a way that would be fatal.

It's encouraging to know that even before we existed, God knew the predicament Satan and our sinful desires would lead us into, and he already had a plan for our deliverance and salvation.

Truth for Today

If God cares enough about us to make provision for our salvation after the first occasion of sin, then how much must he care about our daily lives and concerns today? Bring your concerns to him; he cares for you.

CAN WE TRUST THE STORY OF JONAH?

Now the LORD provided a huge fish to swallow Jonah, and Jonah was in the belly of the fish three days and three nights.

JONAH 1:17

MANY OF US GREW UP HEARING THE STORY OF JONAH, THE prodigal prophet who, after God told him to preach repentance to the people of Nineveh, decided to run from God by boarding a boat for Tarshish—about as far away from Nineveh as he could go.

But then, through a series of events, Jonah ended up being thrown overboard and, as the verse above indicates, was provided free underwater transportation back to Nineveh in the belly of a huge fish. After he finally preached in that city, the people turned from their wicked ways to follow the true God.

It's a great story, but is it *true*? Certainly this is a favorite target for skeptics. They scoff at the seemingly impossible odds of such a thing happening.

Even some theologians have relegated this event to a metaphor. But there's a real problem: this is presented as a factual account in the Old Testament, Jewish people accept it as such, and the New Testament treats it as literal as well.

Specifically, Jesus presented the account of Jonah as a parallel to his coming death and resurrection. He said, "For as Jonah was three days and three nights in the belly of a huge fish, so the Son of Man will be three days and three nights in the heart of the earth" (Matthew 12:40). But if Jonah's story is fictional, why would Jesus appeal to it as a precedent for what he was soon to suffer? He was correlating one historical event (from the past) to another historical event (in the near future).[1]

Some have tried to defend this story by pointing to more recent events in which people have been swallowed by whales and survived. These stories would be fascinating—if they were true. But careful research has shown these accounts not to be credible.[2] As a result, some people conclude that the story of Jonah shouldn't be trusted either.

But their logic isn't sound. Just as with the creation of the universe or the resurrection of Jesus, we don't need similar examples to prove such things can happen. These are *miracles*, after all—we wouldn't expect them just to randomly recur at various points throughout history! And if God can create the heavens and the earth *ex nihilo*, then transporting a wayward prophet via a great fish would be, for him, child's play!

Truth for Today

"I am the Lord, the God of all mankind. Is anything too hard for me?" (Jeremiah 32:27). If God can do miracles, including supernaturally submarining Jonah to a desired location, then he can handle whatever worries you today.

SEEK GOD WHOLEHEARTEDLY

"You will seek me and find me when you seek me with all your heart."

JEREMIAH 29:13

"TRUTH IS SO OBSCURE IN THESE TIMES, AND FALSEHOOD SO established," said seventeenth-century philosopher Blaise Pascal, "that unless we love the truth, we cannot know it."[1]

We must search after God with passion and tenacity. If you already know him, heed the lessons of Psalm 42:1–2: "As the deer pants for streams of water, so my soul pants for you, my God. My soul thirsts for God, for the living God." Are you panting after and thirsting for the living God?

And for our friends who don't know him, the search for God can be perplexing—especially in a world where there are so many spiritual options. With the vast and growing array of religious leaders, teachings, and organizations all vying for their allegiance, how can they sort out what to believe?

Fortunately Jesus promised in Luke 11:9 that if they'll *ask*, they will receive; if they'll *seek*, they will find; and if they'll *knock*, the door will be opened to them. He did not say this would be easy or that truth would be served up on a silver platter. Rather, the answer to their spiritual quest will come if they persistently look for it. The prophet Jeremiah said, "You will seek me and find me when you seek me with all your heart" (Jeremiah 29:13).

This "all your heart" aspect counteracts our tendency toward complacency. It's easy to put off thinking about weighty spiritual matters, to passively accept traditional religious practices, or to simply submit to the teachings of spiritual authorities who want to impress their beliefs upon us. Yielding to these approaches might have been a natural response when we were young, but there comes a point when we must mature in matters of faith and make certain we have embraced the right set of beliefs.

But here's some great news: Jesus didn't just tell us to seek him; he said he also "came to seek and to save" us (Luke 19:10). And he made this promise to anyone who will embrace and hold to his teaching: "Then you will know the truth, and the truth will set you free" (John 8:32).

Truth for Today

God "rewards those who earnestly seek him" (Hebrews 11:6). Even after we've come to know Christ, we still need to pant after and thirst for him. James 4:8 tells us to "come near to God and he will come near to [us]." So seek him today—while helping friends who don't know him learn to ask, seek, and knock.

A SCIENTIST DISCOVERS GOD

*Who has measured the waters in the hollow of his hand, or
with the breadth of his hand marked off the heavens?*

ISAIAH 40:12

ALLAN REX SANDAGE, THE GREATEST OBSERVATIONAL
cosmologist in the world—who deciphered the secrets of the stars,
plumbed the mysteries of quasars, revealed the age of globular clusters, pinpointed the distances of remote galaxies, and quantified
the universe's expansion through his work at the Mount Wilson
and Palomar observatories—prepared to step onto the conference
platform.

Few scientists were as widely respected as this one-time protégé
of legendary astronomer Edwin Hubble. Sandage had been showered with prestigious honors from the American Astronomical
Society, the Swiss Physical Society, the Royal Astronomical
Society, and the Swedish Academy of Sciences, receiving astronomy's equivalent of the Nobel Prize. The *New York Times* dubbed
him the "grand old man of cosmology."[1]

As he approached the stage at this conference on science and
religion, there was little doubt where he would sit. The discussion
would be about the origin of the universe, and the panel would be
divided among those scientists who believed in God and those who
didn't, with each faction sitting on its own side of the stage.

Many of the attenders probably knew the ethnically Jewish
Sandage had been a virtual atheist even as a child. Others undoubtedly believed that a scientist of his stature must surely be skeptical
about God. As *Newsweek* put it, "The more deeply scientists see
into the secrets of the universe, you'd expect, the more God would

fade away from their hearts and minds."[2] So Sandage's seat among the doubters seemed a given.

Then the unexpected happened. Sandage set the room abuzz by turning and taking a chair among the theists. Even more dazzling, in the context of a talk about the big bang and its philosophical implications, he disclosed publicly that he had become a Christian at age fifty.

The big bang, he told the rapt audience, was a supernatural event that cannot be explained within the realm of physics as we know it. Science has taken us to the first event, but it can't take us back to the first cause. The sudden emergence of matter, space, time, and energy pointed to the need for some kind of transcendence.

"It is my science that drove me to the conclusion that the world is much more complicated than can be explained by science," he later told a reporter. "It was only through the supernatural that I can understand the mystery of existence."[3]

Truth for Today

For me, the road to atheism was paved by science, but, ironically, so was my later journey to God. Good information, I am convinced, points us to a good God.

DIVINE CONDESCENSION

*Christ Jesus: Who, being in very nature God, did not
consider equality with God something to be used to his own
advantage; rather, he made himself nothing by taking the
very nature of a servant, being made in human likeness.*

PHILIPPIANS 2:5–7

THIS IS A MIND-BOGGLING TRUTH: THE CREATOR—WHO MADE
the universe and everything in it—humbled himself on our behalf.
Though eternally existing "in very nature God," Jesus was willing
to let go of his heavenly position and privileges. He "made himself
nothing by taking the very nature of a servant, being made in
human likeness."

It's hard to grasp the magnitude of this divine condescension—
God becoming one of us. C. S. Lewis explained:

> The Second Person in God, the Son, became human Himself: was
> born into the world as an actual man—a real man of a particular
> height, with hair of a particular colour, speaking a particular
> language.... The Eternal Being, who knows everything and who
> created the whole universe, became not only a man but (before
> that) a baby, and before that a *foetus* inside a Woman's body. If you
> want to get the hang of it, think how you would like to become a
> slug or a crab.[1]

It's tempting to think that Lewis's example is a bit extreme. But
consider theologian Bruce Ware's words regarding the incarnation
of Christ:

> Would this be like you, fully a human being, joining yourself
> also to the nature of a worm or a slug or a fish? Yes, but . . . no.

No matter how lowly the creature was that you joined with, it still would be one creature being joined to another creature. We simply cannot imagine or understand what God the Son has done in obedience to his Father when he, the eternal and infinite God, Creator of all that is, came and took on also the nature of small, finite, creaturely manhood.[2]

While trying to comprehend *what* God did in becoming human, we should also ask ourselves *why* he went to such drastic measures.

He did it so he could fulfill his mission of "becoming obedient to death—even death on a cross!" (Philippians 2:8) in order to pay the penalty for our sins, with the ultimate goal that "every tongue acknowledge that Jesus Christ is Lord, to the glory of God the Father" (v. 11).

In other words, he did it for *us*. He did it so that we could know him and live with him forever—as our forgiver, leader, and friend.

Truth for Today

God's divine condescension should provoke us to praise: "Thank you, Lord, for going to such incomprehensible lengths to become one of us, so that ultimately you could die for my sins, forgive me, and make me your child."

THE HEAVENS DECLARE

*The heavens declare the glory of God; the skies proclaim
the work of his hands.*

PSALM 19:1

IN HIS 1802 BOOK, *NATURAL THEOLOGY*, WILLIAM PALEY SAID
that if you were walking along a path and found a watch, you would
immediately know that someone must have made it. A watch,
which shows clear evidence of complexity and design, requires a
watchmaker.

This was compelling rationale that pointed to an intuitive
truth: wherever we find design, there must be a designer. This is
commonly referred to as the *teleological argument*.

Two centuries later it's still true. As Mark Mittelberg says, even
today nobody picks up a watch on the beach and says, "Praise the
cosmos! Just look at this wonderful creation that the forces of chance
have tossed together." Our friend Cliffe Knechtle adds, "If you think
the *watch* needs a designer, just glance from the watch to your *hand*. It
is far more complex, has far more moving parts, displays much more
intricate design, and therefore demands a designer that much more."[1]

What many people don't realize, however, is that this argument from design was presented long before the age of science. In
fact, three thousand years ago, King David wrote in Psalm 19:1,
"The heavens declare the glory of God." Haven't you felt that?
Haven't you stood outside in the dark of night gazing at the amazing array of stars lighting up the sky—which are beyond counting
and whose distance from us is unfathomable—and felt an overwhelming sense of the grandeur of creation and the greatness of
the Creator? I certainly have.

It was this awareness, combined with the incredible complexity of the universe and the growing body of evidence related to its origins, that led prominent astronomer Robert Jastrow—who had long been an agnostic—to admit there must be a Creator.

He later wrote the book *God and the Astronomers*, in which he pointed to five lines of evidence that supported his conclusion: "the motions of the galaxies, the discovery of the primordial fireball, the laws of thermodynamics, the abundance of helium in the Universe, and the life story of the stars."[2] These, he said, point us back to "a biblical view of the origin of the world."[3]

No wonder the apostle Paul felt compelled to explain in Romans 1:20, "Since the creation of the world God's invisible qualities—his eternal power and divine nature—have been clearly seen, being understood from what has been made, so that people are without excuse."

Truth for Today

The heavens declare, yet are we listening? More than that, are we helping others hear what God is saying? We're not here just to know God, but also to make him known.

WHO DESIGNED THE DESIGNER?

"Before me no god was formed, nor will there be one after me.
I, even I, am the LORD, and apart from me there is no savior."

ISAIAH 43:10–11

SKEPTICS SOMETIMES RAISE AN OBJECTION: "IF WATCHES NEED watchmakers, and if hands need hand makers, then you've set up an endless regression from which the Christian concept of God can't escape."

Atheistic evolutionist Richard Dawkins wrote, "The designer hypothesis immediately raises the larger problem of who designed the designer."[1] And, "Any God capable of designing anything would have to be complex enough to demand the same kind of explanation in his own right. God presents an infinite regress."[2]

Dawkins seems to be implying that, at best, design in the universe only points to a *finite* designer—not an infinite deity—and therefore that designer needs a designer, who in turn needs his own designer *ad infinitum*.

Mark Mittelberg offers several thoughts:[3]

1. Even if the existence of a finite designer were all we could conclude from the evidence of design, this designer must be *unimaginably old, incredibly intelligent, amazingly powerful,* and *wonderfully wise* to have invented, designed, and produced all of what we see in the universe, including its ten billion galaxies and seventy sextillion stars (that's 70,000,000,000,000,000,000,000).[4] Any being of that creative capacity certainly ought to capture our attention and be listened to.

2. Playing out this line of thinking, though, we shouldn't stop with a finite designer. If the design in the universe compels us to acknowledge a wise and powerful designer, then that same logic, when applied to the designer himself, takes us at least one step further. And the designer-behind-the-designer must be even more mind-boggling. And if *that* designer is limited in any way, we can only *imagine* what the being who made *him* must be like. If we follow this track back far enough, we'll rapidly approach an unlimited God—one uncannily similar to the God of the Bible.

3. What if this intelligent designer actually revealed in other ways what he's like? What if he spoke through chosen prophets, explaining that he's not only an intelligent designer but also the eternal, all-powerful Creator who cares about his creatures and wants a relationship with us?

The evidence from design should lead us to at least consider additional information from divine revelation, the Bible—and revelation can take us the rest of the way home.

Truth for Today

The argument from design doesn't tell us everything, but it tells us a lot—and it ultimately leads us back to the one true God of the universe.

PEOPLE MATTER

What is mankind that you are mindful of them, human
beings that you care for them? You have made them a little
lower than the angels and crowned them with glory and
honor.

PSALM 8:4–5

ADOLF HITLER'S POLITICAL PHILOSOPHY HAS BEEN SUMMED
up to say: "Society's needs come before the individual's needs."[1]
History, of course, tells us how *that* way of thinking worked out.

Similarly, Communism stresses the importance of the political
party over the person. In fact, under Joseph Stalin's collectivization
efforts in the Soviet Union during the early 1900s, peasant farmers
were forced, for the benefit of the state, to give up their land and
animals in order to become part of collective farms. This resulted
in the starvation and death of many millions of innocent people.

In contrast to these philosophies, the biblical worldview holds
that people matter supremely because they matter to God. Genesis
1:26–27 makes it clear that human beings are uniquely created in
the image of God. We therefore have intrinsic value beyond that of
any of the other creatures on earth, and this value is not contingent
on our abilities, quality of life, or perceived worth in society.

Thus, Jesus said that God's greatest commands are to "'Love
the Lord your God with all your heart and with all your soul and
with all your mind. . . . [and] *Love your neighbor as yourself.*' All
the Law and the Prophets hang on these two commandments"
(Matthew 22:37–40, emphasis mine). Jesus also challenged us to
go beyond just loving our neighbors: "You have heard that it was
said, 'Love your neighbor and hate your enemy.' But I tell you, love

your enemies and pray for those who persecute you, that you may be children of your Father in heaven" (Matthew 5:43–45).

It was out of their biblically informed mind-set that the founders of the United States penned these civilization-shaping words of the Declaration of Independence: "We hold these truths to be self-evident, that all men are created equal, that they are endowed by their Creator with certain unalienable Rights, that among these are Life, Liberty and the pursuit of Happiness."

It is usually people who are influenced by the biblical worldview who strive to protect the unborn, fight for the rights of the oppressed, and work to feed, clothe, and lift up those in poverty. These are practical outworkings of the teachings of Jesus, who said in Matthew 25:40, "Truly I tell you, whatever you did for one of the least of these brothers and sisters of mine, you did for me."

Truth for Today

You matter to God, as does every person you know—and those you don't know. Whom might God want you to protect, encourage, or love in his name today?

THE MESSIAH TRIBE

The scepter will not depart from Judah, nor the ruler's staff
from between his feet, until he to whom it belongs shall
come and the obedience of the nations shall be his.

GENESIS 49:10

PREDICTIONS ABOUT THE COMING MESSIAH ARE PEPPERED
throughout the Old Testament. This one in Genesis 49:10 is striking because it told God's people, all the way back in Genesis, that
the Messiah would come through the lineage of Judah, one of
Jacob's twelve sons.

The key phrases in this verse ("The scepter will not depart,"
"the ruler's staff," "the obedience of the nations") make it clear that
not only *a* king, but *the* King, would come from the tribe of Judah.
In other words, the Messiah who would judge all people at the end
of time would be a descendant of Judah.

This prophecy was echoed throughout the Old Testament—
predicting not only that the Messiah would come from the tribe of
Judah, but more specifically that he would come through the house
of David (who was an earlier descendant of Judah; see 2 Samuel
7:12–13). This was finally fulfilled in the New Testament.

When we look at the genealogies of Jesus in Matthew 1:1–17
(the line of Joseph, Jesus' legal father) and Luke 3:23–38 (commonly believed to be the line of Mary, Jesus' mother[1]), we discover
that Jesus did indeed descend from the family of Judah as well as
the house of David.

Further, from Matthew 25:31–46 we see that Jesus will one
day preside over all the nations, and everyone will acknowledge
his authority (see also Isaiah 9:6 and Philippians 2:9–11). This has

not happened yet—but it's important to remember that some of the prophecies point to the first visit of the Messiah, and some point to his return. The first visit was when Jesus came as our suffering servant to give his life "as a ransom for many" (Mark 10:45). The triumphant return of the Messiah is when Jesus will come to judge the earth and to establish his kingdom—when "the obedience of the nations shall be his" (Genesis 49:10).

The prophecy in Genesis clearly points to the future, everlasting kingdom of a son of Judah. Jesus fit this description perfectly.

Truth for Today

When it seems that the countries and kingdoms of this world are invincible, remind yourself of the encouraging news that God has already sent the real King and that he's coming back soon to establish his everlasting kingdom—and we will be part of it!

THE UNIVERSE OFFERS CLUES

*"I am the LORD, the Maker of all things, who stretches out
the heavens, who spreads out the earth by myself."*

ISAIAH 44:24

"ALMOST EVERYONE NOW BELIEVES," DECLARED PHYSICIST
and atheist Stephen Hawking, "that the universe, and time itself,
had a beginning at the big bang."[1]

But that isn't just a belief held by secular scientists. Christian
apologist William Lane Craig explained to me, "Both philosoph-
ically and scientifically, I would argue that the universe and time
itself had a beginning at some point in the finite past. But since something cannot just come out of nothing, there has to be a transcendent
cause beyond space and time which brought the universe into being.

"Now," Craig continued, "this poses a major problem for skeptics."[2] That's because an atheist has to believe that the universe
came from nothing and by nothing. But even the famous skeptic
David Hume said, "I never asserted so absurd a proposition as that
anything might arise without a cause."[3] But that obviously leads to
the question of what that cause could be.

Dr. Craig had formulated an answer to that question in the
form of a strong argument based on the very existence of the universe. Here's how he described it to me:

- "First, whatever begins to exist has a cause.
- "Second, the universe began to exist.
- "And, third, therefore, the universe has a cause."

Then he quickly added, "As the eminent scientist Sir Arthur
Eddington wrote: 'The beginning seems to present insuperable
difficulties unless we agree to look on it as frankly supernatural.'"

"Okay," I interrupted, "that points to a Creator, but does it tell us anything about him?"

"Actually, yes, it does," Craig replied. "[The Creator] must be uncaused, because we know that there cannot be an infinite regress of causes. It must be timeless and therefore changeless, at least without the universe, because it was the creator of time. In addition, because it also created space, it must transcend space and therefore be immaterial rather than physical in nature."

Craig explained that science and logic point us compellingly to a power behind the universe who looks very much like the One we read about in the opening pages of the Bible.

Truth for Today

If both the universe and the Bible point to the same Creator who made all things, isn't it worth our time to learn as much as we can about him and, better yet, to get to know him personally? Take some time now to reach out and talk with him.

SOMETHING FROM NOTHING?

They deliberately forget that long ago by God's word the heavens came into being.

2 PETER 3:5

"IT IS NOT TRUE THAT 'NOTHING COMES FROM NOTHING,'" I heard an atheist say. "In fact, science has observed the emergence of something from nothing in the quantum physic process involving virtual particle pairs. Therefore the emergence of the universe itself could be analogous to this quantum fluctuation of something coming from nothing."

That's an extraordinary claim—universes popping into existence without a cause—but one taken seriously by some skeptics. I asked Christian philosopher William Lane Craig about this. He explained that "virtual particles" are theoretical entities, and it's not even clear that they actually exist as opposed to being merely theoretical constructs.

"However," he continued, "there's a much more important point to be made about this. You see, these particles, if they are real, do *not* come out of nothing. The quantum vacuum is not what most people envision when they think of a vacuum—that is, absolutely nothing. On the contrary, it's a sea of fluctuating energy, an arena of violent activity that has a rich physical structure and can be described by physical laws. These particles are thought to originate by fluctuations of the energy in the vacuum.

"So it's not an example of something coming into being out of nothing, or something coming into being without a cause. The quantum vacuum and the energy locked up in the vacuum are the cause of these particles. And then we have to ask, well, what is the origin of the whole quantum vacuum itself? Where does *it* come from?"

He let that question linger before continuing. "You've simply pushed back the issue of creation. Now you've got to account for how this very active ocean of fluctuating energy came into being. If quantum physical laws operate within the domain described by quantum physics, you can't legitimately use quantum physics to explain the origin of that domain itself. You need something transcendent that's beyond that domain in order to explain how the entire domain came into being. Suddenly, we're back to the origins question."[1]

Apologists Bob and Gretchen Passantino added, "If the atheist can believe that something (e.g., the universe, the material world) can come from nothing, it certainly shouldn't be difficult for him to believe that the universe came about materially from nothing by the agency of an intelligent, purposeful creator."[2]

This, again, brings us back to God—and *his* creation.

Truth for Today

When you get past the technical terms, the claim skeptics are making—that *everything came from nothing, by nothing*—is untenable. Even *The Sound of Music* lyrics refute that idea: "Nothing comes from nothing, nothing ever could." More importantly, science and Scripture say the same thing.

GOD IS ETERNAL?

Before the mountains were born or you brought forth the whole world, from everlasting to everlasting you are God.

PSALM 90:2

IS IT REALLY POSSIBLE THAT GOD EXISTED FOREVER—AS THE verse says, "from everlasting to everlasting"—without a beginning?

Some atheists see what they consider to be a fatal inconsistency here. They don't understand how Christians can say that God, the Creator, could be "uncaused." For instance, atheist George Smith asks, "If *everything* must have a cause, how did god become exempt?"[1] In *The Necessity of Atheism*, David Brooks says, "If everything must have a cause, then the First Cause must be caused and therefore: Who made God? To say that this First Cause always existed is to deny the basic assumption of this 'Theory.'"[2]

"That just misses the point," says philosopher and theologian Dr. William Lane Craig. "I don't know of any reputable philosopher who would say everything has a cause."[3] More than that, it's an argument against a statement nobody is making. Rather, the so-called *kalam* cosmological argument for God's existence states that *whatever begins to exist* has a cause, *not* "everything that exists has a cause." The universe began to exist, and therefore the universe has a cause.

By definition, as the First Cause, God is uncaused. He never *began* to exist, but has always been in existence. "This is not special pleading in the case of God," says Craig. He points out that atheists used to maintain—until scientific evidence contradicted them—that the universe is eternal and therefore doesn't need a cause. "How can they possibly maintain that the universe can be eternal and uncaused, yet God cannot be timeless and uncaused?" he asks.[4]

Others have also pointed out that regardless of what you believe, you're really left with two choices: *either something has always existed,* or *something popped into existence from nothing.* Now, I don't believe that things pop into existence from nothing (and hope you don't either)—so we're left with the idea that something has always existed. Theologian J. Oliver Buswell summed it up well: "Since we must believe that something is eternal, unless something comes from nothing, we shall find that the most reasonable belief in an eternal being is belief in the eternal God."[5]

So even though it stretches our puny minds—which should not be a shock to us—it does make sense logically that God has eternally existed. More than that, he tells us this is true in his revelation, the Bible.

Truth for Today

God has always existed, and he'll always be here. Don't you think he can handle the problems you're wrestling with today? He can—if you'll bring them to him in faith.

ON A RAZOR'S EDGE

Since the creation of the world God's invisible qualities—
his eternal power and divine nature—have been clearly
seen, being understood from what has been made.

ROMANS 1:20

"WHEN SCIENTISTS TALK ABOUT THE FINE-TUNING OF THE universe," said science philosopher Robin Collins, "they're generally referring to the extraordinary balancing of the fundamental laws and parameters of physics and the initial conditions of the universe. Our minds can't comprehend the precision of some of them. The result is a universe that has just the right conditions to sustain life.

"Let's talk about gravity," Collins continued. "Imagine a ruler, or one of those old-fashioned linear radio dials, that goes all the way across the universe. It would be broken down into one-inch increments, which means there would be billions upon billions upon billions of inches.

"The entire dial represents the range of force strengths in nature, with gravity being the weakest force and the strong nuclear force that binds protons and neutrons together in the nuclei being the strongest, a whopping ten thousand billion billion billion billion times stronger than gravity. The range of possible settings for the force of gravity can plausibly be taken to be at least as large as the total range of force strengths.

"Now, let's imagine that you want to move the dial from where it's currently set. Even if you were to move it by only one inch, the impact on life in the universe would be catastrophic."

"One inch compared to the whole universe?" I asked. "What kind of impact could that have?"

"That small adjustment of the dial would increase gravity by a *billion*-fold," he said.

"What would happen to life?" I asked.

"Animals anywhere near the size of human beings would be crushed," he said. "As you can see, compared to the total range of force strengths in nature, gravity has an incomprehensibly narrow range for life to exist. Of all the possible settings on the dial, from one side of the universe to the other, it happens to be situated in the exact right fraction of an inch to make our universe capable of sustaining life.

"Over the past thirty years or so, scientists have discovered that just about everything about the basic structure of the universe is balanced on a razor's edge for life to exist. The coincidences are far too fantastic to attribute this to mere chance or to claim that it needs no explanation. The dials are set too precisely to have been a random accident. Somebody, as [astronomer and cosmologist] Fred Hoyle quipped, has been monkeying with the physics."[1]

Truth for Today

God cared enough to dial in the universe to allow you to live and to flourish, and he also cares about what concerns you today.

DESIGN AT THE
MOLECULAR LEVEL

*All things have been created through him and for him. He
is before all things, and in him all things hold together.*

COLOSSIANS 1:16–17

"DARWIN SAID, 'IF IT COULD BE DEMONSTRATED THAT ANY
complex organ existed which could not possibly have been formed
by numerous, successive, slight modifications, my theory would
absolutely break down,'" said biochemist Michael Behe, a university professor and author of *Darwin's Black Box*.[1]

"And that was the basis for my concept of irreducible complexity. You see, a system or device is irreducibly complex if it
has a number of different components that all work together to
accomplish the task of the system, and if you were to remove one of
the components, the system would no longer function. The illustration I like to use is a mousetrap."

Behe held up a wooden mousetrap for me. "You can see the
interdependence of the parts for yourself," he said, pointing to its
five components. "Now, if you take away any of these parts, then
it's not like the mousetrap becomes half as efficient as it used to be.
It doesn't catch half as many mice. It doesn't work at all.

"[This illustrates] how irreducibly complex biological systems
defy a Darwinian explanation," he continued. "Evolution can't
produce an irreducibly complex biological machine suddenly, all
at once, because it's much too complicated. The odds against that
would be prohibitive. And you can't produce it directly by numerous, successive, slight modifications of a precursor system, because

any precursor system would be missing a part and consequently couldn't function."

I asked, "Are there a lot of different kinds of biological machines at the cellular level?"

"Life is actually based on molecular machines," he replied. "They haul cargo from one place in the cell to another; they turn cellular switches on and off; they act as pulleys and cables; electrical machines let current flow through nerves; manufacturing machines build other machines; solar-powered machines capture the energy from light and store it in chemicals. Molecular machinery lets cells move, reproduce, and process food. In fact, every part of the cell's function is controlled by complex, highly calibrated machines."

Behe motioned toward the mousetrap. "If the creation of a simple device like this requires intelligent design," he said, "then we have to ask, 'What about the finely tuned machines of the cellular world?' If evolution can't adequately explain them, then scientists should be free to consider other alternatives.

"My conclusion," Behe said, "can be summed up in a single word: *design.*"

Truth for Today

God's creativity and wisdom can be seen even at the microscopic level. Don't you think a God like that would have the wisdom and resources needed to help you with your current challenges? Reach out to him and ask for his help.

IF I WERE GUESSING . . .

"But you, Bethlehem Ephrathah, though you are small among the clans of Judah, out of you will come for me one who will be ruler over Israel, whose origins are from of old, from ancient times."

MICAH 5:2

SOME PEOPLE THINK BIBLICAL PROPHECIES ARE MERELY BROAD general statements that could easily be fulfilled by a variety of situations—or are lucky guesses based on high odds of success.

Think again. Take, for example, this prediction in Micah 5:2, in which the prophet foretold the Messiah's birth in the little village of Bethlehem. The town was so diminutive that even Micah described it as "small among the clans of Judah."

Talk about *not* hedging your bets! If I were asked to predict where the hundredth president of the United States would be born, I would play the odds and guess one of the major US cities—such as New York, Los Angeles, Chicago, Houston, or maybe Washington, DC. I wouldn't venture a prediction of a place like Tecumseh, Nebraska; Velva, North Dakota; or Daniels, West Virginia. What would be the chances of *that* happening?

Further, in his book *Science Speaks*, mathematician Peter Stoner and his team of researchers asked the question, "One man in how many, the world over, has been born in Bethlehem?"[1]

Their answer? "The best estimate which we can make of this comes from the attempt to find out the average population of Bethlehem, from Micah down to the present time, and divide it by the average population of the earth during the same period. . . . Since the probable population of the earth has averaged less than two billion, the population of Bethlehem has averaged less than 7,150. Our answer may be expressed in the form that one man in 7,150/2,000,000,000 or one man in 2.8 x 10^5 was born in Bethlehem."[2]

This computes to an estimated chance of 1 to 280,000 that the Messiah would indeed be born in Bethlehem.

So Micah was either an incredibly lucky guesser, or else he really was—as biblical history makes clear—a true prophet of God who received a revelation from the Almighty concerning where the coming Redeemer of mankind would one day be born.

I'm betting on the second option!

Truth for Today

God's plans are never arbitrary or last-minute decisions. Rather, he says, "I make known the end from the beginning, from ancient times, what is still to come" (Isaiah 46:10). In light of that, don't you think he can help you with whatever problems you face today?

THE SUFFERING MESSIAH

He was pierced for our transgressions, he was crushed for our iniquities; the punishment that brought us peace was on him, and by his wounds we are healed. We all, like sheep, have gone astray, each of us has turned to our own way; and the LORD has laid on him the iniquity of us all.

ISAIAH 53:5–6

LOUIS LAPIDES, WHO IS JEWISH, WAS SURPRISED BY THE challenge a street preacher issued to him: "Just read the Old Testament," he said, "and ask the God of Abraham, Isaac, and Jacob—the God of Israel—to show you if Jesus is the Messiah. Because he *is* your Messiah."

"Pretty soon," Lapides told me, "I was reading the Old Testament every day and seeing one prophecy after another. For instance, Deuteronomy talked about a prophet greater than Moses who will come and whom we should listen to. I thought, *Who can be greater than Moses?* It sounded like the Messiah—someone as great and as respected as Moses but a greater teacher and a greater authority. I grabbed ahold of that and went searching for him."

But then Lapides was stopped cold by Isaiah 53. With clarity and specificity, in a haunting prediction wrapped in exquisite poetry, here was the picture of a Messiah who would suffer and die for the sins of Israel and the world—written more than seven hundred years before Jesus walked the earth.

Instantly Lapides recognized the portrait: this was Jesus of Nazareth—the suffering Jesus, the crucified Jesus, the Jesus who he now realized had been "pierced for our transgressions" as he "bore the sin of many" (vv. 5, 12).

As Jews in the Old Testament sought to atone for their sins through a system of animal sacrifices, here was Jesus, the ultimate sacrificial Lamb of God, who paid for sin once and for all. Here was the personification of God's plan of redemption.

So breathtaking was this discovery that Lapides concluded it was a fraud! He believed that Christians had rewritten the Old Testament and twisted Isaiah's words to make it sound as if the prophet had been foreshadowing Jesus.

Lapides set out to expose the deception. "I asked my stepmother to send me a Jewish Bible so I could check it out myself," he told me. "She did, and guess what? I found that it said the same thing! Now I really had to deal with it."

Deal with it he did, and he became a follower of Jesus—and eventually a pastor.[1]

Truth for Today

Jesus' horrific crucifixion was not a mistake or tragedy of history. It was God's plan to utilize the sinful actions of humans to bring about our redemption. Thank him today for his incredible sacrifice and his amazing grace.

PROPHETIC ODDS

*[Jesus said,] "Did not the Messiah have to suffer these
things and then enter his glory?" And beginning with
Moses and all the Prophets, [Jesus] explained to them what
was said in all the Scriptures concerning himself.*

LUKE 24:26–27

IS IT POSSIBLE THAT JESUS FULFILLED THE OLD TESTAMENT
prophecies merely by accident?

"Not a chance" was the confident reply of Louis Lapides,
the Jewish man who, as we've discussed, came to faith in Christ
through the influence of the messianic prophecies. "The odds are
so astronomical that they rule that out. Someone did the math and
figured out that the probability of just eight prophecies being fulfilled is one chance in one hundred million billion. That number
is millions of times greater than the total number of people who've
ever walked the planet!

"He calculated that if you took this number of silver dollars,
they would cover the state of Texas to a depth of two feet. If you
marked one silver dollar among them and then had a blindfolded
person wander the whole state and bend down to pick up one
coin, what would be the odds he'd choose the one that had been
marked?"

With that Lapides answered his own question: "The same
odds that anybody in history could have fulfilled just eight of the
prophecies."

I had studied this same statistical analysis by mathematician
Peter W. Stoner when I was investigating the messianic prophecies
for myself. Stoner also computed that the probability of fulfilling

forty-eight prophecies was one chance in a trillion, trillion, trillion, trillion, trillion, trillion, trillion, trillion, trillion, trillion, trillion, trillion![1]

Our minds can't comprehend a number that big. This is a staggering statistic that's equal to the number of minuscule atoms in a trillion, trillion, trillion, trillion, billion universes the size of our universe!

"The odds alone say it would be impossible for anyone to fulfill the Old Testament prophecies," Lapides concluded. "Yet Jesus—and only Jesus throughout all of history—managed to do it."[2]

The words of the apostle Peter come to mind: "This is how God fulfilled what he had foretold through all the prophets, saying that his Messiah would suffer" (Acts 3:18).

The more I consider the amazing evidence supporting Jesus as the predicted Messiah—as well as the broader evidence that backs up the Christian faith in general—the more my heart echoes the conclusion I reached on the day I gave my life to Christ: "It would take more faith to maintain my atheism than it would to become a Christian!"

Truth for Today

The truth for today is that your faith in Christ is based on overwhelming evidence! Isn't it wonderful to know that your faith is built on a foundation of such amazing facts?

PIERCED

"They will look on me, the one they have pierced, and they will mourn for him as one mourns for an only child, and grieve bitterly for him as one grieves for a firstborn son."

ZECHARIAH 12:10

"MY GOD, MY GOD, WHY HAVE YOU FORSAKEN ME?"

These sobering words, uttered by Jesus on the cross, served two purposes. First, they were an authentic expression of the agony he was suffering as he, "the Lamb of God, who takes away the sin of the world" (John 1:29), was voluntarily made "to be sin for us, so that in him we might become the righteousness of God" (2 Corinthians 5:21).

Second, they were a recitation of Psalm 22:1. "By citing it," says *The Moody Bible Commentary*, "Jesus was probably calling attention to His fulfillment of all that is contained in Psalm 22:1–18."[1]

What's significant about this is that Psalm 22 is filled with allusions to the suffering of the coming Messiah. For instance, verses 7 and 8 read, "All who see me mock me; they hurl insults, shaking their heads. 'He trusts in the LORD,' they say, 'let the LORD rescue him.'" And verse 18 reads, "They divide my clothes among them and cast lots for my garment."

But probably the most significant verse says, "A pack of villains encircles me; *they pierce my hands and my feet*" (v. 16, emphasis mine).[2] This would be a remarkable prediction if it had been written even a few years before the crucifixion of Jesus—but King David wrote it about a thousand years before the time of Christ. What's more, this was some five hundred years before crucifixion had even been invented![3]

And if that weren't remarkable enough, about seven hundred years before Jesus came and died for our sins, Isaiah made a similar prediction when he said, "*He was pierced for our transgressions,* he was crushed for our iniquities; the punishment that brought us peace was on him, and by his wounds we are healed" (Isaiah 53:5, emphasis mine). Also, about five hundred years before the time of Christ, the prophet Zechariah foretold a time when "*They will look on me, the one they have pierced,* and they will mourn for him as one mourns for an only child, and grieve bitterly for him as one grieves for a firstborn son" (Zechariah 12:10, emphasis mine).

These are amazing predictions—made hundreds of years in advance—telling of a time when Jesus would come to fulfill his mission to "give his life as a ransom for many" (Matthew 20:28).

Truth for Today

God's plan from the beginning was to send his Son to be our Savior, allowing him to take the punishment we deserved. What a great reason to worship and follow him today!

IN SEARCH OF NAZARETH

Joseph and Mary . . . returned to Galilee to their own town
of Nazareth. And the child grew and became strong; he was
filled with wisdom, and the grace of God was on him.

LUKE 2:39–40

"WHAT'S FUNNY IS THAT THE EVIDENCE NOW SHOWS THAT Nazareth—the town where Jesus supposedly grew up—didn't even exist in first-century Palestine!"

It was a memorable conversation. My coauthor Mark and I were having breakfast with a couple of prominent atheists. These guys didn't just deny the existence of God; they were out to prove that belief in God is ridiculous.

I left with conflicting thoughts. Part of me knew what was *really* ridiculous was their claim itself. But the other part of me asked, *How do I know for sure? Have I ever really investigated the evidence concerning Nazareth?*

So investigate I did. Do you know what I found out? As I explain in *The Case for Christ*, the evidence for first-century Nazareth is overwhelming—and new data keeps coming in. Scholar Craig A. Evans wrote, "Recent excavations in and around Nazareth—which today is a city of about 60,000—suggest that the village in the time of Jesus may not have been a sleepy, isolated place, as many have imagined."[1]

Also, in 2006 the Nazareth Archaeological Project began excavating beneath the Sisters of Nazareth Convent. The director of the project, Ken Dark of the University of Reading, described the remains of a first-century home that were found there. "Taken together, the walls conformed to the plan of a so-called courtyard house, one of the typical architectural forms of Early Roman-period settlements in . . . Galilee," Dark said.[2]

Archaeologists found doors and windows, cooking pottery, and a spindle whorl used in spinning thread. Fragments of limestone vessels, which Jews believed could not become impure, were also found, suggesting that a Jewish family lived there. "The house must date from the first century AD or earlier," Dark concluded. "No stratified pottery earlier or later than the Early Roman period was discovered in layers associated with the house."[3]

In addition, another first-century house, similar in structure, was discovered nearby in an excavation by Yardenna Alexandre of the Israel Antiquities Authority in 2009.[4]

"The evidence suggests that Jesus' boyhood was spent in a conservative Jewish community that had little contact with Hellenistic or Roman culture," Dark concluded.

In spite of challenges, the case keeps getting stronger that Nazareth did, indeed, exist at the time of Jesus.

Truth for Today

"In a lawsuit the first to speak seems right, until someone comes forward and cross-examines," says Proverbs 18:17. It's natural to feel intimidated when someone questions an aspect of your faith—but looking deeper will make your faith grow stronger.

DID JESUS REALLY DIE?

Jesus cried out in a loud voice, . . . "My God, my God, why have you forsaken me?" . . . With a loud cry, Jesus breathed his last.

MARK 15:34, 37

"THE FACT THAT JESUS IS BELIEVED TO HAVE BEEN SEEN ALIVE after the crucifixion may mean that he survived the attempt on his life, unless we have clear evidence that he died in the process," writes Muslim apologist Shabir Ally. "Rumours of his death have been greatly exaggerated."[1]

This claim—that Jesus didn't die on the cross—is commonly called the Swoon Theory. It was made popular in Hugh Schonfield's 1965 book, *The Passover Plot*.

It's easy to see why this theory would make an intriguing storyline for a novel or movie—but it is quickly demolished by the facts:

- There is no record of anyone surviving a Roman crucifixion.
- Jesus was beaten dozens of times with whips that had jagged bones and balls of lead woven into them. The historian Eusebius described such a flogging: "The sufferer's veins were laid bare, and the very muscles, sinews, and bowels of the victim were open to exposure."
- Then, while Jesus was in hypovolemic shock, the spikes were driven through his wrists and feet, and he was hung on the cross. Crucifixion results in slow asphyxiation because stress on the chest locks the person's lungs into an inhaled position.
- After Jesus "breathed his last," a soldier plunged a spear between his ribs, puncturing his heart, and proving that he was indeed dead.[2]

- "Clearly the weight of the historical and medical evidence indicates that Jesus was dead before the wound to his side was inflicted," concluded the *Journal of the American Medical Association*.[3]
- Each of the four Gospels, which are rooted in eyewitness accounts, makes it clear that Jesus died on the cross (Matthew 27:45–56; Mark 15:33–41; Luke 23:44–49; John 19:28–37).
- The apostle Paul passed on to us one of the earliest creeds of the church: "Christ died for our sins according to the Scriptures . . . [and] was raised on the third day" (1 Corinthians 15:3–4).
- Jesus predicted he would die for our sins (three times in Mark alone: 8:31–33; 9:30–32; 10:32–34), and explained he came to "give his life as a ransom for many" (Mark 10:45).
- Even liberal scholar John Dominic Crossan affirmed, "Jesus' death by execution under Pontius Pilate is as sure as anything historical can ever be."[4] Atheist historian Gerd Lüdemann acknowledged that the historical evidence for Jesus' execution is "indisputable."[5]

The verdict is clear: Jesus really did die on the cross.

Truth for Today

The evidence makes it clear Jesus died. But that doesn't tell us *why* he died. Fortunately Jesus explained it when he said he came to "give his life as a ransom for many" (Mark 10:45). He laid down his life for us.

WAS THE TOMB EMPTY?

As they entered the tomb, they saw a young man dressed in
a white robe sitting on the right side, and they were alarmed.
"Don't be alarmed," he said. "You are looking for Jesus the
Nazarene, who was crucified. He has risen! He is not here."

MARK 16:5–6

"IF THE ROMANS FOLLOWED THEIR NORMAL POLICIES AND customs," wrote agnostic scholar Bart Ehrman, "and if Pilate was the man [who] all our sources indicate he was, then it is highly unlikely that Jesus was decently buried on the day of his execution in a tomb that anyone could later identify."[1]

If Ehrman's assertion is correct, then we would have major problems with the gospel records that tell us Jesus' body was laid in a tomb belonging to Joseph of Arimathea, a member of the Jewish council, and that three days later that tomb was found empty.

How can we respond? New Testament scholar Craig Evans explained in his book *How God Became Jesus* that Ehrman's analysis of Roman policy on crucifixion and burial is "unnuanced and incomplete."[2] He added, "The Gospel accounts describing Jesus' removal from the cross and burial are consistent with archaeological evidence and with Jewish law,"[3] and it is "simply erroneous to assert that the Romans did not permit the burial of the executed, including the crucified."[4]

Evans said, "I conclude that the burial of the body of Jesus in a known tomb, according to Jewish law and custom, is highly probable." He added that "it was the knowledge of the tomb and the discovery that it was empty, in addition to the appearances of Jesus, that led the followers of Jesus to speak in terms of resurrection."[5]

But how did the tomb become empty? The Romans wouldn't have stolen Jesus' body—they wanted him *dead*. The Jewish leaders wouldn't have taken it either—they wanted him to *stay* dead. The disciples? They had neither the courage nor the opportunity to get past the guards, roll back the stone, and steal Jesus' corpse. And even if they had, why would they? So they could live lives of deprivation and suffering—all for a lie?

Perhaps the strongest evidence is that even Jesus' enemies implicitly admitted his tomb was empty. Rather than refute the claims of his resurrection, they made up a cover story to explain *why* the body was missing (Matthew 28:11–15)—thus conceding the tomb was vacant!

The record is clear: on that first Easter morning, Jesus' body was no longer in the tomb.

Truth for Today

The evidence shows that Jesus' tomb was empty. Ask your friends who doubt this what possible explanation—other than the actual resurrection—could account for that.

RESURRECTION NEWS FLASH!

For what I received I passed on to you as of first importance: that Christ died for our sins according to the Scriptures, that he was buried, that he was raised on the third day according to the Scriptures.

1 CORINTHIANS 15:3–4

IT WAS ONCE FASHIONABLE TO SAY THAT THE GOSPELS— Matthew, Mark, Luke, and John—were written too late to give an accurate account of what really happened in the life of Jesus, including the events surrounding his resurrection. Some even said they weren't written until the mid to late second century, more than a hundred years after the events surrounding Jesus' ministry. This discredited the idea that the Gospels were based on eyewitness accounts, and eroded confidence in what they said about Jesus.

However, it is now known that the Gospels were written in the first century—within the lifespan of Jesus' followers.[1]

Also, before the Gospels were recorded, Paul penned his epistles. These letters affirm many details about Jesus' life, including his resurrection. In addition, Paul's epistles relay several earlier creeds, attesting to the beliefs of Jesus' first followers. One of the most interesting is in 1 Corinthians 15:3–7.

Historian Gary Habermas developed a helpful timeline related to this creed. It starts with understanding that Jesus was crucified in either AD 30 or 33. Paul wrote 1 Corinthians in AD 54–55, which puts it within approximately twenty-one and twenty-five years of the crucifixion. But Paul said he had previously passed on the creed to the people of Corinth, so the creed itself dates even earlier.

But there's more. Paul said in 1 Corinthians 15:3: "What I received I passed on to you." When did he receive this creed? He became a Christian one to three years after Jesus' execution. He immediately went to Damascus to meet the disciples. He might have received it then, but it was more likely three years later when he went to Jerusalem and met with Peter and James, both of whom are named in the creed. Paul described this meeting in Galatians 1:18–19, using the Greek term *historesai*, which suggests it was a personal inquiry or investigation.

Either way, this means Paul was given the creed within one to six years of the crucifixion—and it had already been put into creedal form, which tells us these beliefs went back even further.

"This tradition," concluded historian James D. G. Dunn, "we can be entirely confident, was *formulated as tradition within months of Jesus' death*."[2]

Months! The news of Jesus' resurrection was a *news flash* in the ancient world—and it affirmed that the risen Jesus had appeared to many witnesses.

Truth for Today

Many still believe the false rumor that generations had passed before the first Christian accounts were written. Whom should you tell about this exciting early Christian creed?

THE RESURRECTED JESUS APPEARS

*[After his resurrection, Jesus] appeared to Cephas, and
then to the Twelve. After that, he appeared to more than
five hundred of the brothers and sisters at the same
time. . . . Then he appeared to James, then to all the
apostles, and last of all he appeared to me also.*

1 CORINTHIANS 15:5–8

THE ANCIENT CREED THAT WE BEGAN TO EXAMINE IN THE PREVIOUS
reading explains in verses 5–8 not only that Jesus' tomb was empty
but that the risen Jesus appeared to at least 515 people, including
the apostle Paul himself.

In fact, when we look at the broader New Testament, we get
more details of how the resurrected Savior appeared to a variety of
people in a variety of settings—to men and women, some individu-
ally, some in groups, sometimes indoors, sometimes outdoors, to
softhearted people like John, and to skeptical people like Thomas.
And at times Jesus asked them to touch the scars in his hands or
side, or to eat with him, making it clear that he was present physically and not just spiritually.

These appearances occurred over forty days, and Jesus appeared
to the following people:

- Mary Magdalene (John 20:11–18);
- the other women (Matthew 28:8–10; compare Matthew
  28:1; Mark 16:1; Luke 24:10);
- Cleopas and another disciple on the road to Emmaus (Luke
  24:13–32);

- Peter (Luke 24:34);
- ten of the apostles and others, with Thomas absent (Luke 24:36–49; John 20:19–23);
- Thomas and the other apostles (John 20:24–29);
- seven of the apostles (John 21:1–14);
- the eleven apostles (Matthew 28:16–20); and
- the apostles at the Mount of Olives before his ascension (Luke 24:50–52; Acts 1:3–9).

What's more, these reports come from multiple sources, from both inside and outside the New Testament. Historian Michael Licona summarized, "In all, we've got nine sources that reflect multiple, very early, and eyewitness testimonies to the disciples' claims that they had seen the risen Jesus. This is something the disciples believed to the core of their being."[1]

Even the atheist scholar Gerd Lüdemann conceded: "It may be taken as historically certain that Peter and the disciples had experiences after Jesus' death in which Jesus appeared to them as the risen Christ."[2]

The resurrection was the central proclamation of the early church from the very beginning. The earliest Christians didn't just endorse Jesus' teachings; they were convinced they had seen him alive after his crucifixion.

Truth for Today

Jesus said to Thomas in John 20:29, "Because you have seen me, you have believed; blessed are those who have not seen and yet have believed." The evidence for Jesus' appearances is strong—and gives us good reasons to be confident about the reality of the resurrection.

DREAMING DISCIPLES?

"Why are you troubled, and why do doubts rise in your minds? Look at my hands and my feet. It is I myself! Touch me and see; a ghost does not have flesh and bones, as you see I have."

LUKE 24:38–39

SOME HAVE SUGGESTED THAT THE WITNESSES TO JESUS' resurrection were sincere in believing they had seen him, but that they were actually experiencing hallucinations. At first blush, this seems like a possibility. After all, people think they see all kinds of things, right? *Aliens. Bigfoot. Elvis.* Why not *Jesus* too?

This theory, however, is riddled with flaws.

"The disciples were fearful, doubtful, and in despair after the crucifixion, whereas people who hallucinate need a fertile mind of expectancy or anticipation," said scholar Gary Habermas. "Peter was hardheaded, for goodness' sake; James was a skeptic—certainly not good candidates for hallucinations.

"Also," Habermas continued, "hallucinations are comparably rare. They're usually caused by drugs or bodily deprivation. Yet we're supposed to believe that over a course of many weeks, people from all sorts of backgrounds, all kinds of temperaments, in various places, all experienced hallucinations?"[1]

Psychologist Gary Collins added, "Hallucinations are individual occurrences. By their very nature only one person can see a given hallucination at a time. They certainly aren't something which can be seen by a group of people."[2]

This makes sense. When I'm having a dream in the middle of the night about a vacation in Hawaii, I only *wish* I could wake up

Leslie and tell her, "Quick! Let's both go back to sleep and share this dream I'm having about a beach resort in Maui. That way we can skip all the time, money, and effort of actually taking a trip there!"

Dreams, like hallucinations, are not shared events. Yet, as we've seen, the earliest report we have about the resurrection tells us Jesus appeared to more than *five hundred people* at once (1 Corinthians 15:6)! Besides, the disciples claimed they not only saw the risen Jesus but also talked to and even ate with him (Luke 24:36–48).

And if the appearances of Jesus were mere hallucinations, then his body would still be in the tomb, right? Oops! The fact that the tomb was empty only underscores the credibility of the appearance claims.

When you look at all of the data with an open mind, it becomes clear that the disciples and others really did encounter the resurrected Jesus.

Truth for Today

Jesus appeared to his followers alive after the crucifixion. This means he is also alive to forgive, encourage, and lead you. Reach out to the risen Savior and ask him to guide and bless you today.

THE JERUSALEM FACTOR

[Peter said,] "Fellow Jews and all of you who live in Jerusalem, let me explain this to you. . . . God has raised this Jesus to life, and we are all witnesses of it." . . . Those who accepted his message were baptized, and about three thousand were added to their number that day.

ACTS 2:14, 32, 41

DURING MY INTERVIEW WITH HISTORIAN MICHAEL LICONA ABOUT the resurrection of Jesus, he threw out an intriguing phrase: "The Jerusalem Factor."

"The Jerusalem Factor?" I asked. "What's that?"

He replied: "This refers to the fact that Jesus was publicly executed and buried in Jerusalem, and then his resurrection was proclaimed in the very same city. In fact, several weeks after the crucifixion, Peter declared to a crowd right there in Jerusalem: 'God has raised this Jesus to life, and we are all witnesses of the fact' [Acts 2:32]. Frankly, it would have been impossible for Christianity to get off the ground in Jerusalem if Jesus' body were still in the tomb. The Roman or Jewish authorities could have simply gone over to his tomb and viewed his corpse, and the misunderstanding would have been over.

"Instead, what we do hear is enemy attestation to the empty tomb. In other words, what were the skeptics saying? That the disciples stole the body. . . . Here's the thing: Why would you say someone stole the body if it were still in the tomb? This is an implicit admission that the tomb was empty."[1]

My coauthor Mark Mittelberg adds, "The emergence of the church was too tied to claims of the resurrection of Jesus to have been possible without that resurrection really happening. This is not like the rise of Islam or Buddhism or many other religions that are linked to a general set of teachings, rather than to a miraculous make-or-break historical event.

"In light of that, how did the crowd react to Peter's bold claims? The record tells us his words 'pierced their hearts,' and they cried out and asked what they should do. Peter instructed them to 'repent of your sins and turn to God, and be baptized in the name of Jesus Christ for the forgiveness of your sins' [Acts 2:37–38 NLT]. Three thousand people did just that. And this was only the beginning of the rapid emergence and exponential growth of the Christian church. . . . This would never have happened if Peter had not been telling the truth when he so boldly proclaimed his message about Jesus."[2]

Apart from the actual resurrection of Jesus, it really would be hard to explain how the church began in Jerusalem.

Truth for Today

Three thousand spiritually resistant people in Jerusalem believed the evidence for the resurrection and put their trust in Christ. Who do you know who needs to hear the evidence for Jesus' resurrection?

EVIDENCE BEYOND THE BIBLE

What I am saying is true and reasonable. The king is familiar with these things, and I can speak freely to him. I am convinced that none of this has escaped his notice, because it was not done in a corner.

ACTS 26:25–26

A POPULAR CHALLENGE TO THE HISTORICAL CASE FOR THE life, death, and resurrection of Jesus is that it's all based on the testimonies of true believers. "If these things really happened," the argument goes, "then surely there would be records of these events from unbiased, secular sources."

I like what Mark Mittelberg reminds audiences when this comes up in live Q&A events: "There *is* secular evidence, but let's not jump to it too quickly. Have you considered that the true believers might be that *because they were there and actually saw what happened*? Seriously, ruling out the testimonies of the people who were there is like a judge in a court of law saying he wants to hear the testimonies of everyone *except* the eyewitnesses because they would be biased by what they saw!"

Mark makes a great point and, I think, exposes the prejudice some people employ as an excuse to ignore the biblical record. But there is also broader evidence to consider.

According to a leading expert on ancient history, Edwin Yamauchi of Miami University, "We have better historical documentation for Jesus than for the founder of any other ancient religion."[1] Sources from outside the Bible show that there were people who believed Jesus performed healings and was the Messiah; that he was crucified; and that despite this shameful death, his followers, who believed he was alive again, worshiped him as God.

There are thirty-nine ancient sources that corroborate more than one hundred facts concerning Jesus' life, teachings, crucifixion, and resurrection. Seven secular sources and several early Christian creeds concern the deity of Jesus, a doctrine "definitely present in the earliest church," according to Gary Habermas, the scholar who wrote *The Historical Jesus*.[2]

Habermas summarizes: "We should realize that it is quite extraordinary that we could provide a broad outline of most of the major facts of Jesus' life from 'secular' history alone. Such is surely significant. . . . We conclude that ancient extrabiblical sources both provide a broad outline of the life of Jesus and indicate that he died due to the effects of crucifixion. Afterwards he was buried and his tomb was later found empty."[3]

The verdict is in, from both sacred and secular sources, and the record about Jesus stands strong.

Truth for Today

The evidence confirms that the Jesus of history is the same person as the Christ of our faith. You can bet your life on it!

THE CASE FOR THE RESURRECTION

God has raised this Jesus to life, and we are all witnesses of it.

ACTS 2:32

WE HAVE LOOKED AT A NUMBER OF ARGUMENTS FOR THE resurrection of Jesus—each quite persuasive. But the case gets even stronger when we put these pieces together.

Here is a compilation of six facts to shore up your confidence in the resurrection. More than that, these are points you can share with your friends to help them see why they should trust in the risen Savior.[1]

THE SIX E'S OF THE RESURRECTION

1. **Execution—*Jesus really died on the cross***

   Jesus didn't pass out on the cross or fake his death. These were once common theories among skeptics, but they've been thoroughly discredited. The evidence shows that Jesus died even before the spear was thrust into his side to doubly ensure his demise.

2. **Empty Tomb—*Jesus' body was missing***

   On that first Easter morning, women discovered that Jesus' body was gone. Peter and John soon confirmed the empty tomb for themselves. Even Jesus' enemies implicitly admitted this by making up stories to explain why his body was missing.

3. **Eyewitnesses—*The risen Jesus appeared to many***

   Soon the disciples saw the risen Savior for themselves—some of them multiple times. Over forty days Jesus appeared to both individuals and groups in a variety of places and circumstances. We have nine ancient sources, inside and outside the New Testament, confirming the conviction of the disciples that they had encountered the risen Christ.[2]

4. **Early Accounts—*These facts were reported early and often***
Multiple reports of Jesus' resurrection were circulating during the lifetimes of Jesus' contemporaries—people who would have been all too happy to point out the errors if the accounts had not been true. In fact, the earliest report of Jesus' rising comes in a creed that was formulated within months of his resurrection.

5. **Extrabiblical Reports—*There's strong confirmation outside the Bible***
Secular accounts confirm the contours of the New Testament record. Thirty-nine ancient sources provide more than one hundred facts about Jesus' life, teachings, death, and resurrection.[3]

6. **Emergence of the Church—*Its birth in Jerusalem supports its claims***
Apart from the resurrection, it's hard to explain the beginnings of the church, which emerged in the very city where Jesus had been crucified a few weeks earlier. The church grew out of the claim that he had come back to life. If false, it could have been easily disproven.

Truth for Today

Execution, the Empty Tomb, Eyewitnesses, Early Accounts, Extrabiblical Reports, and the Emergence of the Church all point to the truth of Jesus' resurrection. Our belief in this miraculous event is built on the bedrock of solid facts and information!

RESPONDING TO THE RESURRECTION

If you declare with your mouth, "Jesus is Lord," and believe in your heart that God raised him from the dead, you will be saved. For it is with your heart that you believe and are justified, and it is with your mouth that you profess your faith and are saved.

ROMANS 10:9–10

JESUS ROSE FROM THE DEAD. *NOW WHAT?*

I remember pondering that question at the end of my almost two-year search for evidence of the resurrection. I reached the point where I knew that the preponderance of the evidence pointed to the truth of a risen Savior, and then asked myself, *Is that it? Do I just acknowledge this truth and keep on living my life as I did before starting this journey?*

Fortunately a verse came to my mind that a friend had shared with me. It was John 1:12, which says, "As many as received Him, to them He gave the right to become children of God, even to those who believe in His name" (NASB). I realized that this verse had three parts, and these can be put into a simple formula that answers the "Now what?" question:

Believe + Receive = Become

Looking at this, I realized that I had already fulfilled the first part. I had come to *believe* that Jesus is the Son of God and proved it by rising from the dead. But John 1:12 showed me that this was not enough. I also needed to *receive* the gift of forgiveness and eternal life that Jesus purchased for me on the cross.

So I got down on my knees and admitted to God my lifetime of sin, and I told him I wanted—right then and there—to receive Jesus as my forgiver and leader. Do you know what happened? By the time I ended that prayer, I was confident that I had *become* a child of God, just as the verse said.

Then, over time, my philosophy, worldview, attitude, values, character, and motives began to change—all for the better. Do you know what else? Yours can too! And so can those of your friends and family members.

All that you—and they—need to do is to *believe* that Jesus is the Son of God as he claimed to be, that he died to pay for your sins, and that he rose to give you life. Then pray to *receive* him as your forgiver and leader, and you will immediately *become* a child of the heavenly Father.

Truth for Today

You undoubtedly know people who could benefit from the simple but powerful truths of this formula: Believe + Receive = Become. Share it with them, asking God to use your words and to draw them to himself.

THE IMPACT OF EASTER

*If Christ has not been raised, your faith is futile; you are
still in your sins. . . . But Christ has indeed been raised
from the dead.*

1 CORINTHIANS 15:17, 20

"I DON'T BELIEVE IN THE RESURRECTION OF CHRIST!"

John was a hard-hitting businessman who seemed spiritually
open, but he was stymied by his doubts. He was meeting with my
coauthor Mark because he had serious questions—issues that he
said were preventing him from becoming a Christian.

"I'm curious," Mark said. "Why don't you believe Jesus rose
from the dead?"

"It just doesn't make sense to me that a dead person could come
back to life," he explained. "Everything I've ever seen supports the
fact that dead people simply stay in the grave and their bodies rot
there—or get eaten by wild dogs. Why should I believe it was any
different for Jesus?"

Mark probed to find out where John was getting his information. As he suspected, John was listening to liberal scholars in
the media who had made careers out of attacking the miraculous
claims of the Bible.

The two men spent an hour discussing the evidence for Jesus'
resurrection—most of which John hadn't heard before. Then Mark
ended their time together by loaning John a book that included a
chapter presenting the case for the resurrection. Then Mark made
a comment that frankly surprised even him.

"John, I know you're a businessman who relates to challenges
and goals. So let me urge you to read that chapter right away so

you can see how strongly the historical evidence supports the resurrection. Then, assuming you accept this to be true, I want to challenge you to become a Christian before Easter, which is only about a month away. That way you'll finally be able to celebrate the holiday for its real meaning."

The look of intensity in John's eyes communicated that he accepted the challenge. A couple weeks later he sent back the book with a note saying he'd read the chapter, then the entire book, and then he'd purchased copies of it for himself and a few skeptical friends!

He obviously found the evidence convincing too, because about two weeks after that, John put his trust in Christ—just a few days before Easter.

Truth for Today

Even a cursory reading of the book of Acts shows that the early church grew like wildfire. But don't overlook that its main message was that Jesus had risen. Lives were changed by that message— and they are still being impacted today.

THE HOPE OF EASTER

Praise be to the God and Father of our Lord Jesus Christ!
In his great mercy he has given us new birth into a living
hope through the resurrection of Jesus Christ from the
dead, and into an inheritance that can never perish, spoil
or fade. This inheritance is kept in heaven for you.

1 PETER 1:3–4

IT'S EASY TO THINK THAT THE HISTORICAL FACTS SURROUNDING
the life, death, and resurrection of Jesus are just that—dry, intellectual truths.

"Sure," we muse, "it's important to know who Jesus was and
what he did, but I'm too busy to get enmeshed in the nuances of
theological discursion. I need information that will make a difference in my life right here, right now."

Then difficulties come or tragedy strikes, and suddenly the
teachings and truths of the Bible seem much more relevant.

My friend and former colleague Rick Warren, the pastor of
Saddleback Church and the author of *The Purpose Driven Life*, has
taught about the truth and relevance of the Bible for decades. But
in recent years he, together with his wife, Kay, discovered anew
the power of Jesus' resurrection. This happened when they went
through the devastating loss of their twenty-seven-year-old son,
Matthew, who took his own life after battling depression and mental illness for many years.

About a year after this unthinkable loss, Rick said, "I've often
been asked, 'How have you made it? How have you kept going in
your pain?' And I've often replied, 'The answer is Easter.'

"You see, the death and the burial and the resurrection of Jesus happened over three days. Friday was the day of suffering and pain and agony. Saturday was the day of doubt and confusion and misery. But *Easter*—that Sunday—was the day of hope and joy and victory.

"And here's the fact of life: you will face these three days over and over and over in your lifetime. And when you do, you'll find yourself asking—as I did—three fundamental questions:

"Number one, 'What do I do in my days of pain?'

"Two, 'How do I get through my days of doubt and confusion?'

"Three, 'How do I get to the days of joy and victory?'

"The answer is Easter. *The answer . . . is Easter.*"[1]

Truth for Today

When Jesus rose from the dead, he not only proved that his claims were true; he also demonstrated that he has power over everything that hinders and holds us down. What challenge, hurt, or struggle should you bring to the triumphant Savior today?

HOLY BOLDNESS

Salvation is found in no one else, for there is no other name under heaven given to mankind by which we must be saved.

Acts 4:12

PETER AND JOHN, INVIGORATED BY JESUS' RESURRECTION AND filled with the Holy Spirit, ventured into Jerusalem. They encountered a man who had been lame from birth. By God's power they healed the man and then pulled him to his feet so everyone would know God had done a miracle. A miracle *in the name of Jesus.*

Peter and John seized the opportunity to tell the crowd about Jesus—that he was the long-awaited Messiah and that he had been put to death but God raised him to life. They also explained that salvation was available to each of them through this risen Savior.

Peter declared: "Repent, then, and turn to God, so that your sins may be wiped out, that times of refreshing may come from the Lord" (Acts 3:19). The people were receptive, and many trusted in Christ that day (Acts 4:4).

The religious leaders, however, weren't happy. They threw Peter and John in jail, and the next day they questioned them about what they had said and done. But Peter, filled with godly courage, declared, "It is by the name of Jesus Christ of Nazareth, whom you crucified but whom God raised from the dead, that this man stands before you healed. . . . Salvation is found in no one else, for there is no other name under heaven given to mankind by which we must be saved" (vv. 10, 12).

The leaders, who were responsible for Jesus' death, ordered Peter and John to stop speaking in his name. Undaunted, they replied, "Which is right in God's eyes: to listen to you, or to him?

You be the judges! As for us, we cannot help speaking about what we have seen and heard" (vv. 19–20).

Talk about holy boldness! These men were on *fire*, and nobody knew how to put them out.

This didn't escape the attention of their enemies. "They saw the courage of Peter and John and . . . took note that these men had been with Jesus" (v. 13).

Peter and John's response? After being released they went back to their brothers and sisters in Christ and prayed, "Lord, consider their threats and *enable your servants to speak your word with great boldness*," and "the place where they were meeting was shaken" (vv. 29, 31, emphasis mine).

Truth for Today

These men "had been with Jesus," were filled with the Holy Spirit, and spoke boldly for God—and God used them powerfully. If you want to be used by God too, then follow their pattern. Spend time with Jesus, let his Spirit lead you, and speak up for God.

PERFORMANCE PLAN

"Be perfect, therefore, as your heavenly Father is perfect."

MATTHEW 5:48

"GOD HELPS THOSE WHO HELP THEMSELVES." THIS IS ONE OF the best-known and most-loved verses anywhere in the world. It's easy to see why; it just feels so, well, *motivational*. Grab your bootstraps. Pull hard in an upward direction. Improve your lot, and God will recognize that you deserve his assistance and will jump in to help.

There's just one problem. This "verse" is not in the Bible.

Thank goodness that the Bible offers us far better news: God helps those who *can't* help themselves. Those who have given up on trying. Who have lost hope. The ones who, as Jesus described, "are weary and burdened" and in need of soul rest (Matthew 11:28).

When things are going well in our lives, we instinctively put our trust in our efforts to do good, to help others, and perhaps to fulfill some list of spiritual obligations. One could call that the Performance Plan, and it plays perfectly into our sense of pride and independence.

But before we get too excited about the Performance Plan, we should look at what the biblical writer James said: "Whoever keeps the whole law and yet stumbles at just one point *is guilty of breaking all of it*" (James 2:10, emphasis mine). He wasn't trying to make his readers feel bad; he was simply giving a needed warning. If we put our faith in the Performance Plan, we're destined for frustration in this life and for deep regret in the next because we'll always fall short of God's infinite standards (Romans 3:23).

Fortunately there's an alternative. It's called the Grace Plan.

You can't earn it; you'll never deserve it. It's offered freely and must be received with empty hands and a repentant heart. It comes through Christ and his death on your behalf. Hebrews 10:14 explains, "By one sacrifice he has made perfect forever those who are being made holy."

You see, the standard is still perfection. But we'll never gain that perfection through our own flawed performance efforts. Rather, we'll gain it by receiving Jesus' self-sacrificial payment on our behalf, extended to us as free, undeserved favor. In other words, *as a gift of grace.*

Truth for Today

The Grace Plan seems almost too good to be true. In fact, that's why many people don't accept God's grace. They just can't believe it could be that easy. Well, it wasn't easy for Jesus, but fortunately, grace is offered freely. We just need to humble ourselves and accept it like a child getting a gift on Christmas—in no way earning it but wholeheartedly receiving it.

THEY'LL KNOW US BY OUR . . . WHAT?

"If anyone comes to me and does not hate father and mother, wife and children, brothers and sisters—yes, even their own life—such a person cannot be my disciple."

LUKE 14:26

"CHRISTIANS CLAIM THAT JESUS ALWAYS PREACHED LOVE," AN atheist said. "But in Luke 14:26 he told his followers to hate their families, and in Matthew 10:35 he said he came to turn father against son and daughter against mother. So much for being a messenger of love!"

I'll admit these statements can be jolting when you first read them. That is, until you understand that Jesus and the Bible used common literary devices just as we do today. English professor Leland Ryken explains:

> Such overstatements are of course not intended to be taken literally. Jesus was not stating a reasoned ethical position when he said that "if anyone comes to me and does not hate his own father and mother and wife and children and brothers and sisters, yes, and even his own life, he cannot be my disciple" (Luke 14:26 ESV). He was using hyperbole to assert the priority that a person must give to God over other relationships.[1]

This interpretation is supported by the parallel passage in Matthew 10:37, which states the same theme, but without hyperbole: "Anyone who loves their father or mother more than me is not worthy of me; anyone who loves their son or daughter more than me is not worthy of me."

And in Luke 12:53 and Matthew 10:35, Jesus merely noted what happens when he reconciles people to God: family members become divided between those who follow him and those who do not. "We must distinguish between the purpose of Christ's coming to earth and the result of it. His design was to bring peace," writes apologists Norman Geisler and Thomas Howe. "However, the immediate consequence of Christ's coming was to divide those who were for Him and those who were against Him—the children of God from the children of this world."[2]

In a similar way Paul used hyperbole when he wrote, "Just as it is written: 'Jacob I loved, but Esau I hated'" (Romans 9:13). He was saying that the sovereign God has the authority to act in a special way toward one group (those descended from Jacob), rather than toward another group (those descended from Esau), although Esau and his descendants received many blessings from God.

None of these passages teach actual hate, nor should they cause us to doubt that God is love.[3]

Truth for Today

God's followers must never love anything more than they love him. Is there something in your life you need to learn to "hate" in comparison to your love for God?

HOW MANY GODS?

The Lord our God, the Lord is one.

Deuteronomy 6:4

"HERE, THEN, IS ETERNAL LIFE," DECLARED JOSEPH SMITH, the founder of the Mormon faith, "to know the only wise and true God; *and you have got to learn how to be gods yourselves*, and to be kings and priests to God, *the same as all gods have done before you*."[1]

In a world filled with religious teachings telling us there are many gods, as the teachings of Mormonism and Hinduism do, the Bible makes a bold claim: there is only one true God.

Here are five reasons it's so important to understand this truth:

1. *God wants us to know who he is.* He is "a jealous God" (Deuteronomy 6:15)—not in a petty sense, but in the appropriate sense of wanting us to know him and to be faithful to him as our maker and redeemer. The New Testament sometimes refers to us, the members of the church, as Christ's bride.[2] And just as a husband would naturally protect his wife and expect her loyalty, God protects us and desires our loyalty.

2. *God wants us to know there are no other gods.* He tells us plainly in Isaiah 43:10–11, "Before me no god was formed, nor will there be one after me. I, even I, am the Lord, and apart from me there is no savior." I don't know how he could have made it any clearer.

3. *God does not want us to be led astray by false gods.* Deuteronomy 13 says that if someone claims to be a prophet but leads people away to worship other gods, then that person is a false prophet, and both he and his message must be rejected. Similarly, the apostle John warned us in 1 John 5:21, "Dear children, keep

yourselves from idols," and an idol is anyone or anything that pulls us away from the true God.

4. *God wants to protect us from putting our hope in anything that will ultimately disappoint us.* We were created to worship—but worshiping the true God is the only path to fulfillment and to a relationship with the Savior who can forgive our sins, answer our prayers, and guide our lives. No other "god" or mere idol can do that.

5. *It is simply appropriate to give the honor and praise that is due to our Creator.* As the psalmist did in Psalm 150, we should "praise him for his surpassing greatness" (v. 2).

Truth for Today

God loves us enough to tell us the truth about who he is—the one and only true God—and to warn us about the futility of following substitutes. And he wants us to love and trust him in return. What are some practical ways you can do that today?

JESUS IS GOD?

In the beginning was the Word, and the Word was with God, and the Word was God. . . . The Word became flesh and made his dwelling among us.

JOHN 1:1, 14

"SCHOLARS CLAIM THAT THE EARLY CHURCH LITERALLY *STOLE* Jesus from His original followers, hijacking His human message, shrouding it in an impenetrable cloak of divinity, and using it to expand their own power," said Dan Brown's character Teabing in the novel *The Da Vinci Code.*[1]

This is a common claim: Jesus was a good but ordinary man who taught wisdom to all who would listen. But after his death his legend grew and, over time, people began to view him as a god, or the Son of God, exalting him in ways he never intended.

An interesting theory, but is it *true*? Consider:

- Isaiah predicted the coming of the Messiah some seven hundred years before Jesus came. He described him as "Wonderful Counselor, *Mighty God, Everlasting Father*, Prince of Peace" (Isaiah 9:6, emphasis mine). And Isaiah 7:14 predicted, "The virgin will conceive and give birth to a son, and will call him *Immanuel*," which means "God with us." Matthew 1:23 tells us this prophecy was fulfilled in Jesus.
- In the Bible worship is reserved for God and God alone. Yet soon after Jesus' birth, the Magi worshiped him (Matthew 2:11).
- As an adult, Jesus received worship from his disciples after calming the storm (Matthew 14:32–33).

- The religious leaders challenged Jesus concerning Sabbath rules. He defended himself saying, "My Father is always at his work to this very day, and I too am working" (John 5:17). These leaders, understanding exactly what Jesus meant, were immediately offended and "tried all the more to kill him; not only was he breaking the Sabbath, but he was even calling God his own Father, making himself equal with God" (John 5:18).
- When Jesus was on trial, the high priest asked him, "'Are you the Messiah, the Son of the Blessed One?' 'I am,' said Jesus. 'And you will see the Son of Man sitting at the right hand of the Mighty One and coming on the clouds of heaven'" (Mark 14:61–62). This was an undeniable claim that he was the divine person prophesied in Daniel 7:13. That's why the priest immediately tore his clothes, and the chief priests and the Sanhedrin all "condemned him as worthy of death" (Mark 14:64).
- When Thomas, who doubted Jesus' resurrection, realized Jesus had truly risen and was standing in front of him, he exclaimed, "My Lord and my God!" (John 20:28). And what was Jesus' response? He blessed Thomas and everyone else who would believe as he did.

Truth for Today

When you add up all the evidence, Jesus' claim to divinity is clear—and he proved it by rising from the dead (Matthew 12:39–40).

IDENTITY MATTERS

"You are from below; I am from above. You are of this world; I am not of this world. I told you that you would die in your sins; if you do not believe that I am he, you will indeed die in your sins."

JOHN 8:23–24

"SO JESUS CLAIMED TO BE GOD. WHY IS THAT SO IMPORTANT?"

Many people are casual when it comes to understanding the identity and nature of Jesus. To them, weighty discussions about the deity of Christ seem above their pay grade. They'd rather stick to the basics and just live out a faith that's easy to understand.

But understand this: *who Jesus is really matters!* If he were merely a good teacher or a prophet of God, then he would have been a dishonest teacher and a false prophet when he made claims to be divine, like the claims we explored in the previous reading.

Furthermore he, a mere human, would have been incapable of fulfilling the role of "the Lamb of God, who takes away the sin of the world" (John 1:29) or being the One who came to "give his life as a ransom for many" (Mark 10:45). In fact, Psalm 49:7 says, "No man can by any means redeem his brother or give to God a ransom for him" (NASB). If Jesus were just a man, then he could not have been our Savior or our Lord.

But look at the facts:

- Against all odds, Jesus fulfilled numerous ancient messianic prophecies (see "If I Were Guessing . . ." and "Prophetic Odds").
- He made it clear he was both Savior and Lord.

- He backed up his claims by living a sinless life, by performing miracles, and especially by rising from the dead just as he had predicted he would.
- He appeared as the risen Savior, reaffirmed his claims and commands, and then ascended into heaven (see "The Case for the Resurrection").
- And this same Jesus looked people in the eye and declared, "You are from below; I am from above. You are of this world; I am not of this world. I told you that you would die in your sins; if you do not believe that I am he, you will indeed die in your sins."

So, in light of these facts, I have an urgent suggestion: Let's take Jesus at his word. Let's believe him who told us he is the Son of God who shared the divine nature of the Father. And let's follow him wholeheartedly as our Savior and Lord.

Truth for Today

Jesus emphasized the importance of his identity as the Son of God, as deity in humanity. Do you have friends or family members who need this information? When will you gently share it with them?

NON-PROPHETS

Dear friends, do not believe every spirit, but test the spirits to see whether they are from God, because many false prophets have gone out into the world.

1 JOHN 4:1

"I BELIEVE IN JESUS, AND YOU BELIEVE IN JESUS. ISN'T THAT enough?"

Well, as Mark Mittelberg says, "I have an uncle, and you have an uncle—but that doesn't mean we have the same uncle! Just because people say they believe in Jesus doesn't necessarily mean they follow the real Savior."

Mark is right. Knowing who Jesus really is—and trusting in the true Jesus—makes all the difference in this life and in the life to come.

Jesus warned that many imitators would come: "If anyone says to you, 'Look, here is the Messiah!' or, 'There he is!' do not believe it. For false messiahs and false prophets will appear and perform great signs and wonders to deceive, if possible, even the elect. See, I have told you ahead of time" (Matthew 24:23–25).

Paul added, "I am afraid that just as Eve was deceived by the serpent's cunning, your minds may somehow be led astray from your sincere and pure devotion to Christ. For if someone comes to you and preaches a Jesus other than the Jesus we preached, . . . you put up with it easily enough" (2 Corinthians 11:3–5).

According to Jesus, many false messiahs will come, and according to Paul, ordinary people—*like us*—can be deceived by a counterfeit. So what can we do to ensure that we stay true to the real Jesus? A few thoughts:

- Don't take everything at face value. Ask people what they mean by "God" as well as who they believe Jesus is.
- Test what teachers say against what the Bible teaches. Whatever God says today will align with what he has said in the past (Acts 17:11).
- Remember that biblical teachers will affirm both the humanity of Jesus (1 John 4:2–3) and the deity of Jesus (Colossians 1:15–20)—and they will submit to him as Savior (1 John 4:14) and Lord (Luke 6:46).
- Pray, asking God's Spirit to guide and protect you as you seek his truth about these matters (John 16:13).

Jesus said, "Ask and it will be given to you; seek and you will find; knock and the door will be opened to you" (Luke 11:9). If we seek him sincerely, he promises to guide us to the truth.

Truth for Today

You can believe and trust God as he leads you by his Word and by his Spirit. So read the Bible today, seek God sincerely, and obey what he commands.

IS THE HOLY SPIRIT A FORCE?

"When he, the Spirit of truth, comes, he will guide you into all the truth. He will not speak on his own; he will speak only what he hears, and he will tell you what is yet to come."

JOHN 16:13

"THE FORCE IS A RIVER FROM WHICH MANY CAN DRINK," SAID Luke Skywalker, "and the training of the Jedi is not the only cup which can catch it." The Force in *Star Wars* is an invisible power that can be harnessed for good or evil, depending on the intent of the one utilizing it.

Unfortunately, many think the same of the Holy Spirit, whom they incorrectly refer to as an "it" rather than "he." These people see the Spirit as a form of energy, not as a person. They view the admonition to "be filled with the Holy Spirit" as roughly equivalent to "May the Force be with you."

Jehovah's Witnesses teach, for example, "The holy spirit is God's power in action, his active force. God sends out his spirit by projecting his energy to any place to accomplish his will."[1]

Compare this to the Bible, where the Holy Spirit is presented both as a person and as divine. Jesus promised in John 14:16–17, for example, "I will ask the Father, and he will give you another advocate to help you and be with you forever—the Spirit of truth. The world cannot accept him, because it neither sees him nor knows him. But you know him, for he lives with you and will be in you." Notice how Jesus used the personal pronouns *he* and *him*. Jesus was not describing a force, but a person.

In John 16:13 Jesus said the Holy Spirit "will guide [the disciples] into all the truth." And in the following verse he said the

Spirit will glorify him. But an energy field neither guides nor glorifies. Those are things only a person can do.

Also, Paul cautioned in Ephesians 4:30, "Do not grieve the Holy Spirit of God." You can't grieve a force—only a person.

Further, in Mark 3:29 Jesus warned anyone who "blasphemes against the Holy Spirit." This shows that the Spirit is both a person and divine (you can blaspheme only God). This is confirmed in the story of Ananias and Sapphira (Acts 5), where *lying to the Holy Spirit* (v. 3) is used interchangeably with *lying to God* (v. 4).

The Holy Spirit is no mere force; he is a divine person and the third person of the Trinity.

Truth for Today

The Holy Spirit is God, and he wants to "guide you into all the truth." How are you listening today?

TRI-UNITY

"Therefore go and make disciples of all nations, baptizing them in the name of the Father and of the Son and of the Holy Spirit."

MATTHEW 28:19

"HOW CAN YOU BELIEVE IN THE DOCTRINE OF THE TRINITY when the word *trinity* isn't even in the Bible?" This is a common objection, and it seems compelling until you realize that many other terms, like *divinity, omniscience,* and *incarnation* are not in the Bible either, but these concepts are all clearly taught in Scripture. The real question is whether the *concept* of the Trinity is taught in the Bible.

Let's look at four biblical truths:

1. There Is Only One True God

"Hear, O Israel: The LORD our God, the LORD is one" (Deuteronomy 6:4). This is the *Shema*, the central teaching of Judaism (also see Isaiah 43:10–11). Jesus said the same thing in Mark 12:29, and the apostle Paul affirmed that "there is but one God" (1 Corinthians 8:6).

2. The Father Is God

"[Jesus] received honor and glory from God the Father when the voice came to him from the Majestic Glory, saying, 'This is my Son, whom I love; with him I am well pleased'" (2 Peter 1:17). This and many other passages show that the heavenly Father is God.

3. The Son Is God

We saw in the entry "Jesus Is God?" that Jesus claimed divinity and backed it up by rising from the dead. Jesus also said, "Before

Abraham was born, I am!" (John 8:58), affirming his preexistence while also applying to himself the divine "I AM" name for God from Exodus 3:14. He also said, "I and the Father are one" (John 10:30), meaning that they are one in essence or nature.[1]

Jesus is called "our great God and Savior" (Titus 2:13). In him "all the fullness of the Deity lives in bodily form" (Colossians 2:9). Jesus is also described as the Creator in John 1:3 and Colossians 1:16.

4. The Holy Spirit Is God

We saw in "Is the Holy Spirit a Force?" that the Holy Spirit is a divine person. He possesses the attributes of deity (1 Corinthians 2:10–11), and he is associated with God in creation (Genesis 1:2) and with the other members of the Trinity (Matthew 28:19).

The biblical doctrine of the Trinity uniquely accounts for all four of these biblical truths; it shows that God is a "Tri-Unity": "Tri-" (three persons, as in points 2–4 above) in "Unity" (one God, as in point 1 above).

In other words, there is *one God* who eternally exists in *three persons*: Father, Son, and Holy Spirit.

Truth for Today

These four teachings are clear, and they compellingly point to the biblical doctrine of the Trinity. We worship one true God, who eternally exists as Father, Son, and Holy Spirit.

THREE EQUALS ONE?

"For my thoughts are not your thoughts, neither are your ways my ways," declares the LORD. *"As the heavens are higher than the earth, so are my ways higher than your ways and my thoughts than your thoughts."*

ISAIAH 55:8–9

"LET ME GET THIS STRAIGHT," SAID A JEHOVAH'S WITNESS. "You believe the Father is God," he said, grasping his index finger. "And you think that Jesus is God," he continued, grasping a second finger. "And then you say the Holy Spirit is God," he added, grasping a third finger. Then, holding up three fingers he concluded, "It seems you've got three gods!"

"Well, it doesn't really matter what I believe," Mark Mittelberg replied. "What matters is what God has revealed about his nature. And as I've shown you, the Bible teaches that the Father, Son, and Holy Spirit are each God, yet it also teaches that there is only one God. Somehow we've got to hold to all of these biblical truths without compromising any of them. Unfortunately, what you've been taught compromises the deity of Christ as well as the deity and personhood of the Holy Spirit."

"But three cannot equal one," the representative of the Watch Tower Society shot back.

"That's true—and I'm not claiming they do," said Mark. "Rather, I'm trying to show what the Bible reveals: that God is one in essence, yet he exists eternally in three persons. As my mentor used to explain it, 'He is one *what* in three *whos.*'

"It's similar to Genesis 2:24," Mark continued, "where the Bible says when a man and a woman join in marriage, they become one flesh. But obviously they don't become one person. They're still a man and a woman. So, biblically speaking, they have become one flesh but remain two people. Or, as my mentor might have put it, 'one *what* in two *whos*.' It's not a perfect analogy, but it does show how something can be singular in one sense and plural in another."

"That's an interesting illustration," admitted the man, "but I just can't see why God would make it so complicated."

"Keep in mind," explained Mark, "that this isn't an idea God invented for our ease of consumption. It is his revelation of who he actually is. When we realize we're talking about the eternal, almighty Creator of the universe, it shouldn't surprise us that he is a being whose nature is a bit difficult for our finite minds to fully grasp!"

Truth for Today

Our God is a being much greater than we can fully comprehend. Yet his message is so simple even a child can understand it: "Jesus loves me, this I know . . ."

THE IMPLICATIONS OF GOD'S NATURE

May the grace of the Lord Jesus Christ, and the love of God, and the fellowship of the Holy Spirit be with you all.

2 CORINTHIANS 13:14

"I SEE THAT THE DOCTRINE OF THE TRINITY IS TAUGHT IN THE Bible. But how does this affect my life?"

Great question. Let's look at three practical implications of the biblical doctrine of God.

1. Knowing the True God

Jesus said, "Now this is eternal life: that they know you, the only true God, and Jesus Christ, whom you have sent" (John 17:3). But in order to know the true God, we need to understand and embrace what he has revealed about himself even if it's difficult to grasp fully. And as we've seen, he has revealed that he is the Father, the Son, and the Holy Spirit: one God who exists eternally in three persons.

2. Understanding Real Love

The Bible also tells us that God, by definition, is *love* (1 John 4:8). But apart from the truth of the Trinity, it's hard to imagine how this could be. For example, before the creation of the angels and humans, who would there have been for God to love? If he were a singular Being, as the Unitarians claim, then there would have been be no one else to relate to. This is a conundrum for anyone who holds to that viewpoint, but it's not a problem if we embrace the Trinity.

"Love is rooted in God because each person of the Trinity loves and relates to the others. God the Father loves God the Son. The Son loves the Father and the Holy Spirit, and God the Holy Spirit loves both the Son and the Father," said former Muslim Abdu Murray.[1]

Our ability to love genuinely, therefore, flows out of the very nature of God.

3. Understanding the Source of Community

In that same vein, have you ever wondered why we as humans are so incurably relational—and why we are so lost when our relationships are fractured? It's because we were, according to Genesis 1:27, created in the image of God. This means we share certain similarities with the triune God who has forever enjoyed the loving relationship of the three persons in the Godhead.

In other words, he created us to have similar kinds of relationships with him as well as with our fellow human beings.

Truth for Today

There really are important implications in the doctrine of the Trinity: it points us to the true God, to true love, and to the source and model of true community. Knowing this, how can you better reflect his nature in your relationships today?

WHAT IF SCIENTISTS CREATED LIFE?

God made the wild animals according to their kinds, the livestock according to their kinds, and all the creatures that move along the ground according to their kinds. And God saw that it was good.

GENESIS 1:25

WITH ADVANCES IN MODERN SCIENCE, THERE IS INCREASING speculation that scientists will one day be able to produce life in a laboratory.

"Then," some assume, "we'll no longer need to hypothesize that there's a God, since we will have proven that life can emanate without supernatural intervention."

Have you heard this argument? Do you fear that science will make such a breakthrough? Might it cause you to doubt your faith?

Not so fast. This rationale flows from neither good logic nor good theology. On the theological front, Dr. J. Oliver Buswell wrote back in the early 1960s, "The Bible nowhere teaches that man cannot by physical and chemical processes make living, self-propagating organisms out of inorganic material. I am no biochemist. I doubt that men will, as they say, 'create life.' But I have nothing at stake so far as my Christian faith is concerned."[1]

On the logical front, consider what Mark Mittelberg learned in the early 1980s when he heard Dr. A. E. Wilder-Smith, a celebrated European chemist with three earned PhDs, teach in California. "Dr. Wilder-Smith explained," Mark recalls, "that secular scientists often talk as though life came about through this formula:

Matter + Energy + Time = Life

"However," Wilder-Smith went on, "when scientists go into their labs and try to produce life, they add another ingredient—one they often don't think about. The formula they really use is:

Matter + Energy + Time + *Ideas* = Life

"In other words, they're not just throwing all of the ingredients into a blender, switching it to the highest setting, and hoping life will pop out at the end. Rather, they're applying the best of scientific knowledge to selecting the elements necessary for living matter as well as the conditions that will be conducive for life to flourish.

"Putting it another way, Wilder-Smith told us that they are actually following the creation model," Mark continued. "They're trying to replicate what God did. And if they finally succeed, it'll only serve to reinforce what the Bible says—that *God* created life."[2]

So fear not; science is our friend. All truth is God's truth. And, ultimately, the "book of nature" will reveal the same realities as the "book of Scripture."

Truth for Today

Jesus said in John 8:32, "You will know the truth, and the truth will set you free." As followers of God and lovers of truth, we have nothing to fear from what can be learned through science.

FAITH IS . . .

Now faith is confidence in what we hope for and assurance about what we do not see. . . . And without faith it is impossible to please God, because anyone who comes to him must believe that he exists and that he rewards those who earnestly seek him.

HEBREWS 11:1, 6

"FAITH IS," DECLARED ATHEIST SAM HARRIS, "GENERALLY NOTHING more than the permission religious people give one another to believe things strongly without evidence."[1]

I once heard Christian author Jay Kesler say that he often says this to atheists: "Tell me what God you don't believe in. Maybe I don't believe in him either."

He makes a good point. Often what people reject is not the biblical concept of God at all. Rather, it's a caricature of God that has been concocted by culture or even in the person's own mind.

The same is true of *faith*. Many people accept the caricature of faith presented by Harris and other God-deniers—that it is belief "without evidence." Or, as Mark Twain quipped a century earlier, "Faith is believing what you know ain't so."[2]

Paraphrasing Kesler, my response is this: "Tell me what kind of *faith* you don't believe in. Maybe I don't believe in it either." Biblical faith is not irrational trust. It's not a blind leap in the dark nor a willful rejection of evidence in order to cling to a sentimental superstition or tradition.

What is faith? Probably the best synonym for faith is *trust*—we put our trust in something we're convinced is real or true. And how are we convinced as to what we should put our trust in? By reliable information and evidence.

Jesus challenged his listeners to consider the evidence of his miraculous actions: "Do not believe me unless I do the works of my Father. But if I do them, even though you do not believe me, *believe the works*, that you may know and understand that the Father is in me, and I in the Father" (John 10:37–38, emphasis mine).

Later, Jesus convinced the disciples of his resurrection when he "presented himself to them and *gave many convincing proofs that he was alive*. He appeared to them over a period of forty days and spoke about the kingdom of God" (Acts 1:3, emphasis mine). And he was willing to show Thomas the scars in his hands and side in order to give him confidence that he was indeed Jesus, risen from the dead (John 20:26–27).

Truth for Today

We should be careful to trust only in things proven trustworthy. The Bible tells us to "test everything. . . . Hold on to what is good" (1 Thessalonians 5:21 NLT).

BELIEF THAT vs. BELIEF IN

"For God so loved the world that he gave his one and only Son, that whoever believes in him shall not perish but have eternal life."

JOHN 3:16

THIS VERSE IS PROBABLY THE BEST-KNOWN PASSAGE IN THE Bible. It is also one of the most misunderstood.

Many people reduce it in their minds to a superficial understanding of *believing*, as in "I believe Jesus was a historical figure." A good man. A wise teacher. Maybe even a prophet or the long-awaited Messiah. Some will even go so far as to acknowledge Jesus died on the cross and rose from the dead three days later, but they keep it at the intellectual "belief *that*" level.

The problem is, the context of John 3:16 shows that God requires more than just a nodding of our heads in agreement with the basic facts about his Son. Yes, that's an important first step, but we need to go beyond merely believing *that* Jesus is who he claimed he is, to actually believing *in* Jesus. The Greek word that is translated in the verse as *believe* literally means "to be persuaded of . . . to place confidence in, to trust. . . . [It is] reliance upon, not mere credence."[1]

Mark Mittelberg explains this with an illustration that has helped many people. He says, "When this church service is over, I'm heading to the airport to fly back home. But it's not enough for me to sit in the terminal and believe that airplanes fly. Just acknowledging the soundness of aviation science will never get me home. I have to go beyond mere belief *that* airplanes fly to a personal belief *in* the particular airplane that's heading to my city—demonstrated by climbing on board. It's that act of trust that will ultimately get me where I want to go.

"Similarly," Mark continues, "we all need to go beyond merely believing that Jesus is the Son of God who died on the cross for our sins. We must take the next step and trust in him personally, asking him to forgive our sins and to lead our lives. That is the equivalent of 'climbing on board' with Jesus in a way that will ultimately get us where we want to go spiritually."

Truth for Today

Believing *that* Jesus is the Savior of the world is a good start. But we need to make sure we've moved beyond just nodding our heads to the basic facts about Jesus and have actually put our trust *in* him as our forgiver, leader, and friend. Then we need to help our loved ones do the same!

BIBLICAL PROPHETS vs. MUHAMMAD

"This," said the LORD, "is so that they may believe that the LORD, the God of their fathers—the God of Abraham, the God of Isaac and the God of Jacob—has appeared to you."

EXODUS 4:5

GOD'S PROPHETS PERFORMED MIRACLES TO ESTABLISH THEIR credentials.

Moses said to God in Exodus 4:1, "What if they do not believe me or listen to me and say, 'The LORD did not appear to you'?" God told Moses to throw his staff to the ground, and the staff instantly turned into a snake. Then God told him to pick up the snake, and it turned back into a staff. God explained in verse 5, "This . . . is so that they may believe that the LORD, the God of their fathers—the God of Abraham, the God of Isaac and the God of Jacob—has appeared to you."

A similar thing happened to Elijah on Mount Carmel. During his showdown with the prophets of Baal, God sent down fire from heaven to confirm that he was the true God and Elijah was his prophet (1 Kings 18:16–39).

Jesus said, "Do not believe me unless I do the works of my Father. But if I do them, even though you do not believe me, believe the works, that you may know and understand that the Father is in me, and I in the Father" (John 10:37–38). And Jesus *did* the miraculous works he referred to. Even the Pharisee Nicodemus conceded, "Rabbi, we know that you are a teacher who has come from God. For no one could perform the signs you are doing if God were not with him" (John 3:2).

We can see such confirmation repeatedly in the lives of Jesus and the biblical prophets. But it never happened in the life of Muhammad, the founder of Islam. Muhammad believed Jesus was a prophet who performed miracles, including raising the dead. Muslims also believe Moses and Elijah performed miracles.

However, according to the Qur'an, when unbelievers challenged Muhammad to perform a miracle, he refused. He merely said they should read a chapter in the Qur'an (Sura 2:118; 3:181–84; 4:153; 6:8, 9, 37).

So, unlike Jesus, Muhammad never did miracles. It wasn't until approximately 150 to 200 years after Muhammad's death that some of his followers began to come up with stories of miracles and ascribe them to him.[1]

Truth for Today

The biblical prophets—and Jesus in particular—showed with their miracles and their messages that they were from God. Knowing this, we should read and heed what they said.

UNIVERSAL FATHERHOOD?

Who among the gods is like you, LORD? Who is like you—
majestic in holiness, awesome in glory, working wonders?

EXODUS 15:11

"SOME PEOPLE SAY THAT WHEN YOU STRIP AWAY EVERYTHING, all the world religions are essentially teaching the universal fatherhood of God and the universal brotherhood of humankind," I said to Christian apologist Ravi Zacharias. "That would mean that all the world's faith systems are equally valid."[1]

Zacharias shook his head, his face registering dismay. "Only someone who doesn't understand the world religions would claim they basically teach the same thing," he said. "What do they mean by the universal fatherhood of God when Buddhism doesn't even claim that there is a God? What do we mean by the fatherhood of God when Shankara, one of the most respected Hindu philosophers, said theism is only a child's way to ultimately get to the top, where you find out God is not distinct from you? What then does the fatherhood of God mean?" Zacharias continued. "It's an illusion. This fatherhood of God is not a trans-religious doctrine.

"Secondly, the brotherhood of humanity—yes, we are brothers and sisters as fellow human beings, but the only reason we are is because we have been fashioned by God. Once you take that foundation away," he said with a chuckle, "then brotherhood ends up with more hoods than brothers! In sum, Islam, Buddhism, Hinduism, and Christianity are not saying the same thing. They are distinct and mutually exclusive religious doctrines. They all cannot be true at the same time."

However, Zacharias concluded, "Jesus Christ has made it clear that the eternal truths of God may be known. Jesus Christ is the center-piece of the gospel—in him, all of truth came together. So while there may be aspects of truth elsewhere, the sum total of truth is in Christ."

It was clear in my conversation with Zacharias that he is a very wise man. And, as I reflected on this last comment about Jesus and truth, I concluded that Jesus' wisdom would agree with him. Jesus was, after all, the One who said, "I am the way and *the truth* and the life. No one comes to the Father except through me" (John 14:6, emphasis mine).

Truth for Today

The other faith systems may not teach the truth about God the Father, but ours does. Why not spend some extra time today getting to know him better?

THE PROBLEM OF EVIL

The LORD is close to the brokenhearted and saves those who are crushed in spirit.

PSALM 34:18

"GOD IS GREAT AND GOD IS GOOD, AND WE THANK HIM FOR our food. *Ah-men.*"

Mark Mittelberg remembers singing this prayer with his family before meals as he was growing up. "The tune was monotonous," he recalls, "but the message was profound. God is both good and great—and he is worthy of our thanksgiving and praise."

Yes, the message is profound and, these days, under attack. The late Christopher Hitchens wrote a bestselling book titled *God Is Not Great.* And many people today question God's goodness as well.

The doubts usually come under the banner of the problem of evil: If God were really good, then he would not want evil to exist. And if he were really great, then he would have the power to vanquish evil. But evil abounds, so God must lack goodness or greatness—or not exist at all.

Thus many people have lost their confidence in the God of the Bible, and some of them have turned to agnosticism or atheism. The presence of evil is an important question, and we'll address it over a number of readings.

For today, let me just say this: If you're in the midst of pain or some kind of suffering, then what you need most are not intellectual answers. Discussions about why God allows these things might just make you feel worse. What you need right now are not ideas about God, *but God himself.*

Jesus said in John 16:33 that when we're struggling with troubles in our lives, we can take heart because, ultimately, he has overcome this world. He said in Matthew 11:28 that when we're burdened and weary, we can come to him for rest. Psalm 34:18 reminds God's people that "The Lord is close to the brokenhearted and saves those who are crushed in spirit." And Hebrews 4:15–16 assures us that Jesus can empathize with our struggles and that, when we come to him, we will "receive mercy and find grace to help us in our time of need."

In the next reading we'll begin to explore answers to the problem of evil. But when you are hurting, what you need most is to draw close to the One who has already suffered, who overcame, and who stands ready to comfort and help you during your time of difficulty.

Truth for Today

Ultimately the answer to pain, suffering, and evil is not an answer at all. It's a person. Jesus understands your pain, he loves you, and he wants to walk with you through your season of grief. "Come near to God," James 4:8 encourages us, "and he will come near to you."

JESUS TOLD THE TRUTH

"I have told you these things, so that in me you may have peace. In this world you will have trouble. But take heart! I have overcome the world."

JOHN 16:33

WE LIVE IN A WORLD THAT IS MARKED BY TRAGEDY, PAIN, AND suffering. This is not something we can resolve with a tidy answer that will make us feel good about our trying situation. However, as I've contemplated that problem of pain, I've found what I sometimes refer to as "five points of light" that have helped illuminate this challenging matter. I'll share those thoughts in the readings that follow this one.

But first let me share an insight from my friend Mark Mittelberg. He reminds us that evil and suffering, as painful as they can be, are exactly what Jesus predicted we would experience. "In this world you will have trouble," Jesus said in John 16:33. He didn't say we *might* have trouble; he guaranteed it.

This statement, of course, reflects the broader biblical worldview that tells us when Adam and Eve sinned back in the garden, their act brought a curse upon the earth (Genesis 3). This curse has resulted in untold pain and suffering throughout the ages. Ever since then "the whole creation has been groaning" (Romans 8:22), waiting for the day when Christ will return and bring things back to his original plan: a planet without sin, pain, or suffering. At that time, "He will wipe every tear from their eyes. There will be no more death or mourning or crying or pain, for the old order of things has passed away" (Revelation 21:4).

This comforting truth, of course, does not take away our

current troubles, but it puts them in perspective and gives us the assurance we're following an honest Savior. He is unlike the Eastern religious teachers who tell us pain and suffering are illusory and that we can overcome them with positive beliefs alone. All we have to do is reflect upon our own lives and the lives of the people we know—not to mention watching the evening news—to know Jesus was right and suffering is real.

It is much better, therefore, to follow the One who tells us the truth and who then helps us "take heart" because he has "overcome the world" (John 16:33).

Truth for Today

Proverbs 27:6 tells us, "Wounds from a friend can be trusted, but an enemy multiplies kisses." Jesus treats us like friends when he tells us the truth about the world we live in, and then he helps us overcome the trials we face.

FOLLOW THE LIGHT

*How long, Lord? Will you forget me forever? How long will
you hide your face from me?*

Psalm 13:1

THE QUESTION OF WHY THERE IS EVIL GOES BACK THOUSANDS
of years. Job and the writers of the Psalms asked it, and it was
just as relevant during the twentieth century when we witnessed
two world wars, the Holocaust, genocides in the Soviet Union
and China, devastating famines in Africa, the killing fields of
Cambodia, the emergence of AIDS, the genocide in Rwanda, and
the ethnic cleansing of Kosovo. The twenty-first century hasn't
started any better. There was 9/11, slaughters in Syria and Iraq, and
the ongoing fighting throughout the Middle East.

Why all of *this* if there's a loving and powerful God?

Several years ago I commissioned a national survey and asked
people what they'd say if they could ask God one question. Their
top response: "Why is there suffering in the world?"

I can't stand in the shoes of God and give a complete answer.
"For now we see only a reflection as in a mirror; then we shall see
face to face," Paul said. "Now I know in part; then I shall know
fully, even as I am fully known" (1 Corinthians 13:12).

When we ask why certain things happen, we may not get the
full answer in this world. But even though we can't understand
everything about suffering, we *can* understand *some* things.

One time Leslie and I were driving from Chicago to Door
County, Wisconsin. We were motoring up the highway in the dark
when it started raining heavily. We hit dense fog, and I could barely
see the white stripe on the edge of the road. I couldn't stop because

I was afraid someone might come along and rear-end us. It was a tense situation.

Then a truck appeared in front of us, and we could clearly see his taillights through the haze. He had fog lamps in front and was traveling at a confident and deliberate pace. So I knew if we could just follow those taillights, we'd be headed in the right direction.

The same is true in understanding tragedy and suffering. We may not be able to make out all the peripheral details of why, but there are some key biblical "points of light" that we can follow. They will lead us in the right direction, toward some conclusions that I believe can help satisfy our hearts and souls.

We'll look at those points of light in the readings that follow.

Truth for Today

Evil is real, and its effects are ugly. We may not comprehend why God allows it, but we can trust and follow him as he leads us through it.

POINTS OF LIGHT, PART 1

This is the message we have heard from him and declare to you: God is light; in him there is no darkness at all.

1 JOHN 1:5

POINT 1: GOD IS NOT THE CREATOR OF EVIL AND SUFFERING.

People ask: "Why didn't God just create a world without tragedy, pain, and suffering?" The answer is, *He did!* Genesis 1:31 says: "God saw all that he had made, and it was very good."

But if God is not the author of these things, where did they come from? When God created humans, he made us beings who could give and receive love. But this entailed giving us the freedom *not* to love. Why? Because love always involves a choice.

When my daughter was little, she had a doll with a string in its back, and when you pulled it, the doll said, "I love you." Did that doll love my daughter? Of course not. It was programmed to say those words. To really experience love, the doll would need to have been able to choose genuinely to love or not to love.

So in order for us to experience real love, God bestowed on us free will. But, unfortunately, humankind has abused this freedom by rejecting God and walking away from him. And that has resulted in the introduction of two kinds of evil into the world: *moral evil* (sin and the direct results of it) and *natural evil* (things like wildfires, earthquakes, tornadoes, and hurricanes that cause suffering to people). But these too are the indirect result of sin being allowed into the world.

As Cliffe Knechtle explained, "When we human beings told God to shove off, he partially honored our request. Nature began to revolt. The earth was cursed. Genetic breakdown and disease began. Pain and death became part of the human experience."[1]

The Bible says it's because of sin that nature was corrupted and "thorns and thistles" entered the world. Romans 8:22 says, "We know that the whole creation has been groaning as in the pains of childbirth right up to the present time." In other words, nature itself longs for redemption.

Let's make this clear once more: God did not create evil and suffering, though he did create the potential for evil to enter the world. That was the only way to create the potential for genuine love. But it was people, abusing their free will, who brought that potential evil into reality.

Truth for Today

James 1:13 tells us, "When tempted, no one should say, 'God is tempting me.' For God cannot be tempted by evil, nor does he tempt anyone." So we can't blame God for sin. But we can turn to him for help in overcoming it.

POINTS OF LIGHT, PART 2

We know that in all things God works for the good of those
who love him, who have been called according to his purpose.

ROMANS 8:28

POINT 2: THOUGH SUFFERING ISN'T GOOD, GOD CAN USE IT TO ACCOMPLISH GOOD.

God does accomplish good through our suffering by fulfilling his promise in Romans 8:28. Notice the verse doesn't say God *causes* evil and suffering but that he promises to bring good out of it. And the verse doesn't say we will see immediately or even in this life how God has caused good to emerge. Remember, we see things only dimly in this world. And notice that God doesn't make this promise to everyone. He pledges to take the bad circumstances that befall us and cause good to emerge *if* we're committed to following him.

The Old Testament gives a great example of this in the story of Joseph, who went through terrible suffering: He was sold into slavery by his brothers, unfairly accused of a crime, and falsely imprisoned. Finally, after an extended time in prison, he was placed in a role of great authority where he could save the lives of his family and many others.

This is what Joseph said to his brothers in Genesis 50:20: "You intended to harm me, but God intended it for good to accomplish what is now being done, the saving of many lives." And if you're committed to God, he promises he will take whatever pain you're experiencing and draw something good from it.

You might say, "Not in my circumstances. The harm was too great; the damage, too extreme; the depth of my suffering, too crushing. In my case there's no way God can cause any good to emerge."

But listen to what a wise man told me: "God took the very worst thing that has ever happened in the history of the universe—*deicide*, or the death of God on the cross—and turned it into the very best thing that has happened in the history of the universe: the opening up of heaven to all who follow him."

If God can take the very worst circumstance imaginable and turn it into the very best situation possible, can he not take the negative circumstances of your life and create something good from them?

He can, and he will.

Truth for Today

God can use our suffering to draw us to himself, to mold and sharpen our character, to influence others for him. He can draw good from our pain in a myriad of ways if we trust and follow him.

POINTS OF LIGHT, PART 3

The Lord is not slow in keeping his promise, as some
understand slowness. Instead he is patient with you, not
wanting anyone to perish, but everyone to come to repentance.

2 PETER 3:9

POINT 3: THE DAY IS COMING WHEN SUFFERING WILL CEASE AND GOD WILL JUDGE EVIL.

People often ask, "If God has the power to eradicate evil and suffering, then why doesn't he do it?" The answer is that just because he hasn't done it yet doesn't mean he won't do it. I recently wrote my first novel, *The Ambition.* How do you think I'd feel if someone read only half of it, and then slammed it down and said, "Well, Lee did a terrible job with that book. There are too many loose ends with the plot. He didn't resolve all the issues with the characters."

I'd protest, "Hey! You read only half the book!"

And the Bible says that the story of this world isn't over yet. It says the day will come when sickness and pain will be eradicated and people will be held accountable for the evil they've committed. Judgment Day is coming, and justice will then be served in a perfect way. That day will arrive, but it's not here yet.

Fortunately, the God who will bring judgment is also patient. He said to Moses, "Yahweh! The LORD! The God of compassion and mercy! I am slow to anger and filled with unfailing love and faithfulness. I lavish unfailing love to a thousand generations. I forgive iniquity, rebellion, and sin. But I do not excuse the guilty" (Exodus 34:6–7 NLT).

So what's holding God up? One answer might be *you* or some-one you know. He's actually delaying the consummation of history in anticipation that we, or some of our friends, will yet put our trust in him and spend eternity in heaven with him. He's delaying everything out of his love for people.

That is why Peter told us, "The Lord is not slow in keeping his promise, as some understand slowness. Instead he is patient with you, not wanting anyone to perish, but everyone to come to repentance" (2 Peter 3:9).

To me, that's strong evidence of a loving God; he cares that much for us and for others in our lives.

Truth for Today

Are you in the midst of a hard time? Listen, and heed what he says. Hebrews 3:7–8 tells us, "The Holy Spirit says: 'Today, if you hear his voice, do not harden your hearts.'" Keep trusting in God, and he will ultimately bring you through your time of suffering.

POINTS OF LIGHT, PART 4

I consider that our present sufferings are not worth comparing with the glory that will be revealed in us.

ROMANS 8:18

POINT 4: OUR SUFFERING PALES COMPARED TO WHAT GOD HAS IN STORE FOR US.

I don't want to minimize pain and suffering, but it helps to take a long-term perspective. Paul, who suffered through beatings, stonings, shipwrecks, imprisonments, rejection, hunger, thirst, and homelessness, began 2 Corinthians 4:17 like this: "For our light and momentary troubles . . ."

Wait a second. *Light and momentary troubles?* Five times Paul was whipped with thirty-nine lashes; three times he was beaten to a bloody pulp by rods. But he said, "For our light and momentary troubles are achieving for us an eternal glory that far outweighs them all."

Paul also wrote, "I consider that our present sufferings are not worth comparing with the glory that will be revealed in us" (Romans 8:18).

Think of it this way. Let's say on the first day of the year you had an awful day. You had an emergency root canal at the dentist, and the office ran out of painkillers. You crashed your car and had no insurance. Your stock portfolio took a nosedive. Your spouse got sick. A friend betrayed you. It was like that children's book *Alexander and the Terrible, Horrible, No Good, Very Bad Day.*

But then every other day for the rest of the year is terrific. Your relationship with God is close and real. A friend wins the lottery and gives you $100 million. You get promoted to your dream job. *Time* magazine names you "Person of the Year." You have your first child, and he's healthy and strong. Your marriage is idyllic, your health is fabulous, and you take a six-month vacation in Tahiti.

Then next New Year's Day someone asks, "So, how was your year?"

You'd say, "It was wonderful!"

And they'd say, "But didn't it start out bad?"

You'd think back and say, "You're right. But when I put everything in context, it's been a great year."

Maybe that's a good analogy for heaven. This is not to deny the pain in your life. It might be terrible. Maybe you're suffering from a physical ailment or heartache. But in heaven, after 354,484,545 days of pure bliss—and infinitely more to come—if someone asked, "So, how has your existence been?" you'd say, "It has been absolutely wonderful! Words can't describe the joy and fulfillment!"

Truth for Today

God promises a time when there will be no more crying, no more tears, and no more pain and suffering—a time when we will be reunited with God in perfect harmony forever. Isn't that worth hanging on for?

POINTS OF LIGHT, PART 5

See to it, brothers and sisters, that none of you has a sinful, unbelieving heart that turns away from the living God. But encourage one another daily, as long as it is called "Today," so that none of you may be hardened by sin's deceitfulness.

HEBREWS 3:12–13

POINT 5: WE DECIDE WHETHER TO TURN BITTER OR TURN TO GOD FOR PEACE AND COURAGE.

We have all seen how the same suffering that causes one person to reject God and to become hard, angry, and sullen can cause another person to turn to God—to become gentler, more loving, and more tender, willing to reach out compassionately to help people who are in pain. One person who loses a child to a drunk driver turns inward in chronic rage and despair; another turns outward to help others by founding Mothers Against Drunk Driving.

As one thinker said: "I believe all suffering is at least potential good, an opportunity for good. It's up to our free choice to actualize that potential. Not all of us benefit from suffering and learn from it, because that's up to us."

We make the choice either to run away from God or to run to him. But what happens if we run to him? We looked earlier at what Jesus said: "I have said this to you, so that in me you may have peace. In the world you face persecution. But take courage; I have conquered the world!" (John 16:33 NRSV).

In other words, Jesus offers us the very things we need when we're hurting: *peace* to deal with our present and *courage* to deal with our future. How? By overcoming the world! Through his own suffering, death, and resurrection, he has deprived this world of its ultimate power over us.

But we must make the decision to trust him. British church leader Galvin Reid tells about meeting a young man who is a great example of this. The young man had fallen down a flight of stairs as a baby and shattered his back. He had been in and out of hospitals his whole life—and yet he made the astounding comment that he thinks God is fair. Reid asked him, "How old are you?" The boy said, "Seventeen." Reid asked, "How many years have you spent in hospitals?" The boy said, "Thirteen years." The pastor said with astonishment, "And you think that is fair?" The boy replied with buoyant enthusiasm: "Well, *God has all eternity to make it up to me.*"

Truth for Today

Like the boy in the story, we must reject bitterness and look to God for his peace and courage. What problems do you need to bring to him today?

THE ULTIMATE LIGHT

"I have come into the world as a light, so that no one who believes in me should stay in darkness."

JOHN 12:46

I HOPE THESE FIVE POINTS OF LIGHT HAVE HELPED GIVE YOU perspective and hope in the midst of the pain and struggles in your life.

Let me finish the story of Leslie's and my drive through the fog in Wisconsin. We were following the taillights of that truck when the fog slowly began to lift, the rain began to let up, and we entered a town. Things were becoming clearer, and we could see better. As we rounded a curve, silhouetted against the night sky, guess what we saw. We saw the steeple of a church topped by the cross of Christ.

After driving through the confusion of the fog for so long, that image struck me with poignancy I'll never forget. After all, it was through the cross that Jesus conquered the world for us.

A wise man once told me that God's ultimate answer to suffering isn't an explanation; it's the incarnation. Suffering is a personal problem, and it demands a personal response. God isn't some distant, detached, and disinterested deity; he entered into our world and personally experienced our pain. Jesus is there with us at the lowest places of our lives.

Are you broken? He was broken, like bread, for us. *Are you despised?* He was despised and rejected. *Do you cry out that you can't take any more?* He was a man of sorrows and acquainted with grief. *Did someone betray you?* He was sold out by his friend. *Are your most tender relationships broken?* He loved and he was rejected. *Did people turn from you?* They hid their faces from him. *Does he descend into all of our hells?* Yes, he does. From the depths of a Nazi death camp, Corrie ten Boom wrote, "There is no pit so deep that God's love is not deeper still."[1] Every tear we shed becomes his.

Then this wise man explained that God doesn't just know about your troubles and sympathize with you in them. After all, any close friend can sit beside you, comfort you, and empathize with you. No, Jesus is much closer than your closest friend. If you've put your trust in him, then he is *in* you. Therefore your sufferings are his sufferings; your sorrow is his sorrow.

Truth for Today

When tragedy strikes, as it will; when suffering comes, as it will; when you're wrestling with pain, as you will; and when you make the choice to run into his arms, here's what you're going to discover: *peace* to deal with the present, *courage* to deal with your future, and the incredible *hope* of eternal life with God in heaven.

THE DENIAL OF EVIL

*In those days there was no king in Israel; everyone did
what was right in his own eyes.*

JUDGES 17:6 NKJV

WE'VE BEEN ADDRESSING THE PROBLEM OF EVIL OVER A NUMBER
of days. I hope this has shed some light, and brought some comfort, regarding a very difficult issue—one that, as I said before, is
never solvable with a tidy solution that makes us feel good.

That said, I think it's worth pointing out something Mark
Mittelberg often talks about at churches and universities. He
points out that this is a challenging issue for *everyone*, not just for
Christians. Some people don't like the answers we offer from our
Christian worldview, so Mark asks them what their alternative
solution is. Usually they haven't thought of one.

To drive home his point, he explains that there are two
major competing worldviews to Christian theism—*atheism* and
pantheism—and he shows how these two points of view deal with
the problem of evil. We'll look at the answer from atheism today,
and that of pantheism in the next reading.

The problem with atheism is that, with its denial of God's
existence, there's a loss of any ultimate moral basis by which to
declare something good or evil. So atheists are left without any
objective standard by which to judge something as being right or
wrong. Instead, they're left with mere preferences. I have mine. You
have yours. Rape and murder may not be my cup of tea, but they
may be somebody else's. And who are we to say that what others
choose to do is wrong?

Don't misunderstand. Mark is not saying an atheist cannot

live a moral life; he's saying that an atheist *cannot define what morality is.* Atheist Jean-Paul Sartre acknowledged, "Everything is indeed permitted if God does not exist."[1] And atheist Bertrand Russell defined something as "*moral* when the agent would judge it to be *right* after an appropriate amount of candid thought."[2] In other words, rightness is determined by the individual and whatever standards he or she decides to adopt. Atheist John D. Steinrucken acknowledged this problem when he challenged fellow skeptics to come up with "the immutable moral laws of secularism" and then admitted there simply are none.[3]

So without any objective standards, atheism ultimately denies the reality of evil. Therefore it can lead, and has led, to all kinds of atrocities.

Yet we know unmistakably and undeniably that evil is real and that some things are simply wrong. And this brings us back to a transcendent moral lawgiver. One we worship as God.

Truth for Today

The denial of God leads to the denial of evil. Yet we know evil is real and leads to great damage. This knowledge provides a strong reason to reject atheism and to trust in the righteous God who loves and redeems us.

THE DEIFICATION OF EVIL

*Although they knew God, they neither glorified him as God
nor gave thanks to him. . . . [They] exchanged the glory of
the immortal God for images made to look like a mortal
human being and birds and animals and reptiles.*

ROMANS 1:21, 23

IN THE PREVIOUS READING WE SAW THAT FOR ATHEISTS THERE
is no God so there are no objective moral standards, and consequently their worldview ultimately denies the existence of evil.

The second alternative is *pantheism*, which is the view that
everything that exists is part of an all-encompassing, impersonal
god. We see this view reflected in Hinduism and Buddhism as well
as New Age teachings in the West. But if everything is part of god,
then what we call evil is actually part of that god as well.

Thus we observe the example of Kali, the Hindu goddess of
death, who is seen in statues and paintings wearing a necklace of
human skulls. She is evil personified as a god. Thus, some of her
more radical devotees have committed murders and even child
sacrifices in her name, and some of these practices continue today.[1]

We also see deified evil in the *Star Wars* movies. They present
the Force, which sometimes manifests as a benevolent power, for
example, through the Jedi Knights. But we also see the destructive "dark side of the Force" manifesting itself in Darth Vader. So
this godlike Force is both good and evil. This reflects the pantheistic beliefs of *Star Wars* creator George Lucas, who subscribes to
Buddhist thought.[2]

But if everything is part of an all-encompassing, impersonal
god, as it is in the pantheistic worldview, then evil and suffering

are part of that god too. This is the very god, or ultimate reality, that Eastern philosophy says we're supposed to strive to become more like and eventually to become one with.

This presents a tremendous problem: we're supposed to join with the very entity that contains evil within itself!

So in light of the *denial of evil* we find inherent in atheism and the *deification of evil* we see in Eastern pantheism, I'm feeling much better about living with the *problem of evil* that we have in Christianity—and the points of light we've discussed related to that problem.

Truth for Today

The existence of evil raises challenging questions, but we can be thankful that our Christian faith addresses those questions in a cogent way, without ever denying evil or making it part of the God we worship.

EVIL AS EVIDENCE OF GOD?

The light shines in the darkness, and the darkness has not overcome it.

JOHN 1:5

YEARS AGO MARK MITTELBERG AND I HOSTED A NOW-FAMOUS debate between atheist Frank Zindler and Christian apologist William Lane Craig. Zindler leveled the standard challenge of the problem of evil—that evil in the world is strong evidence against the existence of the Christian God.

I'll never forget Dr. Craig's response. Using some kind of spiritual jujitsu, he turned Zindler's argument against him: "No logical inconsistency has ever been demonstrated between the two statements 'God exists' and 'evil exists.'" Besides, he added, in a deeper sense the presence of evil "actually demonstrates God's existence, because without God there wouldn't be any [moral] foundation for calling anything evil."

C. S. Lewis was an atheist, convinced that because of the problem of evil there could be no God.[1] But then Lewis realized that if there is no God, then nothing can really be considered evil—and his whole case against God fell apart. Lewis explained:

> My argument against God was that the universe seemed so cruel
> and unjust. But how had I got this idea of *just* and *unjust*? A man
> does not call a line crooked unless he has some idea of a straight
> line. What was I comparing this universe with when I called it
> unjust? If the whole show was bad and senseless from A to Z, so
> to speak, why did I, who was supposed to be part of the show,
> find myself in such violent reaction against it? . . .

Thus in the very act of trying to prove that God did not exist—in other words, that the whole of reality was senseless—I found I was forced to assume that one part of reality—namely my idea of justice—was full of sense. Consequently, atheism turns out to be too simple. If the whole universe has no meaning, we should never have found out that it has no meaning: just as, if there were no light in the universe and therefore no creatures with eyes, we should never know it was dark. *Dark* would be without meaning.[2]

And so, ironically, the very problem that had caused Lewis to reject God ended up changing his mind and helping him to see that there *had* to be a God—One who established the standard by which we inevitably know good from evil. This was a vital step in Lewis's fascinating journey toward faith in Christ.

As Craig explained in the debate, the reality of evil, rather than being an argument against God, is yet another reason to believe *in* God!

Truth for Today

Probably the strongest argument against God is the one based on the problem of evil. But when you see how even *that* argument rests on assumptions that require God's existence, you begin to realize just how strong the case for God's existence is. You really can have a confident faith in him!

TRUTH PREVAILS

"The reason I was born and came into the world is to testify to the truth. Everyone on the side of truth listens to me."

JOHN 18:37

IN THE PREVIOUS READING I MENTIONED THE DEBATE MARK Mittelberg and I hosted in Chicago. We called it "Atheism vs. Christianity: Where Does the Evidence Point?"[1]

It was an amazing event. The news media, stunned that a church was unafraid to confront the toughest objections by skeptics, was quickly abuzz. The *Chicago Tribune* wrote four articles on the upcoming event. Soon I began getting calls from radio stations across the country. "Can we broadcast this debate live?" they asked. "Uh, sure," I said. To our astonishment, we soon had 117 stations from coast to coast.

On the night of the debate, traffic became gridlocked around the church as people flocked to the event. When we opened the doors a full hour before the start time, people ran down the aisles to get seats, filling the main auditorium in minutes and then several other rooms that were linked by video. In all, 7,778 people showed up. The atmosphere was electric.

William Lane Craig began by spelling out an array of powerful arguments for God and Christianity. Despite Craig's repeated challenges, Frank Zindler, arguing against this avalanche of evidence, came up empty in trying to offer a compelling case for atheism. Instead, he charged that biological evolution "is the death knell of Christianity"; that there's no convincing evidence Jesus actually lived; and that the existence of evil argues against God (a charge we addressed in the previous reading).

At the end of the two-hour debate, I asked members of the audience to set aside their personal beliefs and vote for whichever side had presented the stronger case. When I was handed the results to announce, I found that 97 percent declared that the Christian case prevailed!

A cynic might object, "Well, of course. This took place in a church." However, we asked people to record their spiritual position *before* the debate and then *after* they heard the evidence. Of the people who marked that they were definitely *not* Christians, an overwhelming 82 percent concluded that the evidence offered for Christianity was more compelling.

And—*get this!*—47 people indicated that they had walked in as unbelievers, heard both sides, and were walking out as believers! *And not a single person became an atheist.*

It was a stunning affirmation of the persuasive evidence for Christianity. And it reminded me that we have an unfair advantage in the marketplace of ideas: *we have truth on our side.*

Truth for Today

I hope this story emboldens your faith. Christianity is defensible because it is *true*. We can stand on that truth, and we can confidently declare it to the people we know.

BAD NEWS, GOOD NEWS

For the wages of sin is death, but the gift of God is eternal life in Christ Jesus our Lord.

ROMANS 6:23

IMAGINE THIS: YOU'RE OUT IN THE OCEAN ON A SUNNY SUMMER day, about a mile from the shore with a group of friends who are having fun together swimming near the boat. You, however, are standing on the deck, concerned for their safety. So you throw out a rope with a life preserver tied to it and shout to them to grab it so you can pull them up into the boat.

How do your frolicking friends respond? "Lighten up!" they playfully call back to you. "The water's warm and the swimming's great. Why don't you just jump in and join us!"

Maybe I should reconsider my strategy, you think to yourself. *Maybe they would be more interested in my offer if I first told them about the sharks that are encircling them!*

It's true that lifelines become much more relevant when we realize that our lives are actually in jeopardy. People don't get cancer-killing radiation treatments unless they know they have the disease. Nobody gets heart surgery until they find out they have a cardiovascular problem. We don't cry for help until we've hit bottom and face the fact that we're helpless.

The apostle Paul understood this principle well. That's why he unabashedly laid out the bad news first. He spelled it out for almost the entire first three chapters of Romans, summarizing it in 3:23: "For all have sinned and fall short of the glory of God." Paul explained that, morally speaking, we're in serious trouble. We're in deep water, the sharks are encircling, and we're about to go down for the last time. Once we grasp that, we'll be ready to hear about the solution to our spiritual dilemma.

That solution is made clear in the next verse, Romans 3:24: "All are justified freely by his grace through the redemption that came by Christ Jesus."

The sharks are real, but so is the life preserver. And to whom is that lifeline made available? Romans 10:13 tells us, "Everyone who calls on the name of the Lord will be saved."

Truth for Today

If you've never admitted that you "fall short of the glory of God," then this would be a great day to acknowledge the truth. Then you can be "justified freely by [God's] grace through the redemption that came by Christ Jesus." If you've already done this, then pray for opportunities to share this bad news and good news with others.

GOD SPEAKS

"My sheep listen to my voice; I know them, and they follow me."

JOHN 10:27

MOST PEOPLE BELIEVE IN GOD, BUT THEY DON'T EXPECT HIM to show up at their doorstep or speak to them personally. But if God created the universe and all the life in it, why wouldn't he be able to talk to us too?

Surely God *can* speak. The question is whether he's willing—and whether we're really listening and discerning whether it's his voice we're hearing.

Acts 10 is a fascinating study in how God is able to communicate with people. First he talked to Cornelius, a God-fearing Roman military leader, through an angel. The angel told Cornelius to send for a man named Peter, who would come and teach him.

Then, while Cornelius was sending messengers for Peter, God spoke to Peter through a dream, which prepared him to go speak to Cornelius and his family. And while Peter was figuring out the dream, God spoke to him in yet another way, this time directly through the Holy Spirit. He told Peter not to be afraid of the three men at the door looking for him, but to go with them immediately. (Talk about a divine setup!)

So Peter traveled with the men back to the home of Cornelius and met with Cornelius's family and friends who were assembled there. As Peter explained the gospel to them, the Holy Spirit came upon them in a way that was obvious—and they ended up becoming followers of Jesus just like Peter and his companions (Acts 10:34–43).

But that was during Bible times, you might be thinking. *Does*

God speak to us in similar ways today? He certainly can! And he usually speaks to those who, like Cornelius and Peter, turn to him regularly (Acts 10:2, 9).

Even if you struggle with spiritual doubts, you can seek God and ask him to speak to you. Pray the "skeptic's prayer" that the man in Mark 9:24 cried out to Jesus: "I do believe; help me overcome my unbelief!" If you are sincere and really want to hear and follow God, I'm confident he'll find a way to communicate his love and truth to you. It might be through the message of the Bible, the way he usually speaks to us, or it could be in more direct ways through his Spirit; but remember God's Spirit will always agree with God's Word, the Bible.

Truth for Today

Jesus said in today's verse that his sheep listen to his voice; he knows them, and they follow him. Will you listen for his voice today? He wants to guide and encourage you.

DIVINE INTERRUPTIONS

As Jesus and his disciples . . . were leaving the city, a blind
man, Bartimaeus, . . . was sitting by the roadside begging.
When he heard that it was Jesus of Nazareth, he began to
shout, "Jesus, Son of David, have mercy on me!"

MARK 10:46–47

MY LIFE IS BUSY. I'LL BET YOURS IS TOO. SO IT'S EASY, EVEN
for committed Christians, to think we're too busy to serve
Christ—at least right now. "After things settle down a bit," we tell
ourselves, "I'll find ways to make a difference in God's kingdom."

Jesus was busy too. In fact, without the modern conveniences
we enjoy today, it's easy to imagine he was far busier than we are—
not because he had 456 TV channels to choose from, but because
every detail of life had to be sorted out by hand.

Yet have you ever noticed that much of Jesus' ministry happened in the midst of interruptions? As he was "leaving the city,"
for instance, a blind man called out to him. It would have been easy
for Jesus to say to his disciples, "Sorry, guys, it's not on the agenda.
We have other obligations to fill, so tell him it'll have to wait."

Can you imagine? Instead, Jesus asked the man what he
wanted, and he ended up restoring the man's sight. All on his way
out of town!

In Acts 3 we read that "Peter and John were going up to the
temple at the time of prayer" when a man who was lame asked
them for money (v. 1). They could have decided prayer meetings
were more important and kept on walking. Instead, they reached
out to him, healed him, and changed his life forever.

And in Acts 16 Paul was looking for a prayer meeting down by a river. Apparently he never found it but instead "sat down and began to speak to the women who had gathered there" (v. 13). This led to one of those women, named Lydia, along with her entire household, trusting in Christ (vv. 14–15).

See a pattern? No, we can't meet every need or stop every time someone wants to talk—and neither could Jesus and his followers. But like Jesus and these early Christian leaders, we need to stay open, always watching for divine interruptions that God might be opening up to us while we're on our way to do other things.

Truth for Today

God might have a divine interruption planned for you today. Look for it. Don't let busyness keep you from making "the most of every opportunity" (Colossians 4:5).

WHAT IS

"You will know the truth, and the truth will set you free."

JOHN 8:32

"TRUTH IS WHATEVER WORKS FOR YOU," MANY PEOPLE SAY. "Besides," they add, "I have my truth and you have your truth—so let's just get along!"

I'm an ardent supporter of getting along. But the idea that reality changes according to one's beliefs just doesn't work for me—and I hope it doesn't work for you either.

In his book *Confident Faith*, Mark Mittelberg comments, "Call me old-fashioned, but truth is just what's real. Not my own private reality—or yours—but the way things actually are. Truth is *what is*—what exists really exists, and what doesn't exist really doesn't exist—whether we like it or not, whether we can prove it or not, whether we have different perceptions about it, or whether we think about it or believe in it at all."[1]

Mark goes on to explain that a person's refusal to believe in the existence of trucks won't prevent him from getting flattened by one when stepping into an intersection without looking. Or the sincere conviction that drinking gasoline is good for you won't make doing so safe. Or deciding the sign for mile marker 110 by the side of the highway is actually your speed limit won't prevent you from getting a hefty speeding ticket.

Beliefs, even sincerely held, have no power to change reality. As Mark likes to say, "Whatever is . . . is!" And what's true for crossing intersections, choosing a beverage, and driving on the highway is also true for spiritual matters. If God really exists, then ignoring or denying him isn't going to get rid of him.

And, as you're seeing in these readings, the evidence shows that God certainly does exist. Knowing this is the first step, but it's not enough. We also need to know him in a personal way.

In today's verse Jesus said, "You will know the truth, and the truth will set you free." He also declared, "I am the way and the truth and the life. No one comes to the Father except through me" (John 14:6).

Yes, Jesus believed and taught that there are objective truths— the "what is" kind that squares with reality—that we must know and embrace if we're to be his true followers. In the next five readings we're going to look at some of these truths as they relate to four areas: *God, people, Christ,* and *you.*

Truth for Today

Jesus said in Matthew 7:7, "Ask and it will be given to you; seek and you will find; knock and the door will be opened to you." What can you do to seek or live out this truth better today?

THE GOSPEL TRUTH: GOD

"Now this is eternal life: that they know you, the only true God."

JOHN 17:3

MUCH CAN BE SAID ABOUT THE ONE TRUE GOD, BUT FOR TODAY we'll focus on three essential characteristics that affect his relationship with us, the people he created.[1]

GOD IS *LOVING*

God, by his very nature, is love. We're told in 1 John 4:16, "God is love. Whoever lives in love lives in God, and God in them." Most people are happy to hear this—and they want to stop the conversation right there.

Let's just leave it at that, they think. *God loves me, and he smiles on pretty much everything I do.*

They view God as some sort of a benevolent grandpa in the sky who exudes sweetness and warmth, but who would never challenge, correct, or punish us for what we do.

But we know that this is an inadequate view of God because *loving* isn't all he is.

GOD IS *HOLY*

"Holy, holy, holy is the LORD Almighty; the whole earth is full of his glory," says Isaiah 6:3. "Just as he who called you is holy," adds 1 Peter 1:15–16, "so be holy in all you do; for it is written: 'Be holy, because I am holy.'"

What does it mean to be holy? It means to be absolutely pure.

Anything sinful or in any way impure stands in stark contrast to a holy God, since he is without sin or impurity of any kind. And the brilliant, shining light of his holiness exposes and rejects anything that falls short of his perfect moral standards.

GOD IS *JUST*

The Bible tells us that "God is just" (2 Thessalonians 1:6) and that "the LORD is known by his acts of justice" (Psalm 9:16). This means that God is a good and perfect judge.

So not only does God's holiness expose and reject anything impure or sinful, but his justice has to deal with it. He must punish rebellion and sin because a good judge must uphold the law and not let lawbreakers go without paying for their misdeeds.

We are moral lawbreakers, so it's hard for us to know how to view these attributes of God, at least initially. It is sobering to hear that God is both holy and just, but encouraging to remember that he is also love. Fortunately there's more to the story, which we'll continue in tomorrow's reading.

Truth for Today

God is loving, holy, and just. None of these attributes cancel out the others. Which of these three attributes of God do you most need to reflect upon and respond to today?

THE GOSPEL TRUTH: PEOPLE

*We all, like sheep, have gone astray, each of us has turned
to our own way.*

ISAIAH 53:6

WE'VE EXAMINED THREE ATTRIBUTES OF GOD THAT AFFECT
our relationship with him. Today we'll look at three characteristics
of ourselves as people that also impact this relationship.[1]

WE WERE CREATED GOOD BUT BECAME *SINFUL*

God cannot sin, nor could he ever create or cause sin. He originally
made us humans morally good. But we became sinful, at least initially, as a result of Adam and Eve's disobedience to God (Genesis
3). But the disobedience didn't stop there. That was just the beginning of the human race's rebellion against God—a rebellion in
which all of us are active participants. As Romans 3:23 plainly puts
it, "For all have sinned and fall short of the glory of God."

WE DESERVE *DEATH*

Because of our spiritual rebellion—our sin—we have each incurred
a moral debt before God. And Romans 6:23 explains that the
"wages," or penalty, for this debt is "death," which doesn't just
mean physical death but also spiritual death, which is separation
from God for eternity in a real place called hell.

Wow, you're probably thinking. *This sure is gloomy information you're sharing with me! I thought the gospel was supposed to be
good news!"*

The gospel *is* good news, and we'll get to that part soon. But first we need to understand our predicament.

WE ARE SPIRITUALLY *HELPLESS*

"All of us have become like one who is unclean," Isaiah 64:6 declares, "and all our righteous acts are like filthy rags."

Our friend Bill Hybels explains the situation by saying we are "morally bankrupt."[2] In other words, we have incurred a spiritual debt that must be paid, and there are no funds in our moral bank account to pay that debt or to buy our way off spiritual death row.

Yes, this is bad news, but it is vital that we—and our friends— understand this reality. If we don't, then we'll never grasp the urgency, relevancy, or beauty of the gospel message for our lives.

Truth for Today

We are desperately needy sinners. It's tempting to avert our eyes from that reality, but we must not. We need to own the fact that we are rebels before a holy and just God. Only then will we be able to receive his remedy humbly. What, if anything, do you need to own and admit to God right now?

THE GOSPEL TRUTH: CHRIST, PART 1

"Now this is eternal life: that they know you, the only true God, and Jesus Christ, whom you have sent."

JOHN 17:3

WE HAVE SEEN THAT GOD IS *LOVING*. BUT HE IS ALSO *HOLY,* SO he can't ignore or overlook anything that is unholy—including us and our actions. And he is *just*, which means he must punish our unholiness and disobedience.

In addition, we were created good, but became *sinful*, and every human being has disobeyed God. This has earned us a penalty of *death*, both physical and spiritual, which must be paid. And we are in a moral predicament that we are *helpless* to resolve on our own. Thankfully, there's good news.

Enter Jesus Christ, our Savior. He alone provides the opportunity for forgiveness and reconciliation between God and us. He is the only One who can solve our dilemma.

Here are three important facts about him.[1]

CHRIST IS *GOD*, WHO ALSO BECAME MAN

As we've seen in earlier readings, not only is Jesus God, but he also became human. The Creator actually became one of us and lived among us. "Christ Jesus . . . though he was God . . . was born as a human being" (Philippians 2:5–7 NLT). This uniquely qualified him to "be the offering for our sin, so that we could be made right with God through Christ" (2 Corinthians 5:21 NLT).

CHRIST DIED AS OUR *SUBSTITUTE*

"Christ also suffered once for sins, the righteous for the unrighteous, to bring you to God" (1 Peter 3:18). This is the central idea of the gospel: The death penalty we owed has been paid by Christ, who died in our place. Jesus will give us his righteousness, forgiveness, and life in exchange for our sin, our guilt, and the death sentence we deserve.

What do we need to do to obtain this?

CHRIST OFFERS HIS FORGIVENESS AS A *GIFT*

"It is by grace you have been saved, through faith—and this is not from yourselves, *it is the gift of God*—not by works, so that no one can boast" (Ephesians 2:8–9, emphasis mine; see also Romans 6:23).

In spite of the enormity of our debt and the high cost Jesus paid to buy us forgiveness and new life, this amazing gift of grace is offered freely to all who are willing to humble themselves, give up on their own efforts to earn God's acceptance, and receive it (John 1:12).

Truth for Today

Jesus paid for our sin so we can have salvation. This is good news worth embracing, and then sharing with everyone we know!

THE GOSPEL TRUTH: CHRIST, PART 2

"The Son of Man came not to be served but to serve others and to give his life as a ransom for many."

MARK 10:45 NLT

BEFORE WE PROCEED TO "THE GOSPEL TRUTH: YOU," LET'S ADDRESS a couple important questions that people sometimes ask about Jesus being our substitute.[1]

The first question is this: "Why did a price have to be paid, and can't God just forgive and forget like we can?"

Suppose your neighbor accidentally ran into your brand-new car that you had parked in front of your home. Now, you could forgive your neighbor and release him from any responsibility to fix your car. In that sense you could forgive and forget. But don't overlook the fact that you would still have a dented car, and that means you'd have to pay for the repairs yourself!

In the same way, our sins have done moral damage that must be paid for. God can forgive and forget our sins, but then he is left holding the debt—the spiritual death penalty that we owed. That's why Jesus came to "give his life as a ransom for many" by dying on the cross to pay our penalty for us.

The second question is: "But why did *Jesus* have to die? What kind of justice is there in having him, an innocent bystander, suffer instead of me?"

Some people have even compared Christ to a whipping boy. Whipping boys were part of an unjust system of punishment practiced in medieval times. When a young son in a royal family broke

142

the rules, the child's teachers dared not discipline the prince directly. Instead, they would bring a young slave boy into the presence of the prince and whip that boy in front of him. This was supposed to make the prince feel bad enough to change his behavior and start following the rules. But this practice was not only ineffective; it was blatantly unfair.

This illustrates why Jesus' identity, which we discussed in the previous reading, is so important. He was not some unwilling bystander God forced onto the scene as a whipping boy to take our punishment. No, he is the very God we have sinned against, the second person of the Trinity, who says to us, "I love you, I'm willing to forgive you, and I'll pay the death penalty that you owe so you can be set free."

Truth for Today

Jesus willingly became "the offering for our sin, so that we could be made right with God through Christ" (2 Corinthians 5:21 NLT). Knowing this, we should wholeheartedly receive what he has done for us and enthusiastically share it with others.

THE GOSPEL TRUTH: YOU

Examine yourselves to see whether you are in the faith; test yourselves.

2 CORINTHIANS 13:5

EVEN IF WE KNOW ALL ABOUT THE FIRST THREE GOSPEL TRUTHS— about God's loving, holy, and just character; about our predicament as sinners before a righteous judge; about Jesus and his sacrificial death on our behalf—we can still end up facing the spiritual death penalty if we don't say yes to God's gracious offer of salvation. That is why today's three points are so important.[1]

YOU AND I MUST *RESPOND*

The apostle Paul said, "Everyone who calls on the name of the Lord will be saved" (Romans 10:13). Salvation is not automatic. It has been offered to everyone, but each of us must respond by receiving it.

There are many people, even in churches, who understand the truths we've been discussing but have never entered into a relationship with Christ by accepting the gift he has offered. In fact, Jesus warned in Matthew 7:21–23 that on Judgment Day many people will be shocked to discover that their religious knowledge and activities have not gained them God's acceptance.

WE MUST ASK CHRIST TO BE OUR *FORGIVER* AND *LEADER*

The gospel of John explains, "*As many as received Him*, to them He gave the right to become children of God, even to those who believe in His name" (John 1:12 NASB, emphasis mine). John later added, "If we confess our sins, he is faithful and just and will forgive us our sins and purify us from all unrighteousness" (1 John 1:9).

As our forgiver, Christ applies his death on the cross to us, freeing us from the penalty we owe and giving us eternal life. As our leader, he begins to guide us in ways that will honor him and fulfill his purposes in our lives.

THE RESULT IS A SPIRITUAL *TRANSFORMATION*

"Do you not know that your bodies are temples of the Holy Spirit, who is in you, whom you have received from God? You are not your own; you were bought at a price" (1 Corinthians 6:19–20).

When we ask Christ to be our forgiver and leader, a spiritual transformation takes place in us. The Holy Spirit comes into us, and he begins to change us from the inside out, helping us to follow, honor, and serve Christ.

Truth for Today

When we get a gift on Christmas, it's not really ours until we reach out and receive it. Similarly, we must respond to God's offer of salvation by asking Christ to forgive our sins and lead our lives. Are you sure you've done that? Who else needs to understand this information?

AN ANTI-GOD BIAS

Paul . . . spoke boldly . . . , arguing persuasively about the
kingdom of God. But some of them became obstinate; they
refused to believe and publicly maligned the Way.

ACTS 19:8–9

SOME PEOPLE HAVE HONEST SPIRITUAL DOUBTS. THESE ARE
based on legitimate questions and can usually be alleviated with
good information. What often sounds like doubt, however, is actually bias. Some people don't *want* to know the truth because they
realize it will challenge their lifestyle or beliefs.

Some of Paul's listeners, after hearing him explain and defend
God's truth, "became obstinate; they refused to believe" (Acts
19:9). They were no longer just doubting; they were stonewalling.
Whether they realized it or not, they were biased against God's
truth.

Paul also described people who "perish because they refused
to love the truth and so be saved" (2 Thessalonians 2:10). And he
warned about God's wrath that will be poured out against those
who "suppress the truth by their wickedness" (Romans 1:18). Paul
went on to explain that "although they knew God, they neither
glorified him as God nor gave thanks to him, but their thinking
became futile and their foolish hearts were darkened. Although
they claimed to be wise, they became fools" (vv. 21–22).

We see willful ignorance throughout our culture. People know
what God says about sexual purity, for example, but they give in to
illicit desires anyway and downplay the importance of God's command. Or they shade the truth in business dealings, knowing it's a
sin to lie, and they justify their dishonesty.

Bias doesn't just occur in moral areas, however. It affects the intellectual realm as well. Scientists, for example, often refuse even to consider possible supernatural causes behind the phenomena they observe, claiming that such causes would not be scientific. Historians often do the same, discounting credible reports of the miraculous and explaining they can't even *consider* anything beyond the natural.

This is known as "methodological naturalism," but let's call it what it is: *intellectual prejudice*. It's deciding up front, prior to looking at the evidence, that nothing could be supernatural. It says, in effect, "Whatever happened, we know that God—if he exists at all—was not involved. So now let's figure out what occurred!"

Contrary to all this, we need to do what I learned in journalism school: investigate the truth with an open mind, and then follow the facts wherever they lead. And from my experience, they ultimately lead back to God.

Truth for Today

In many ways our culture is geared to suppress the truth by substituting almost anything for the knowledge of God. It takes courage and wisdom to challenge that culture and to help reopen people's minds to him. Get ready. God wants you to speak for him.

GOD EXCURSIONS

*God, who got you started in this spiritual adventure, shares
with us the life of his Son and our Master Jesus. He will
never give up on you. Never forget that.*

1 CORINTHIANS 1:8–9 THE MESSAGE

WHEN MOST PEOPLE CONSIDER FOLLOWING CHRIST, THEY THINK
of words like *obedience*, *service*, and *ministry*.

Me? I think of *adventure*! As I look at the stories of the Bible
as well as my own experience, my conclusion is that a life given to
God is one filled with thrills—thrills that fulfill.

Don't get me wrong. I'm not saying the path God leads us
down will necessarily be safe or comfortable. My coauthor Mark,
who lives in Colorado, experienced an interesting leading from
God this evening. He was out riding his mountain bike just before
dusk—the time when black bears often begin to roam. As he was
approaching an area where he had previously encountered a large
bear, Mark sensed an inward nudge, which he believed to be from
God, telling him to turn down the path to the left, thus avoiding
what might be a danger zone.

"But then, after less than a minute of pedaling down that alternative route," Mark reported, "I came upon a big black bear! It was
then that I realized God had probably nudged me in that direction
so that I would see the bear, feel the rush of adrenaline, and understand anew that his guidance is often away from tranquility and
toward adventure."

Unharmed, and chuckling to both himself and God, Mark
turned around and went back the way he had originally intended
to go—but with a much better story to tell!

Remember what God told the man he sent to pray over Saul, the recently converted persecutor of the church who became the apostle Paul?

"Go!" God said to Ananias. "This man is my chosen instrument to proclaim my name to the Gentiles and their kings and to the people of Israel. I will show him how much he must suffer for my name" (Acts 9:15–16).

Translation: "I'm going to take Paul on the adventure of a lifetime—but it's not going to be easy for him!"

Certainly Joseph in the Old Testament went through a labyrinth of challenges in order to experience finally the rush and reward of being exalted to the second most powerful position in Egypt, right next to the pharaoh, enabling him to save his family and people.

God's guidance will take us down some dangerous and even painful paths, but if we'll trust him, he'll also fill it with thrills—the kind that fulfill.

Truth for Today

Do you know the path God wants to lead you down? It may seem scary, but life is ultimately better when we wholeheartedly seek and follow him.

PREPARED

In your hearts revere Christ as Lord. Always be prepared to give an answer to everyone who asks you to give the reason for the hope that you have. But do this with gentleness and respect.

1 PETER 3:15

IF YOU'RE A FOLLOWER OF CHRIST, THEN GOD HAS CALLED YOU to be ready to defend your faith to the people around you, respectfully striving to help them see and understand the truth for which you stand.

Peter made this clear in 1 Peter 3:15. Here are four lessons we can draw from this verse.

1. Revere Christ as Lord

Before we can be effective spokespeople for Christ, we need to be authentically *his*. Only as we let him lead and guide our lives will our character reflect his truth in ways that honor him and attract people to his message.

2. Always Be Prepared

When someone challenges our faith, it's tempting to fire back, even if we don't have all the ammunition we need! Zeal without knowledge often does more damage than good. We need to make the effort ahead of time to study and really understand our faith and the realities that support it. As Paul admonished, "Do your best to present yourself to God as one approved, a worker who does not need to be ashamed and who correctly handles the word of truth" (2 Timothy 2:15).

3. Give an Answer

Revering Christ as Lord and being prepared to defend our faith are ongoing processes in the Christian life. They help us get ready to "give an answer" whenever the opportunity arises. It's interesting that in the original Greek, the word Peter used for *answer* is *apologia*, from which we get our word *apologetics*. It literally means we are to be ready to give a speech of defense—a well-thought-out account of why our faith in Christ makes sense. Now, we'll never feel fully prepared, but even so, God wants to use us in the midst of our own growth process to help answer questions about our faith and reach others for him.

4. Show Gentleness and Respect

Peter ended his admonition with an important qualifier: As we're giving reasons for the hope we have in Christ, it's important that we watch our attitude and approach. We should be confident but never cocky. Rather, attributes such as humility, love, gentleness, and respect—character traits of Jesus himself—will help people become open to the answers we present to them on his behalf.

Truth for Today

God wants to use you as his spokesperson. Are you ready? Which of these four challenges from Peter do you most need to act on today?

REMOVING OBSTACLES

*We demolish arguments and every pretension that sets
itself up against the knowledge of God, and we take captive
every thought to make it obedient to Christ.*

2 CORINTHIANS 10:5

"YOU CAN'T ARGUE SOMEONE INTO GOD'S KINGDOM." YOU MAY
have heard that said, but is it true?

The answer is yes. And no!

Let me explain. In order for people to receive salvation, the
Holy Spirit must draw them to him and convict them of sin; they
must understand the gospel message that, according to Romans
1:16, is "the power of God that brings salvation to everyone who
believes"; and they must turn from their sins to follow Christ.
Arguments alone will never produce these results.

That said, I'm also convinced many people will not come to
Christ without hearing convincing arguments and seeing persuasive evidence. God can use this kind of information—what we
present in Christian apologetics—to clear the path for the gospel.
Apologetics can remove obstacles that keep people from consider-
ing the powerful message of grace and forgiveness through Christ.

It's in this spirit that Paul explained, "We demolish arguments
and every pretension that sets itself up against the knowledge of
God, and we take captive every thought to make it obedient to
Christ." And it's why "every Sabbath [Paul] reasoned in the syna-
gogue, trying to persuade Jews and Greeks" (Acts 18:4), and again
he "tried to persuade them about Jesus" (Acts 28:23).

The result? "Some were convinced by what he said, but others
would not believe" (v. 24). So it's clear that Paul used arguments

and persuasion as he presented the message of Christ. It is also clear that God used Paul's efforts, leading many to himself.

Likewise, as we've seen, Peter said we need to "be prepared to give an answer to everyone who asks you to give the reason for the hope that you have" (1 Peter 3:15). In the original language this means that we need to be ready to give an *apologetic*—a verbal defense—to anyone who is open to discussing our beliefs.

So, can we argue people into God's kingdom? Well, with God's help we can present information that will remove intellectual barriers, helping people move one step closer to faith in Christ.

And *that* is worth arguing for!

Truth for Today

If good arguments and evidence can help people move toward faith in Christ, then it's certainly worth our efforts to master this kind of information. So keep reading and learning, and ask God to give you opportunities to help others with the knowledge you've gained.

DYING FOR HOPE

*Hope deferred makes the heart sick, but a longing fulfilled
is a tree of life.*

PROVERBS 13:12

"PEOPLE IN MANY NATIONS APPEAR TO BE SEARCHING WITH A
new intensity for spiritual moorings," observed pollster George
Gallup. "One of the key factors prompting this search is certainly a
need for hope in these troubled times."[1]

Can't you feel it? With the increase in violence, terrorism,
conflict, and economic uncertainty, there seems to be a corre-
sponding increase in hunger for hope. "What does it all mean?"
people wonder. "Isn't there more to life than just getting by and
hoping things won't blow up?"

We have good news: God offers a hope so powerful it can
transform a person's life and future. But it's not the kind of hope
we usually think about. Much of what we call "hope" falls into
three categories: *wishful thinking, blind optimism,* and *hopeful
dreams.*

WISHFUL THINKING

Wishful thinking is trying to change reality with our thoughts.
We blow out the candles on our birthday cake and say, "I hope
I stay healthy for another year." It's the superstitious feeling that
maybe, somehow, some way, our sincere desires will help things go
the direction we want them to, even though we really don't have
any power to make that happen.

BLIND OPTIMISM

Another hopeful attitude we commonly see is blind optimism. It's good to have a positive outlook, but some optimists paper over their problems as if those problems don't exist; they avert their eyes from the ugly aspects of the world; they act as if, for them, everything will be fine all the time. This might seem admirable, but, again, it doesn't change reality.

HOPEFUL DREAMS

Hopeful dreams are lofty goals we set out to achieve. The problem is that these are restricted by our limitations. I could fantasize about becoming the next big NBA star, but that wouldn't change the fact that my vertical leap has to be measured in millimeters! I can dream all I want, but it's just not going to happen. Our earnest belief in our dreams does not guarantee they'll ever become reality.

Thankfully, God offers us something greater.

BIBLICAL HOPE

Biblical hope is the confident expectation that God will fulfill his promises to those who trust in him. The apostle Peter wrote, "In [God's] great mercy he has given us new birth into *a living hope* through the resurrection of Jesus Christ from the dead, and into an inheritance that can never perish, spoil or fade. This inheritance is kept in heaven for you" (1 Peter 1:3–4, emphasis mine).

Truth for Today

People are dying for hope. Fortunately, Jesus died to *give us* hope—the kind "that can never perish, spoil or fade." It's available to everyone; let's spread the news!

FIRSTHAND

But these are written that you may believe that Jesus is the Messiah, the Son of God, and that by believing you may have life in his name.

JOHN 20:31

IT'S ENCOURAGING TO KNOW THE GOSPELS OF JESUS ARE BASED on direct or indirect eyewitness testimonies. The early disciples were with Jesus as he walked, taught, did miracles, died, and rose from the grave. Their accounts were not based on myths, speculation, or hearsay. They're not later compilations that had been hopelessly corrupted by the development of legends.

John explained that his writings about Jesus were based on his own direct experiences with him (for example, John 21:24). It's hard to imagine what else John could have said to make this any clearer. Throughout his gospel and in his first letter (1 John 1:1–3), John wrote that he had personally seen and heard and touched what he was describing. It's as if John were grabbing us by the collar, staring us in the eye, and speaking to us emphatically, "Look, I was there! I experienced with my five senses what Jesus did and taught. This information is real. Listen to what I'm telling you. Apply it to your lives!"

And Luke, not an eyewitness himself, described how he collected the information from those who were eyewitnesses for his gospel: "Many have undertaken to draw up an account of the things that have been fulfilled among us, just as they were handed down to us by those who from the first were eyewitnesses and servants of the word. With this in mind, since I myself have carefully investigated everything from the beginning, I too decided to write an orderly account . . . so that you may know the certainty of the things you have been taught" (Luke 1:1–4).

Also, prior to his crucifixion, Jesus assured the disciples they would have supernatural assistance in recalling and writing down what he had said and done. "All this I have spoken while still with you," Jesus told them. "But the Advocate, the Holy Spirit, whom the Father will send in my name, will teach you all things and will remind you of everything I have said to you" (John 14:25–26).

Other readings in this book explain the reasons we can be confident about the early dates and authentic authorship of the four biblical Gospels: Matthew, Mark, Luke, and John. But for now remember what John said in today's verse: "These are written that you may believe that Jesus is the Messiah, the Son of God, and that by believing you may have life in his name."

Truth for Today

The Gospels were written by people who gave up everything to relay Jesus' message to us. Isn't it worth our effort to read and heed what they wrote?

UNDESIGNED COINCIDENCES

When Jesus looked up and saw a great crowd coming toward him, he said to Philip, "Where shall we buy bread for these people to eat?"

JOHN 6:5

CRITICS OF THE BIBLE OFTEN ACCUSE THE GOSPEL WRITERS of colluding with one another in order to get their stories straight. The underlying assumption is that the details of Jesus' life were exaggerated or even fabricated.

There are many problems with such theories. One of the most interesting responses in recent years comes from philosopher Tim McGrew, and it involves what he calls "undesigned coincidences."

One of many examples is in John 6:1–7, where we read the account of Jesus' feeding the five thousand. We are told in verse 5, "When Jesus looked up and saw a great crowd coming toward him, he said to Philip, 'Where shall we buy bread for these people to eat?'"

"Now, Philip is a fairly minor character in the New Testament," said apologist Jonathan McLatchie, summarizing McGrew's argument. "And one might, naturally, be inclined to wonder why Jesus hasn't turned to someone a little higher in the pecking order (such as Peter or John). A partial clue is provided in John 1:44: *'Philip, like Andrew and Peter, was from the town of Bethsaida.'*

"And what is so significant about Philip being from the town of Bethsaida?" McLatchie continued, "We don't learn this until we read the parallel account in Luke's gospel (9:10–17). At the opening of the account (verses 10–11) . . . we are informed by Luke that the event was actually taking place in Bethsaida—the town Philip was from! Jesus thus turns to Philip, [who], he believed, would be familiar with the area. Notice too that Luke does not tell us that Jesus turned to Philip.

"What makes this even more intriguing," McLatchie concluded, "is that the parallel account in Mark's gospel (6:30–42) states, in verses 30–31 that

> The apostles gathered around Jesus and reported to him all they had done and taught. Then, *because so many people were coming and going* that they did not even have a chance to eat, he said to them, "Come with me by yourselves to a quiet place and get some rest." [emphasis mine]

"Why were there many coming and going? Mark doesn't tell us. The answer lies in John's account. John 6:4 explains that 'the Jewish Passover Festival was near.'"[1]

Undesigned coincidences like this one show us how the claims of the biblical writers fit together like a jigsaw puzzle, often making complete sense only when the various pieces are examined together.

Truth for Today

Undesigned coincidences are no mere coincidences. They are the earmarks of authentic historical writings—and they give us more reasons to trust the Bible!

TOO NARROW?

"Enter through the narrow gate. For wide is the gate and broad is the road that leads to destruction, and many enter through it. But small is the gate and narrow the road that leads to life, and only a few find it."

MATTHEW 7:13–14

MANY PEOPLE HAVE ACCUSED JESUS OF BEING NARROW-MINDED. "How can he claim that he's the only way to God," they say, "and that his spiritual path is the only path to take?"

They also think it was exclusivistic for him to say in John 14:6, "I am the way and the truth and the life. No one comes to the Father except through me," as if he were unnecessarily restricting our spiritual options and trying to compete with all the other religions in order to amass more followers.

But I like what Mark Mittelberg often tells audiences when we teach together.

"I don't know about you," Mark says, "but whenever I fly somewhere, I'm always glad that our pilot is narrow-minded. I mean, we don't want a pilot who is looking around for fresh ideas about where he might try landing the plane.

"I'm sure it would be possible to put it down on a field or a beach—or worse yet, on the side of a hill or in a mountain valley. But creativity isn't a characteristic I'm looking for in a pilot. I'd rather have an old-fashioned pilot who insists he's going to land the jetliner on 'that narrow path that leads to life,' called the runway."

Don't you prefer a predictable pilot like that as well?

Then Mark drives his message home by explaining you really could plop down an airplane just about anywhere—unless, that is, you prefer to stay alive!

Similarly, there are many religious teachers, prophets, and gurus out there. But only one leader came with the credentials to show he was the Son of God. Only One came to lay down his life as a ransom for his friends. Only One paid the penalty for our sins by dying in our place. Only One proved it all to be true by rising from the dead. And that only One, Jesus, said we must "enter through the narrow gate" by putting our trust in him.

In light of all he said and did, being narrow-minded is sounding pretty good to me.

Truth for Today

Sometimes truth is narrow. Are you willing to follow the One who said that he alone was the way, the truth, and the life? Are you willing to take risks to explain to others why they should do the same?

SWEATING BLOOD?

Being in anguish, [Jesus] prayed more earnestly, and his
sweat was like drops of blood falling to the ground.

LUKE 22:44

WHEN, AS A SKEPTIC, I FIRST ENCOUNTERED THIS PASSAGE claiming that Jesus' "sweat was like drops of blood falling to the ground" as he prayed prior to his crucifixion, I assumed it was a figure of speech. I thought it was like today when someone has gone through a very stressful situation, and they say they were "sweating bullets." We understand what this means without taking it literally.

But years later I started my research for *The Case for Christ*. I went to California to interview Dr. Alexander Metherell, a physician, research scientist, and expert on the crucifixion of Jesus.

"This is a known medical condition called *hematidrosis*. It's not very common, but it is associated with a high degree of psychological stress," he told me.

"What happens is that severe anxiety causes the release of chemicals that break down the capillaries in the sweat glands. As a result, there's a small amount of bleeding into these glands, and the sweat comes out tinged with blood. We're not talking about a lot of blood; it's just a very, very small amount."[1]

Interestingly, it was the physician Luke who noted this phenomenon. He reported in Luke 22:44: "Being in anguish, [Jesus] prayed more earnestly, and his sweat was like drops of blood falling to the ground."

Jesus' anguish and passionate prayers over his impending torture and death could certainly have been enough to trigger this medical phenomenon. The *Journal of Medicine* analyzed seventy-six cases of hematidrosis and concluded that the most common causes were acute fear and intense mental contemplation.[2]

I asked Dr. Metherell what effect this bloody sweat would have had on Jesus. "What this did," he replied, "was set up the skin to be extremely fragile so that when Jesus was flogged by the Roman soldier the next day, his skin would have been very, very sensitive."

What could have prompted Jesus to endure willingly the misery of Gethsemane, the brutality of the flogging, and the unspeakable torment of the cross?

"Well," said Dr. Metherell, "I suppose the answer can be summed up in one word—and that would be *love*."[3]

Truth for Today

When we understand what Jesus suffered for us, even prior to the actual crucifixion, we get a better grasp of the meaning of passages like Romans 5:8: "God demonstrates his own love for us in this: While we were still sinners, Christ died for us." What love! What a God! What a Savior to worship, serve, and share with others!

JESUS OR NO ONE

When the set time had fully come, God sent his Son, born of a woman, born under the law, to redeem those under the law, that we might receive adoption to sonship.

GALATIANS 4:4–5

CONVINCED THAT JESUS WAS NOT THE "ANOINTED ONE," MANY Jewish people still look for the long-awaited Messiah. But according to Michael Brown, a scholar and messianic Jew, Jesus—and Jesus alone—fit the Old Testament's description of the coming Messiah.

That's a bold claim, so I asked him to explain.

"In 2 Chronicles 7, God says if Israel's sin reaches a certain level, he'll destroy the temple, exile the people, and leave them in a state of judgment," Brown said. "Sure enough, this comes to pass. The prophet Daniel prays in Daniel 9 that God would have mercy. God gives him a revelation about the temple being rebuilt. Before this new temple is destroyed, Daniel is told, several things are going to take place, including the bringing of everlasting atonement—the final dealing with sin.

"The prophet Haggai says the glory of the second temple will be greater than the glory of the first temple," Brown continued. "God will fill the second temple with his glory. Then the prophet Malachi says the Lord will come to his temple. He uses a Hebrew term that always refers to God himself: the Lord—*he* will come to that temple.

"Keep in mind the second temple was destroyed in AD 70," Brown said. "Atonement for sin had to be made and the divine visitation had to take place before the second temple was destroyed.

"So . . . if it's not Yeshua, which is the Jewish name for Jesus, then throw out the Bible," Brown concluded, "because nobody except him accomplished what needed to be done prior to AD 70. What divine visitation did take place if not for Yeshua? When else did God visit the second temple in a personal way? Who else atoned for sin? How else was the glory of the second temple greater than the first?

"Either the Messiah came two thousand years ago, or the prophets were wrong and we can discard the Bible. But they weren't wrong. Yeshua is the Messiah—or nobody is."[1]

I found Brown's explanation fascinating and faith-affirming—and vital information for Jewish people to know. If they long for their true Messiah, this can help lead them to *Jesus*.

Truth for Today

You don't have to read much of the Old or the New Testament to realize that Jewish people have a special place in God's heart. Which of your friends might find this information helpful? Take a risk and share it with them!

WITH ALL YOUR MIND

"Love the Lord your God with all your heart and with all your soul and with all your mind and with all your strength."

MARK 12:30

A TEACHER OF THE LAW ONCE ASKED JESUS, "OF ALL THE commandments, which is the most important?" (Mark 12:28).

Jesus' reply, seen above in Mark 12:30, made it clear that the most important thing for us to do is to love God with everything we've got. But it was interesting that he broke it down into four categories. Three of those four were repeated from the command given to Moses in Deuteronomy 6:5, which said, "Love the LORD your God with all your heart and with all your soul and with all your strength."

Jesus, however, added a fourth category: "Love the Lord your God . . . *with all your mind*" (emphasis mine). This is important. Jesus was saying, in effect, that contrary to popular opinion, right religion is not just about heart, feelings, or emotions, but it also involves the intellect.

Here are some practical ways this should play out in our lives as Christians:

- We should study the Scriptures as 2 Timothy 2:15 commands: "Present yourself to God as one approved, a worker who does not need to be ashamed and who correctly handles the word of truth."
- We should study biblical theology in order to understand better the nature of God and embrace him for who he truly is.
- We should learn and apply sound logic to spiritual questions, knowing that logic flows from the very nature

of God and that it helps us to understand and interpret his revelation, the Bible.

- We should scrutinize truth claims to see if they square with God's previously revealed truth (Acts 17:11; Galatians 1:8–9).
- We should actively apply all we've learned to train other believers concerning who God is and what he desires in our lives (2 Timothy 2:2).
- We should prepare ourselves to "give an answer" to everyone who asks about our faith and why it makes sense (1 Peter 3:15).
- We should worship God in ways that involve clear thinking about who he is and what he has revealed. As Jesus said, we should worship him "in the Spirit *and in truth*" (John 4:24, emphasis mine).

Truth for Today

God wants us to use our minds to know and understand truth and to apply it to our lives in order to love and honor him better. On which of the areas above do you need to focus?

IS IT WRONG TO BE RIGHT?

"You will know the truth, and the truth will set you free."

JOHN 8:32

"YOU CHRISTIANS ACT LIKE YOU'RE RIGHT, AND EVERYONE ELSE is wrong." It's a common complaint in our culture.

The part that concerns me most is the phrase "act like." It seems to indicate an attitude of arrogance or superiority, neither of which is acceptable for a Christian. Rather, our attitude should be like that of Jesus, who "humbled himself" even though he really was superior to any mere human, and chose to love and serve us self-sacrificially (Philippians 2:8).

But what about the rest of the accusation—that we think we're right and others are wrong? Is that bad?

Mark Mittelberg offers some interesting analysis: "What's fascinating is that the people who condemn Christians for acting as if they're right and others are wrong are, in that very action, acting as if they themselves are right and Christians are wrong. So they are at that moment doing the very thing they say is wrong. When you think about it, it's pretty silly to condemn people for thinking they are right—because aren't you simultaneously thinking you are right in saying they are wrong?

"Or, broadening the point a bit, who in their right mind doesn't consistently think that they are right? Seriously, if a sane person thinks he is wrong, doesn't he immediately change his thinking and begin to believe what he now thinks is actually right? If so, then doesn't he once again think he is right and that anyone who contradicts his new belief is, by the very nature of logic, wrong? Don't we all think that way? I think we do!

"Therefore, for two reasons, no one should condemn Christians for thinking they're right and others are wrong: (1) Everybody else does the same thing, and (2) Christians might really be right after all."[1]

Mark also adds that Jesus, though completely humble, knew he was right when he said in John 14:6, "I am the way and the truth and the life." He also said in John 8:32 that "you will know the truth, and the truth will set you free." If, as Jesus said, we can know the truth, then that truth must be right; and, logically, whatever contradicts it must be wrong.

I would simply add: *I think that's right!*

Truth for Today

As Christians, we should be confident in truth but humble in spirit.

CAN'T WE JUST COEXIST?

If it is possible, as far as it depends on you, live at peace with everyone.

ROMANS 12:18

IF YOU'VE PAID ATTENTION TO BUMPER STICKERS IN RECENT years, you know a lot of people think we simply need to *coexist*.

How do you react to that message? My initial response was a bit negative. *We're not here to coexist*, I thought. *We're here to point people to Jesus!* Of course that's true.

But is it really an either/or situation? Maybe we should ask the people with those stickers what they're really saying. They could mean that we need to *compromise*, or they might just mean we need to *cooperate*.

If it's the second option, meaning they believe we need to learn to get along better and be tolerant of each other's beliefs, then I would agree. It was, after all, the apostle Paul who told us in Romans 12:18, "If it is possible, as far as it depends on you, live at peace with everyone."

Who wouldn't like to see Muslims, Christians, and Jews better coexist in the Middle East and around the world? Who wouldn't prefer to see the East and the West better cooperate? And wouldn't we all love to see the ultimate of blood feuds—between Democrats and Republicans—simmer down?

My response changes, however, if we are asked to compromise our beliefs or our mission as Christians. Then we must draw the line. You see, today's statements of "tolerance" all too often say that *everyone* is right and that it's wrong to disagree with or challenge anyone else's thinking. This is coexisting in the sense of compromise.

Here's a great irony: that very viewpoint is one that they insist we must fall in line with—or else! Isn't it interesting that some of the people who talk the loudest about being tolerant turn out to be the most intolerant people of all when we don't accept what they're saying?

The problem is that this new view of tolerance is meddling with the very idea of truth. And ultimately, I hope, we all want truth. More than that, the Bible tells us to be lovers of truth (Zechariah 8:19; 2 Thessalonians 2:10).

So the answer is not to pretend everybody is right. Rather, the answer is to love, seek, and embrace what's true while loving and living in peace with those who disagree.

Truth for Today

We must do our best to coexist with people who believe differently than we do, but we must also reject the new understanding of tolerance. Everybody can't be right. When two ideas contradict, at least one of them must be wrong.

QUESTIONS WELCOME

When John, who was in prison, heard about the deeds of the Messiah, he sent his disciples to ask him, "Are you the one who is to come, or should we expect someone else?"

MATTHEW 11:2–3

JOHN THE BAPTIST WAS BOLD, BRASH, AND CONFIDENT. According to the Gospels, God used this eccentric prophet to prepare the way for Jesus, the Messiah. John announced Jesus' arrival and even baptized him in the Jordan River at the beginning of Jesus' ministry (Matthew 3). If anyone understood Jesus' identity and mission, it was John the Baptist.

How shocking, then, to later see John begin to question whether Jesus was the one the Jewish people had been waiting for. John had been isolated in prison for almost a year at that point, and today's verse reports that he sent his disciples to double-check with Jesus, asking, "Are you the one who is to come, or should we expect someone else?"

John's questions may have stemmed from his being alone, which is when doubts often creep in. He might also have had some misconceptions about what the Messiah would actually do. John had predicted God's judgment. Perhaps he was confused by Jesus' patience and gentleness as well as his delay of judgment.

Whatever the reason for John's doubts, Jesus' response was fascinating: Jesus didn't shame him, scold him, and try to scare him back into line. He didn't blurt out: "For goodness' sake, John, what's wrong with you? God told you who I was, and then you told everyone else. You baptized me and even heard my Father's voice from heaven affirming my identity, and now you're getting all double-minded on me?"

On the contrary, Jesus was gracious and kind. He provided evidence for his messianic work (Matthew 11:5, prophesied seven hundred years earlier in Isaiah 61:1–2) and gently urged John not to turn away from him (Matthew 11:6). What's more, Jesus went on to tell the people who had heard this seemingly embarrassing exchange what a great prophet John was—even proclaiming "Truly I tell you, among those born of women there has not risen anyone greater than John the Baptist" (v. 11).

Isn't it encouraging to know that doubters were—and are—welcomed by Jesus? It's intellectually inspiring to see that he fulfilled prophecies and did miracles, but it's personally affirming to discover that he understands, empathizes with, and gently reassures those of us who seek to know him but who have doubts and questions on our journey of faith.

Truth for Today

We don't need to be afraid of spiritual questions. We just need to take them to our gracious and kind Savior and to seek the truth that he can show us.

WHO HAS FAITH?

"You have forgotten me and trusted in false gods."

JEREMIAH 13:25

"NO DOUBT ABOUT IT. YOU LIVE YOUR LIFE BY FAITH EVERY day, even in the mundane details," said my coauthor Mark Mittelberg. "What is faith? My broad definition is *beliefs and actions that are based on something considered to be trustworthy— even in the absence of absolute proof.*

"You believed the food was safe, so you ate it; you trusted the chair would hold you, so you sat in it; you've had luck in the past with computers, random canines, and commutes home—so why not try them again? You didn't have conclusive evidence that any of these things would work out, but the odds seemed to be in your favor, so you went for it. All of us do similar things—routinely.

"We live by faith not only in the small, everyday details of ordinary experience but also in the bigger issues related to religion, God, and eternity. We all adopt 'beliefs and actions' related to these areas 'based on something considered to be trustworthy—even in the absence of absolute proof.' So if you are a Christian, you're trusting in the teachings of Christ; if a Muslim, you're trusting in the teachings of Muhammad; if a Buddhist, you're trusting in the teachings of Buddha.

"Even nonreligious people live in the trust that their non-religious beliefs are accurate and that they won't someday face a thoroughly religious Maker who actually did issue a list of guidelines and requirements that they failed to pay attention to.

"Even well-known atheists like Richard Dawkins and Sam Harris live their lives accepting an unproven assumption that there is no God and that the opinions they express about these matters are ultimately helping and not harming people. They don't *know* they are correct—they just *believe* and *act* as if they are."[1]

What Mark is saying is that faith is *trust* and that no one is belief-neutral. All people trust in something, even if that something is themselves. The ultimate question that people need to ask, then, is whether or not what they're trusting in is, in fact, *trustworthy*.

As one who spent almost two years investigating the Christian faith as an atheist, and who was compelled to follow God's truth even when I didn't want to, I'll tell you with great assurance that the claims of Christ are true and worth trusting in completely.

Truth for Today

We all trust in something. Have you examined your beliefs to make sure they're trustworthy? Whom can you help walk through such a process, helping them to see that they can confidently put their faith in Christ?

FAITH SUBSTITUTES

Test all things; hold fast what is good. Abstain from every form of evil.

1 THESSALONIANS 5:21–22 NKJV

"ALL YOU NEED IS FAITH!" IT'S BEEN SAID SO MANY TIMES IT almost sounds true. Usually you're not told what you're supposed to have faith *in*. People treat faith like magic, as if just believing strongly in something—*in anything*—will make the difference.

Here are some misguided forms of faith.[1]

- SUPERSTITIOUS FAITH. This is the magical approach. According to this view, sincerity is what counts. It overlooks the fact that many people are sincere, but sincerely wrong. The truth is, belief has no power to change the truth.
- THERAPEUTIC FAITH. This is believing in something because it makes you feel better. "My faith is real because it helps me," proponents say. The problem is that you can trust in something that brings temporary relief but is ultimately misleading and destructive.
- BLIND FAITH. This is belief in something without evidence or reason. It's the "leap before you look" approach, and it leads people into all kinds of harm.
- IRRATIONAL FAITH. This is belief that goes *against* reason and facts. It's believing something even though you know in your heart it couldn't possibly be true.

Thankfully, the Bible doesn't speak in such misguided ways. Yes, it advocates faith, but makes it clear that faith is only as good as what it is focused upon. Biblical faith is a rational faith in a divine Being who has proven himself worthy of our trust.

The Bible tells us to be open to what might be messages from God, but not in careless or naive ways. Rather, today's verse tells us to "Test all things; hold fast what is good. Abstain from every form of evil."

How can we test claims to spiritual truth? At the very least we need to make sure the message squares with what God has already said in the Bible. Thus, "the Berean Jews were of more noble character than those in Thessalonica, for they received the message with great eagerness and examined the Scriptures every day to see if what Paul said was true" (Acts 17:11).

Wise, biblical faith is a commitment of trust in the God of the Bible. It's based on solid evidence that he is the one and only true God and that Jesus is his only begotten Son.

Truth for Today

"The righteous will live by faith" (Romans 1:17). Knowing our faith is grounded in a wealth of facts and evidence, we can give ourselves wholeheartedly to living that faith and sharing it with others.

A DOUBTER'S BLESSINGS

Jesus told him, "Because you have seen me, you have believed; blessed are those who have not seen and yet have believed."

JOHN 20:29

FOR SOME PEOPLE, BELIEVING COMES EASILY. SOMEBODY TELLS them what's true, and they readily accept it. But for many of us, skepticism runs deep, and claims of the miraculous are, well, hard to swallow. So we approach religion cautiously, not wanting to fall for any tricks or buy into any fables. "I'm going to need some solid evidence before I put stock in that story!" we say.

If that's how you approach claims of the supernatural, then you've got a friend in Thomas. He earned the title Doubting Thomas by his unwillingness to merely accept the testimonies of his fellow disciples when they told him they had seen the risen Savior.

To Thomas's credit, he was a skeptic (one with doubts), but not a cynic (someone who scoffs at spiritual ideas). He didn't rule out the possibility that his friends were right, but he said, "Unless I see the nail marks in [Jesus'] hands and put my finger where the nails were, and put my hand into his side, I will not believe" (John 20:25).

But then, importantly, he hung around the places where that divine encounter would most likely happen. Jesus was more than willing to meet him halfway. The One who had bled and died suddenly showed up alive in the room with Thomas.

That got Thomas's attention! He was probably shaking in his sandals, not only because Jesus was alive but because Thomas had been so hesitant to believe. Rather than expressing anger, Jesus gently encouraged him to look at his hands and to touch the wound in his side.

That was good enough for Thomas. He didn't need to investigate further or ask any more questions. Abruptly and wholeheartedly, Thomas turned from skeptic to Christ-follower. He accepted not only the reality of Jesus' resurrection but also the truth about who Jesus claimed to be. "Thomas said to him, 'My Lord and my God!'" (John 20:28).

And get this: Jesus actually blesses people everywhere who, like Thomas, are willing to ask hard questions, search for real answers, and have the courage to follow the facts all the way back to him. "Because you have seen me, you have believed," Jesus said in verse 29. "Blessed are those who have not seen and yet have believed."

Truth for Today

To doubt is human. But God's blessings await those who approach their doubts with diligent investigation, a sincere search for truth, and a willingness to seek the One who showed that he was the truth.

PATHWAYS TO BELIEF, PART 1

I have become all things to all people so that by all possible means I might save some. I do all this for the sake of the gospel.

1 Corinthians 9:22–23

HAVE YOU EVER TRIED TO TALK WITH A FRIEND ABOUT YOUR faith but felt you were speaking a different language? Maybe you were! In *Confident Faith*, Mark Mittelberg explores six approaches or "faith paths" people tend to follow.[1] Understanding these paths, along with their strengths and weaknesses, can help you discuss your faith with all kinds of people.

1. **Relativistic Faith Path**

   Some people arrive at their beliefs via the *relativistic* path; they assume whatever they believe becomes true for them. You'll hear them talk about "their truth" versus "your truth." This approach can be alluring, but its mind-over-matter thinking quickly collapses when confronted with reality.

2. **Traditional Faith Path**

   Others take the *traditional* path, passively accepting the teachings passed down to them by parents or teachers. This is a natural way to begin a journey to faith, but traditions may or may not promote truth. We must "test them all; hold on to what is good" (1 Thessalonians 5:21). Only then can we be confident in our beliefs.

3. **Authoritarian Faith Path**

   The *authoritarian* path leads people to submit to the ideas of a powerful leader or organization. These beliefs could be correct, but the credentials and message of those authorities need to be weighed against logic, evidence, and the truth of the Bible. Jesus warned about malicious leaders who would deceive people, so we must be cautious (Matthew 24:4–5, 11).

4. Intuitive Faith Path

Then there's the *intuitive* faith path, which relies on inner instincts. Instincts can sometimes be helpful, but without further information they can also lead you down blind alleys. Solomon warned, "There is a way that appears to be right, but in the end it leads to death" (Proverbs 14:12).

5. Mystical Faith Path

People on the *mystical* path believe what they think God has told them. But though God *can* speak to us, the Bible warns, "Do not believe every spirit, but test the spirits to see whether they are from God" (1 John 4:1).

We will encounter these paths when speaking to others about God, but the truth is, none of them alone is optimal. In the next reading, we'll explore a more effective way to test and confirm beliefs.

Truth for Today

Paul worked to "become all things to all people . . . for the sake of the gospel" (1 Corinthians 9:22–23). We too need to try to understand our friends and how they arrived at their beliefs. Then we'll be better equipped to help them consider the truth of Christ.

PATHWAYS TO BELIEF, PART 2

"Do not believe me unless I do the works of my Father. But if I do them, even though you do not believe me, believe the works."

JOHN 10:37–38

WE HAVE EXAMINED A VARIETY OF WAYS PEOPLE FORM THEIR beliefs. These included what Mark Mittelberg calls the relativistic, traditional, authoritarian, intuitive, and mystical faith paths. Some of these can be helpful, but all have their weaknesses. They all need to be tested. The pathway we'll look at today provides tools to do that testing.[1]

6. Evidential Faith Path

The *evidential* path relies on logic and evidence to help us determine what to believe. Logic and evidence are two inescapable, God-given tools for determining what is true.

First, logic. We can't think, evaluate ideas, or make decisions without it. Some will claim they don't trust logic—but then they'll use logic to try to make their point! And do we even need to argue for the importance of evidence, which is experienced through our five senses? Scientific research relies on it; it's the foundation of our justice system; it's what we use every day to figure out what is true.

Logic and evidence really are inescapable, so we might as well learn to use them well. More than that, the Bible—itself supported by reason and evidence—tells us to test or prove truth claims using these tools, as Jesus did in the passage above. To verify his claims, he often pointed to evidence, including fulfilled prophecies, miracles, his sinless life, and his resurrection from the dead. He also warned us to examine the fruit of those who claim to be prophets to see whether the evidence supports their claims.

Now, I'm not saying we can rely on our intellects alone to get to God. He must reveal himself to us, and his Holy Spirit must draw us. Ultimately our faith needs to be in God and his Word, but logic and evidence help us know *who* God is and *which book* is his revelation.

Looking back over the other five paths, we can see that this mix of logic and evidence in the evidential path helps us evaluate the relativistic faith path, detecting its departure from reality. It provides the tools to test our traditions for determining which ones are worth keeping and for assessing the credentials of the authorities in our lives. It also helps us to size up our intuitive instinct, and to confirm or disconfirm mystical encounters.

Truth for Today

God has graciously given us the tools to evaluate and determine truth. We need to master them for ourselves in order to better point others to him.

COOL CHRISTIANS

We know that we have come to know him if we keep his commands. Whoever says, "I know him," but does not do what he commands is a liar, and the truth is not in that person.

1 John 2:3–4

"SO, MARK, ARE YOU A CHRISTIAN?"

Terry's simple question was actually quite intimidating to Mark Mittelberg in that era of his life. He was nineteen years old and living large. Thoughts of God, church, and religion were at that time low on his list of concerns.

Then on that fateful day, his friend from high school walked into the store where Mark worked, ready for a confrontation.

"Sure, I'm a Christian, Terry. What about it?" Mark replied, somewhat defensively.

Terry responded to his claim with another question: "How can you call yourself a Christian and yet do so many things that Christians don't do?"

"Well," Mark said flippantly, "I guess I'm just a *cool* Christian!"

Without batting an eye, Terry shot back, "Oh, really? Don't you know there's a word for 'cool Christians'?"

Mark shook his head, though Terry wasn't really waiting for a reply.

"They're called hypocrites!" Terry spit out.

Ouch.

Mark was not very receptive to this challenge and managed to end the conversation fairly quickly, but even after Terry left, his words lingered. At first Mark felt angry, but he soon realized why: Terry was right!

Gradually Mark's anger turned to reflection, and within a few days that reflection turned into repentance. Finally, after this and a combination of other divinely orchestrated influences, Mark committed his life to Christ. That decision changed the trajectory of his life and eternity and put him on an unexpected spiritual adventure unlike anything he had ever experienced.[1]

I relay this story because the truth I want to share today is sobering but essential: Many people who claim to be Christians are really just "cool Christians." They use the name of Christ and they sometimes go to church, but they aren't really walking with God. Ultimately, as the verses above explain, their life is a lie—to themselves, to others, and to God.

Jesus asked in Luke 6:46, "Why do you call me, 'Lord, Lord,' and do not do what I say?" Yes, we are saved by faith in Jesus alone—but real faith changes us. It turns us into genuine and obedient followers of Christ. So let's not fool ourselves, and let's not let our loved ones be fooled either.

Truth for Today

The apostle Paul urged each of us to "examine yourselves to see whether you are in the faith; test yourselves" (2 Corinthians 13:5). There's no lasting joy or adventure in being a "cool Christian," so let's make sure we're *real* Christians instead.

DO vs. DONE

*He saved us, not because of righteous things we had done,
but because of his mercy.*

TITUS 3:5

OUR ACTIONS MATTER. JAMES SAID, "FAITH BY ITSELF, IF IT IS
not accompanied by action, is dead" (James 2:17).

But Paul explained, "It is by grace you have been saved, through
faith—and this is not from yourselves, it is the gift of God—not by
works, so that no one can boast" (Ephesians 2:8–9).

So what does the Bible really teach about salvation and how
to access it? Our tendency is to think we have to earn everything.
We *earn* our reputation. We *earn* our wages. We *earn* our place in
society. So we naturally think we must *earn* the favor of God.

It was the same in Jesus' day. That's why the people asked him,
"What must we do to do the works God requires?" (John 6:28).

Jesus' answer was telling: "The work of God is this: to believe
in the one he has sent" (v. 29). In other words, don't *do* anything;
just trust in the One who does it for you.

Bill Hybels explains that there's a "difference between religion
and Christianity. Religion is spelled D-O, because it consists of the
things people *do* to try to somehow gain God's forgiveness and favor.
The problem is that you never know when you've done enough. . . .
Worse yet, the Bible tells us in Romans 3:23 that we *never* can do
enough. We always fall short of God's perfect standard.

"Thankfully," Bill continues, "Christianity is spelled differently. It's spelled D-O-N-E, which means that what we could never
do for ourselves, Christ has already done for us. He lived a perfect
life we could never live, and he willingly died on the cross to pay
the penalty we owed for the wrongs we've done."[1]

No wonder they call it good news! We don't need to earn anything. We simply need to put our faith in the One who laid down his life as a ransom for us and then cried out, "It is finished" (John 19:30). He has done everything on our behalf.

After we trust in Christ, we'll naturally want to do works of service, not to earn anything, but out of gratitude to God and as an expression of our new nature. In fact, Paul added this: "For we are God's handiwork, created in Christ Jesus to do good works, which God prepared in advance for us to do" (Ephesians 2:10).

Truth for Today

Christ has done everything needed for your salvation. Trust in him, thank him, and then serve him wholeheartedly. Oh, and explain to others the exciting news of *DO* versus *DONE*.

MESSENGERS OF GOD?

*If we or an angel from heaven should preach a gospel other
than the one we preached to you, let them be under God's
curse!*

GALATIANS 1:8

THE BIBLE RECORDS A NUMBER OF INCIDENTS WHERE PEOPLE
were visited by angels. Many people have reported angelic visitations throughout history since then. Imagine an angel of God
standing in front of you, telling you what God wants you to know
or do. You'd listen carefully and respond to everything it told you,
right?

Hold on. As amazing as such an experience might be, the Bible
warns that it may not be what it seems. Why? Because even if the
angel is real, that doesn't necessarily mean it speaks for God. In
fact, some are fallen angels who are God's enemies.

The apostle Paul was so concerned about this he warned about
it twice in Galatians 1:8–9: "But even if we or an angel from heaven
should preach a gospel other than the one we preached to you, let
them be under God's curse! As we have already said, so now I say
again: If anybody is preaching to you a gospel other than what you
accepted, let them be under God's curse!"

Paul was telling us to test every teacher—human or otherwise—by carefully weighing what they say against what is already
known from the Scriptures. New revelations, if they are really from
God, may bring new or more personal information, but they will
never contradict his prior revelations. Isn't it interesting, in light of
these warnings, that the religion of Islam started when Muhammad
listened to the teaching of an angel? Similarly, Mormonism began

after Joseph Smith claimed he was visited by an angel (or group of angels). In both cases the messages conveyed were different "gospels" from the ones God had revealed in Scripture.

Elsewhere Paul was explicit about why he gave these warnings: "Satan himself masquerades as an angel of light. It is not surprising, then, if his servants also masquerade as servants of righteousness" (2 Corinthians 11:14).

We must, therefore, be very careful whom we listen to—without ruling out the possibility that God may communicate to us in extraordinary ways. In fact, Peter predicted such things on the day of Pentecost (Acts 2:16–21). And Paul admonished, "Do not quench the Spirit. Do not treat prophecies with contempt but test them all; hold on to what is good" (1 Thessalonians 5:19–21).

Truth for Today

Hebrews 3:15 warns: "Today, if you hear his voice, do not harden your hearts." God usually speaks to us through the Bible, but he might also lead you in other ways consistent with the Bible. Keep your ears, and your heart, open to him.

WINSOME REPRESENTATIVES

Be wise in the way you act toward outsiders; make the most of every opportunity. Let your conversation be always full of grace, seasoned with salt, so that you may know how to answer everyone.

COLOSSIANS 4:5–6

IF YOU ARE A FOLLOWER OF CHRIST, YOUR LIFE IS NOT YOUR own. It belongs to God for his purposes. And Jesus spelled out his central purpose for each of us when he told his original disciples—and, through them, *us*—to go into all the world and make more disciples (Matthew 28:18–20).

I was tempted to say that this command was not just for missionaries, but that would have been incorrect. It actually *was* just for missionaries—and we're all missionaries! As Mark Mittelberg likes to remind people, "According to the Bible, we're all strangers in a strange land, residing in a spiritually foreign culture—even if you still live in the hometown where you grew up. And therefore we're all missionaries on assignment to bring the love and truth of Christ to everyone around us!"

How are we to do this?

First, we need to own the truth that this really is our mission from God. In fact, the primary reason he has us on this planet is to spread his gospel to other people (see Luke 19:10; John 20:21).

Second, we must get prepared to explain what we believe and to "give an answer to everyone who asks you to give the reason for the hope that you have" (1 Peter 3:15). That's why evangelism and apologetics training are so important; they help us think through what we can say to make our message clear.

Third, we need to follow Paul's example to "become all things to all people so that by all possible means I might save some. I do all this for the sake of the gospel, that I may share in its blessings" (1 Corinthians 9:22–23). In other words, we need to learn to translate the unadulterated biblical message into language that people will understand. In missionary terms, we need to contextualize the message to the culture without compromising that message.

Fourth, we must foster the winsome attitude encouraged in Colossians 4:5–6: "Be wise in the way you act toward outsiders; make the most of every opportunity. Let your conversation be always full of grace, seasoned with salt, so that you may know how to answer everyone."

Truth for Today

God wants you to be his winsome representative. Do what it takes to get ready. Know what you believe and why, and learn how to say it in plain language. Then "make the most of every opportunity" to tell others about Christ.

GOD'S UNIQUE LOVE

God is love.

1 JOHN 4:8

IT SEEMS SO SIMPLE: *GOD IS LOVE.* THIS IS A THEOLOGICAL truth many of us have heard for most of our lives, so we mark it off of our checklist for Christian orthodoxy.

"Got it," we say, and we move on.

But did you know that most other worldviews and religions diminish or deny this idea? Atheism, of course, denies that God exists at all, so there is nobody out there to love us. Eastern religions generally hold to a pantheistic view that says everything is part of an impersonal *All.* But when everything is god, you no longer have a personal God who can relate to us as people and certainly not One who can love us.

Even Islam, a religion that believes in one God, downplays the idea that God is love. The Qur'an does describe him a few times as being loving, but this is minimized by the fact that a number of other passages in the Qur'an "qualify Allah's love significantly," explains Christian philosopher David Wood. "While Allah is said to love those who do good deeds (2:195), those who are pure (2:222), those who are righteous (9:7), and those who fight in his cause (61:4), the Qur'an is equally clear that Allah has no love for transgressors (2:190), ungrateful sinners (2:276), the unjust (3:57), or the proud (4:36).

"Even more significantly," Wood continues, "the Qur'an states that Allah does not love non-Muslims: 'Say [O Muhammad]: If you love Allah, then follow me, Allah will love you and forgive you your faults, and Allah is Forgiving, Merciful. Say: Obey Allah and the Apostle; but if they turn back, then surely *Allah does not love the unbelievers*' (Qur'an 3:31–32)."[1]

Muslim apologist Shabir Ally summarized it like this: "The proper response to God is to love Him, and in response God will love us as well."[2] But the apostle Paul said just the opposite: "God demonstrates his own love for us in this: While we were still sinners, Christ died for us" (Romans 5:8).

Once you see how many ways various belief systems around the world tend to minimize God's love, Christian truths about the God of Scripture jump out in stark and satisfying contrast.

Truth for Today

Try to push through the fog of the familiar to realize anew the uniqueness of the God of the Bible. *He loves us.* We matter so much that he sacrificed his Son to pay for our sins and to pave the way back to him. This is a God to be followed, worshiped, and, yes, loved in return.

GOD'S PERSONAL LOVE

*I pray that you, being rooted and established in love, may
have power, together with all the Lord's holy people, to grasp
how wide and long and high and deep is the love of Christ,
and to know this love that surpasses knowledge—that you
may be filled to the measure of all the fullness of God.*

EPHESIANS 3:17–19

MOST CHRISTIANS UNDERSTAND GOD'S LOVE ON A GRAND
scale. Growing up, we learned from John 3:16 that "God so loved the
world"—and he does. He loves all people and, as we saw earlier, he
demonstrated that love by sending Jesus to die for us (Romans 5:8).

For many of us it's easier to comprehend and accept this grand-
scale love than it is to grasp the fact that he loves us as individuals.
He loves *you*. He loves *me*.

"Jesus loves me, this I know, for the Bible tells me so," says the
Sunday school song you may have learned growing up. But have
you ever let that really soak in?

It's an age-old exercise, but sometimes it helps just to take a
verse like John 3:16 and personalize it. Put your name in place of
the broader terms like "the world." Try it now, preferably out loud,
and include verse 17 at the same time:

> "For God so loved [*my name*] that he gave his one and only Son,
> that [*if I believe in him, then I*] shall not perish but have eternal
> life. For God did not send his Son into the world to condemn
> [*me*], but to save [*me*] through him."

Think about that. The eternal, almighty, all-knowing Author
of the universe loved *you and me* enough to sacrifice his very own

Son in order to pay the penalty we owed for our sin and to open the door of heaven to us. We are truly loved in ways that go beyond words! Or, as today's passage puts it, in a way that "surpasses knowledge."

In fact, let's take those verses and personalize them as well:

> I pray that [*I*], being rooted and established in love, may have power, together with all the Lord's holy people, to grasp how wide and long and high and deep is the love of Christ, and to know this love that surpasses knowledge—that [*I*] may be filled to the measure of all the fullness of God. (Ephesians 3:17–19)

Truth for Today

God is not just the Creator of the universe; he's the One who lovingly knit you together in your mother's womb. He's not just the redeemer of humankind; he's the lover of your soul who came in the person of Christ to pay your ransom and adopt you into his family. "Yes, Jesus loves [*your name*]!"

SPIRITUAL CONFIDENCE

I write these things to you who believe in the name of the
Son of God so that you may know that you have eternal life.

1 JOHN 5:13

MANY PEOPLE SIMPLY GUESS WHEN IT COMES TO THEIR STANDING
before God and their prospects of getting into heaven. They figure
that as long as they're living a more-or-less moral life, observing a
few religious practices, and doing better than the next person, then
God will give them a pass into paradise after they die—or at least
they hope he will.

Hope is the operative word in their calculations—because they
don't really have an objective basis for their assumptions or any
way of measuring whether they're really right with God. That hope
erodes, though, in moments of personal awareness when they realize they're not all that moral after all, at least when it comes to their
true thoughts, desires, motives, and intents—let alone their inconsistent outward actions. When this track record is mixed with an
understanding of what Jesus taught about the performance level
necessary to pass God's bar of entry, namely perfection (Matthew
5:48), then despair often sets in.

Hopelessness, ironically, is a more honest emotion than hope,
given the reality of the situation. The truth is that if we were left to
fend for ourselves before an unwaveringly holy God based on our
own spiritual performances, all we'd be left with is despair.

We should be thankful we don't have to fend for ourselves
or bank on our own spotty spiritual performance. Instead, if
we confess our sins and turn to God to receive his forgiveness
and cleansing (1 John 1:9), then "we have an advocate with the

Father—Jesus Christ, the Righteous One" (1 John 2:1). And because of Christ in our lives, we can know that "God has given us eternal life, and this life is in his Son" (1 John 5:11).

Once we're clear that we have asked Jesus for his forgiveness and leadership, this next confidence-building verse applies to us: "I write these things to you who believe in the name of the Son of God so that you may *know* that you have eternal life" (1 John 5:13, emphasis mine).

Christianity was never meant to be a "hope-so" faith; it is a "know-so" faith that's based on what Jesus, our Advocate, has done for us.

Truth for Today

God wants us to have spiritual confidence both for today and for eternity, but it must be grounded in a right relationship with Jesus. "Whoever has the Son has life; whoever does not have the Son of God does not have life" (1 John 5:12).

THE ULTIMATE DOORWAY

"Here I am! I stand at the door and knock. If anyone hears my voice and opens the door, I will come in and eat with that person, and they with me."

REVELATION 3:20

FROM OUR PERSPECTIVE, WE CAN DO MUCH TO SEARCH FOR and discover the true God. Jesus said: "Ask and it will be given to you; seek and you will find; knock and the door will be opened to you" (Luke 11:9). His assumption is that God has given us everything we need to find and follow him.

But other verses make it clear that our seeking after God is actually a response to his first seeking after us. In fact, left to our own propensities, Romans 3:11 explains, none of us would look for God. Our ability to move toward him is enabled by his first moving toward us. He awakens in us the necessary spiritual desire. So think about this: if we are sincerely seeking God today, it's evidence that he is already working in our lives.

Further, even though Jesus told us to seek and to knock, in Revelation 3:20 he assured us he is already on the other side of the door, knocking and calling out to us in the hope we'll hear his voice and open the door to an authentic relationship with him.

Whom is Jesus knocking for? Anyone who realizes he is spiritually "wretched, pitiful, poor, blind and naked" (Revelation 3:17). That describes all of us because of our sins against God. This reality ought to break us of spiritual self-reliance or the thought that we can somehow earn our way back to God. Our sins are offenses against a holy God, and our efforts fall far too short of his perfect standard.

Fortunately, Jesus said to all of us in Revelation 3:20, "Here I am! I stand at the door and knock." Can you hear him? Do you sense his presence? Do you recognize your spiritual need? Whether you've never responded to him before or you've simply drifted away from him, he is extending to you his gifts of grace and guidance.

Truth for Today

Jesus is knocking. Will you humble yourself, turn from your sins, and ask for his help and strength? In other words, will you stand up, grasp the handle, and fling open the door? Let Jesus in and you will immediately experience his forgiveness, his friendship, and a whole new sense of purpose for your life.

THE LIFE-CHANGING GOSPEL

I am not ashamed of the gospel, because it is the power of God that brings salvation to everyone who believes.

ROMANS 1:16

MARK MITTELBERG HAD BEEN TEACHING A ROOMFUL OF LEADERS about the gospel—how Jesus died for our sins so we could have God's forgiveness and new life in him. He also went through some principles related to sharing one's story of coming to know and follow Christ.

During a break a man came up to ask Mark a question. His name was Steve, and he wanted to clarify some things he'd been hearing.

As Mark explained to him what he meant about all people needing to make sure they had put their faith in Christ and let God lead their lives, suddenly something unexpected happened: Steve burst into tears!

Realizing the message had struck a nerve, Mark suggested that they spend the upcoming lunch break together so they could discuss Steve's concerns.

As soon as the group broke for lunch, the two dashed to Mark's car, where they ended up spending most of the break talking.

Steve shared how he had been involved in a variety of church programs over the years, but he had never actually asked Jesus to be his Savior. He was religious, but he now realized he didn't have a genuine relationship with Christ. This was very troubling to him.

Mark explained to Steve that many people were in this situation, and he urged Steve not to stay in it any longer. Mark then explained the gospel one more time, and Steve affirmed that he believed it. After they'd talked for a while, Steve also affirmed that he wanted to be forgiven for his sins and to know he was a true member of God's family.

So right then and there, sitting in Mark's car in the parking lot next to the deli where they were going to have lunch, the guys prayed together. Steve sincerely asked Jesus to be his forgiver and his leader.

This was a turning point in Steve's life. Since then Steve has grown immensely in his faith, written a couple of devotional books, and even served for a season as the pastor of a church.

All this happened because Steve heard and responded to the life-changing message of the gospel.

Truth for Today

In many ways our message is simple: God loves us; we blew it; Christ died for us; we must receive him. But don't let its simplicity make you think this truth is not potent, because, as today's verse says, it is "the power of God that brings salvation to everyone who believes." So share this message boldly, and watch God use it.

IMPOSSIBLY LARGE ROCKS

"I am the LORD, the God of all mankind. Is anything too hard for me?"

JEREMIAH 32:27

"YOU BELIEVE GOD CAN DO ANYTHING AND EVERYTHING, RIGHT?" goes a common objection. "Then do you believe that God can create a rock so heavy that he can't lift it? If you say no, then he can't *create* everything. But if you say yes, then he can't *lift* everything. Either way, you no longer have an all-powerful God!"

This is a question Mark Mittelberg and I have heard many times during Q&A sessions. Here are a few thoughts:

- First, let's be clear: there are things God *can't* do. The Bible says, for example, that God cannot lie (Titus 1:2, Hebrews 6:18). It also teaches that he cannot sin in any way because sin goes against his very nature (James 1:13). So God cannot do all things.

- But someone might ask, "Don't you believe that God is *omnipotent*, meaning all-powerful?" The answer is yes. "I am the LORD, the God of all mankind. *Is anything too hard for me?*" (Jeremiah 32:27, emphasis mine). Anything that can be done with power, God can do. That's what omnipotence means.

- However, there are many things that power can't do. It can't make two plus two equal five; it can't make a circular square; it can't force logical fallacies to make sense. All of these are logical contradictions, and God can't contradict logic because it flows out of his very nature. Therefore, God cannot create things so complicated that he can't understand them, or so far away that he can't reach them, or so heavy that he can't lift them.

So nothing is impossible for God—except for self-contradiction and illogical nonsense. J. Warner Wallace summarizes it well: "Those who ask logically incoherent questions of this kind are requiring God to *violate* His nature (His logical coherency) in order to *demonstrate* His nature (His power)."[1]

Fortunately God does another difficult thing well: "He is patient with you"—including our friends who try to undo him with silly logical conundrums—"not wanting anyone to perish, but everyone to come to repentance" (2 Peter 3:9).

Truth for Today

The Bible makes it clear that while God can't contradict himself by creating rocks so large he can't lift them, he *can* move mountains (Mark 11:23–24). What mountains, or even moderately large hills, do you need to bring to God for his help today?

THE BENEFIT OF THE DOUBT

"Truly I tell you, whatever you did not do for one of the least of these, you did not do for me."

MATTHEW 25:45

ARNIE SKEIE AND HIS YOUNG DAUGHTER, JEAN, WERE DRIVING down a rural North Dakota highway in the early 1940s when they noticed a cardboard box on the road ahead of them.

Arnie pulled off the road near the box. But as he got out of his car to pick it up, he and Jean saw something they'd never forget. Suddenly a small child popped out of the box, giggling with delight at surprising these strangers.

After getting over their shock, they returned the child to his nearby home. Years later, Jean related this story to Mark Mittelberg and his wife, Heidi, who is Jean's daughter. "My father told me, 'Whenever you're unsure about situations like that, it's always better to give the benefit of the doubt and play it safe. You might be wrong, but you might save someone's life.'"

We all have the opportunity to help save lives. A battle is raging for the rights of the unborn. The medical evidence that life starts at conception is in, and it only gets stronger as technology improves. These are precious, developing children who are being destroyed in the womb. The other side has even admitted this. In her *Salon* article "So what if abortion ends life?" Mary Elizabeth Williams chillingly writes that she believes that "life begins at conception. . . . The fetus is indeed a life. A life worth sacrificing."[1]

Contrary to this, the Bible says God lovingly forms and shapes us in our mothers' wombs (Psalm 139:13), and Jesus said one of the marks of his followers is that they look out for the rights of "the least of these" (Matthew 25:45). Who could be more "least of these" than innocent, not-yet-born children who are completely dependent on our love and protection?

But what if our friends are still only half convinced these fetuses are human lives? Well, if Arnie and Jean saw the box in the road and thought there was half a chance a child was hiding inside it, would they ignore or run over the box? Of course not! Even if they thought there was a chance of one in ten thousand, they'd stop and move it.

This is precisely what we need to do when it comes to unborn children. We should follow Arnie's example: grant these unborn children the benefit of the doubt and protect what the evidence overwhelmingly shows to be living human beings.[2]

Truth for Today

This is a hard subject in our culture, especially when so many have already participated in abortions directly or indirectly. We need to speak the truth boldly but also extend grace and compassion.

REST FOR THE WEARY

"Come to me, all you who are weary and burdened, and I will give you rest. Take my yoke upon you and learn from me, for I am gentle and humble in heart, and you will find rest for your souls. For my yoke is easy and my burden is light."

MATTHEW 11:28–30

I READ A POIGNANT INTERVIEW WITH A PROMINENT AMERICAN athlete, and a portion of it reminded me of what Augustine said so many years ago about God's purpose for every person: "You have made us for yourself, and our heart is restless until it rests in you."[1]

Here's the part of the interview that grabbed me:

"Where do you call home now?" I ask.

"My heart," he says. "Wherever my heart is and I can have peace of mind. Life can seem nomadic because I don't know if I'm embracing it or running from it. I can go anywhere, but I don't know where I want to be.

"I'm searching," he says. "I'm searching, but I don't know for what. I can't see what I'm looking for. I just, like, reach out and hope I grab something. But I don't know what it will be because I don't know what I'm searching for."

"Happiness?" I ask.

"More than that," he replies. "But that would be real nice."

"What do you think about on a daily basis?" I ask. . . .

"I think about a lot," he says. . . . "I think all the time—about everything. My kids, my wife. But mostly I think about the mind. My mind. There's so much going on. So many thoughts. I think about this life. About me. Who I could be. Who I was. Who I am. Who *am* I?"[2]

206

When I was a young atheist, I was so busy building my career and climbing my way through the ranks of the newspaper that I rarely reflected on the deeper meaning—or, at that time, the lack thereof—in my life. But every once in a while I would have those rare, lie-awake-and-stare-at-the-ceiling moments when the bigger questions would seep up from my subconscious, leaving me wondering what my life was supposed to be about.

Fortunately, God didn't leave me aimless and confused for very long. He reached my wife, Leslie, and then through her and her church he reached me.

But my heart goes out to people who say, "I'm searching, but I don't know for what. I can't see what I'm looking for. I just reach out and hope I grab something. . . . Who am I?"

Jesus came for people like that. Like me. And like you. And our hearts are restless until they find their rest in him.

Truth for Today

We all know people who are searching, even if they're not sure what they're searching for. We have the great honor of introducing them to the One who can give them answers and rest.

MAKING ROOM FOR DOUBT

Be merciful to those who doubt.

JUDE V. 22

"I USED TO BE A CHRISTIAN." THOSE WERE THE STUDENT'S FIRST words. He had called because someone told him Mark Mittelberg would take his doubts seriously.

"I don't want to offer quick-fix answers over the phone," Mark told him. "How about coming to my office so we can really work through some of your questions?" The guy seemed surprised by Mark's openness but met with him that afternoon, bringing a friend with him.

As their story unfolded, Mark learned they'd been part of a nearby church that taught the Bible but didn't welcome questions. The problem was that these guys *had* questions—and kept asking them. Their youth leader tried to shut them down by telling them they just "needed to believe" and their doubts would go away. Then, during their summer church camp, the director told them more or less the same thing.

Their response? "Well, we concluded that the Bible couldn't be trusted and the Christian faith teaches things it can't prove. So we basically abandoned our belief in God," they said. In addition, they had turned a Bible study that met in one of their homes into what they now called their "Skeptics Group." There they shared with those attending the evidence they were learning *against* the Bible and Christianity.

"That's . . . fascinating," Mark said, trying to stay calm. "Well, I'm really glad you're here—and I'm willing to do whatever it takes to help you get answers to your objections."

With that, they launched into a three-hour conversation about their main areas of concern. By the end, Mark could tell their doubts were already beginning to dissipate.

"Before we go, can I make a request?" the young man asked. "I was wondering if you'd be willing to come to our Skeptics Group meeting at my house to explain some of this information to our friends. I think they'd be interested in what you have to say."

That was an easy decision. About a week later Mark and I sat with a roomful of sincere but spiritually confused teenagers. For four hours we shared our testimonies, answered questions, and challenged their thinking.

By the end of the evening, the original student had recommitted his life to Christ, and a couple weeks later the friend he had brought to Mark's office became a believer.

And, maybe the best part, they converted their Skeptics Group back into a Bible study!

Truth for Today

Students are asking spiritual questions at earlier and earlier ages. According to 1 Peter 3:15, we must be ready to give them good answers, but do so with gentleness and respect. Today's reading shows what a difference doing this can make.

WHEN ANSWERS EVADE YOU

*Since in the wisdom of God the world through its wisdom
did not know him, God was pleased through the foolishness
of what was preached to save those who believe.*

1 CORINTHIANS 1:21

"EXIT-STENCIL-*WHAT*?" MARK MITTELBERG ASKED.

"It doesn't derive from the word *exit*," Kyle explained, "but
from the word *exist*. It's called *existentialism*, and it was promoted
by thinkers like Jean-Paul Sartre, Friedrich Nietzsche, and even
the Christian philosopher Søren Kierkegaard."

"Okay," Mark said, straining to understand. "And how does
this relate to your questions about God?"

Kyle tried to explain, but Mark finally decided to move the conversation in a different direction. Fresh out of high school, new in his
relationship with Christ, and years before Mark decided to get his
master's degree in philosophy, he felt out of his league—especially
since Kyle had been one of the smartest guys in their high school.

"I'll tell you what, Kyle," Mark interjected. "You might be able
to help me understand this *existent—um,* the philosophy you're
studying, but for now there's some basic information about Jesus
that's important for you to understand. And since I'm fairly new to
all of this, I'd like to play you a talk a Christian speaker gave that I
thought was helpful. It's about the message of the Bible and how we
can know God personally. Okay with you?"

"Sure," Kyle responded.

When the recording finished, Mark let a moment of silence go
by to allow the powerful message of the gospel to sink in. "Well,
Kyle, what do you think?"

"I've never heard anything like that before," Kyle said. "That was really powerful."

Since Kyle seemed so receptive, Mark decided to ask him point-blank: "Where do you see yourself right now in terms of your relationship with God?"

Kyle's next words amazed Mark. "I think I need to do what that guy was talking about and ask for God's forgiveness."

Wow, Mark thought. *What happened to all of his philosophical questions?* Now that those questions seemed to have dissolved, Mark just went with the flow. He led Kyle in a prayer of commitment to Christ right then and there.

This led to big changes in Kyle's life. The last time Mark saw him, Kyle was heading overseas for the chance to serve people in a different culture and to tell them what it means to follow Jesus.

Truth for Today

There will always be questions we don't feel equipped to answer. Sometimes it's best to study up, get better answers, and come back to the person later. Other times God will lead us to bypass their questions and go straight to the simple message of the gospel.

DIVINE ACCESS

*Let us then approach God's throne of grace with
confidence, so that we may receive mercy and find grace to
help us in our time of need.*

HEBREWS 4:16

"ISN'T IT INTERESTING," MARK MITTELBERG SAYS, "THAT ON A
human level, the higher a person's position, the harder he is to
access? If you're having problems with a salesclerk, you can ask for
a manager, and they'll probably find one for you. But talking to
that manger's supervisor is a bit more challenging. And getting the
ear of the CEO or the owner of the corporation—good luck! There
are layers of bureaucracy and red tape between you and those sen-
ior leaders that make them almost impossible to get to.

"In light of that," Mark continues, "isn't it amazing that no
matter who we are or what we've done, we can *all* have immediate
and direct access to the almighty sovereign of the world?"

Think about it! The King of the universe has provided every
one of us a direct hotline into his throne room, and we can talk
to him day or night. More than that, he *wants* us to call—not just
in emergencies or for occasional holiday greetings, but on a daily
basis so we can discuss things that are happening in our lives, both
big and small, and have regular times of fellowship together.

Many of us grew up so surrounded by prayer that we've come
to view it as commonplace—an obligation even, rather than the
supreme opportunity and privilege that it is. Let me encourage you
to think about it again in a fresh way: *The God of the universe wants
to have regular conversations with you!*

He told Jeremiah, "Call to me and I will answer you and tell you great and unsearchable things you do not know" (Jeremiah 33:3). Paul admonished followers of Christ: "In everything by prayer and supplication, with thanksgiving, let your requests be made known to God; and the peace of God, which surpasses all understanding, will guard your hearts and minds through Christ Jesus" (Philippians 4:6–7 NKJV).

But let me add a caution from James, who encouraged us to "come near to God and he will come near to you," but pointed out the need to "wash your hands, you sinners, and purify your hearts, you double-minded" (James 4:8). We must approach God with humility and repentance, fully accepting the grace of Christ, the "one mediator between God and mankind" (1 Timothy 2:5).

Truth for Today

God wants to spend time with you today. Don't miss your divine appointment. It's a supreme privilege, and it will bless both you and him!

AN EXCLUSIVE CLUB?

In Christ Jesus you are all children of God through faith,
for all of you who were baptized into Christ have clothed
yourselves with Christ.

GALATIANS 3:26–27

A NETWORK REPORTER CALLED TO INTERVIEW ME ABOUT spirituality in America. The interview went well—until I commented that I hoped everyone would find faith in Christ. He objected that it sounded "elitist" to him when Christians claim that Jesus alone can bring eternal life.

Unfortunately, some Christians do project an air of arrogance when dealing with others. This is never acceptable, and it poorly represents Christ who, in spite of being God's Son, was "gentle and humble in heart" (Matthew 11:29). We need to show humility, love, and tolerance while at the same time upholding truth. Real Christianity is anything *but* arrogant.

Imagine two country clubs. The first has a strict set of rules and allows in only people who have earned their membership. Members have to accomplish something, obtain superior wisdom, or fulfill a long list of demands and requirements to qualify for entry. Despite their best efforts, lots of people won't make the grade and will be excluded. In effect, this is what other religious systems are like: acceptance is predicated on performance.

The second country club is different. It throws its doors open and says, "Anybody who wants membership is invited inside. Rich or poor, regardless of religious background, race, ethnic heritage, or where you live, we would love to include you. Entry is based not on your efforts or qualifications but only on accepting this invitation because your membership has already been paid. So we'll leave it up to you. You decide. But remember, if you seek admittance, we will not turn you away." That's what Christianity is like.

It's true that Jesus said, "I am the way and the truth and the life. No one comes to the Father except through me" (John 14:6). He is the one way to God. But the Bible also adds, "The Spirit and the bride say, 'Come!' And let the one who hears say, 'Come!' Let the one who is thirsty come; and let the one who wishes take the free gift of the water of life" (Revelation 22:17).

So which country club is restrictive? True Christians aren't being exclusive, but inclusive. They're not being haughty, but egalitarian. They're not pretending to be better or more accomplished than anyone else. D. T. Niles summarized Christianity this way: it's "one beggar telling another beggar where to find food."[1]

Truth for Today

Paul said Jesus "came and preached peace to you who were far away and peace to those who were near" (Ephesians 2:17). We need to reflect his inclusive spirit by showing love and hospitality to others and viewing every person as someone for whom Jesus died.

AN AVALANCHE OF SCIENTIFIC INFORMATION

Every house is built by someone, but God is the builder of everything.

HEBREWS 3:4

IT WAS CHALLENGING TO INTERVIEW THE EXPERTS, SIFT THROUGH the data, and write *The Case for a Creator*.[1] But as I reviewed the avalanche of information from my investigation, I found the evidence for an Intelligent Designer to be credible, cogent, and compelling.

In fact, I determined that the findings from cosmology (related to the origins of the universe) and physics (related to the fine-tuning of the universe) alone were sufficient to support the design hypothesis. The other data simply built an even more powerful case that ended up overwhelming any objections I might have had at the beginning.

But who or what is this master Designer? Like in a connect-the-dots puzzle, each one of the scientific disciplines I investigated contributed clues to help unmask the identity of the Creator.

As scholar William Lane Craig explained, the evidence of cosmology demonstrates that the cause of the universe must be an uncaused, beginningless, timeless, immaterial, personal being endowed with freedom of will and enormous power. In the area of physics, philosopher and physicist Robin Collins established that the Creator is intelligent and has continued to be involved with his creation after the big bang, especially in fine-tuning it to support life.

The evidence from astronomy shows that the Creator was incredibly precise in creating a livable habitat for his creatures, logically implying his care and concern for them. Also, astronomer Guillermo Gonzalez and philosopher Jay Richards presented evidence that the Creator has built at least one purpose into his creatures—to explore the world he has designed and therefore to perhaps discover him through it.

Not only do biochemistry and the existence of biological information affirm the Creator's activity after the big bang, but they also show he's incredibly creative. And the evidence of consciousness, as philosopher J. P. Moreland explained, helps establish that the Creator is rational, gives us a basis for understanding his omnipresence, and even suggests the credibility of life after death.

This evidence, as we'll see in the next reading, draws from science to paint a picture of the Creator that in many ways parallels that of Scripture. If you're interested in going deeper, I would urge you to read *The Case for a Creator*, where detailed discussions on all of the above points can be found.

Truth for Today

Whether you're a science buff or someone whose eyes glaze over with too much scientific information, I hope you see that the evidence of God's existence is growing by the day—and we have great reasons to be confident in our Creator.

UNCANNY PARALLELS

*The heavens declare the glory of God; the skies proclaim
the work of his hands. Day after day they pour forth
speech; night after night they reveal knowledge. . . . Their
voice goes out into all the earth, their words to the ends of
the world.*

PSALM 19:1–2, 4

FOR THOSE OF US WHO KNOW CHRIST, VERSES LIKE THESE
affirm our faith in God. However, if we're to influence friends who
don't share our faith, often it is more effective to start with areas
they already trust—like science—and then show how that information points in the same direction as Scripture.

So, picking up our discussion from the previous reading, let
me show how the portrait of the Creator that is suggested by the
scientific data (the terms in italics) is uncannily consistent with the
description of God in the pages of the Bible (the verses that follow).

- *Creator?* "In the beginning you laid the foundations of the
  earth, and the heavens are the work of your hands." (Psalm
  102:25)
- *Unique?* "You were shown these things so that you might
  know that the LORD is God; besides him there is no other."
  (Deuteronomy 4:35)
- *Uncaused and timeless?* "Before the mountains were born
  or you brought forth the whole world, from everlasting to
  everlasting you are God." (Psalm 90:2)
- *Immaterial?* "God is spirit." (John 4:24)
- *Personal?* "I am God Almighty." (Genesis 17:1)

- *Freedom of will?* "God said, 'Let there be light,' and there was light." (Genesis 1:3)
- *Intelligent and rational?* "How many are your works, LORD! In wisdom you made them all; the earth is full of your creatures." (Psalm 104:24)
- *Enormously powerful?* "The LORD is . . . great in power." (Nahum 1:3)
- *Creative?* "For you created my inmost being; you knit me together in my mother's womb. I praise you because I am fearfully and wonderfully made; your works are wonderful, I know that full well." (Psalm 139:13–14)
- *Caring?* "The earth is full of his unfailing love." (Psalm 33:5)
- *Omnipresent?* "The heavens, even the highest heaven, cannot contain you." (1 Kings 8:27)
- *Purposeful?* "For everything, absolutely *everything*, above and below, visible and invisible, . . . everything got started in him and finds its purpose in him." (Colossians 1:16 THE MESSAGE)
- *Life-giving?* "He will swallow up death forever." (Isaiah 25:8)

As the apostle Paul wrote two millennia ago: "Since the creation of the world God's invisible qualities—his eternal power and divine nature—have been clearly seen, being understood from what has been made, so that people are without excuse" (Romans 1:20).

Truth for Today

Isn't it fascinating to see how the "book of nature" aligns with the "book of Scripture"? Let this encourage and embolden you in your faith today.

FROM SCIENCE TO GOD

God chose the foolish things of the world to shame the wise;
God chose the weak things of the world to shame the strong.

1 CORINTHIANS 1:27

NO ONE WAS MORE SURPRISED BY THE SCIENTIFIC EVIDENCE
for God than the soft-spoken, silver-haired physician sitting across
from me. Viggo Olsen is a brilliant surgeon whose life has been
steeped in science. In fact, he attributed his spiritual skepticism to
his knowledge of the scientific world.[1]

"I viewed Christianity and the Bible through agnostic eyes," he
said. "My wife, Joan, was a skeptic too. We believed there was no
independent proof that any Creator exists."

The problem was Joan's parents, both devout Christians. When
Viggo and Joan visited them, they got an earful of religious information. In late-night discussions, Viggo and Joan would patiently
explain why Christianity was inconsistent with contemporary science. Finally, in frustration one night, they agreed to examine the
evidence for themselves.

"My intent was not to do an objective study at all," Olsen recalled.
"Just like a surgeon incises a chest, we were going to slash into the
Bible and dissect out all its embarrassing scientific mistakes."

Viggo and Joan labeled a piece of paper: "Scientific Mistakes in
the Bible," figuring they could easily fill it. Well, problems quickly
emerged—but not the kind they were anticipating. "We were having trouble finding those scientific mistakes," he said.

Then a student gave Viggo an old book called *Modern Science
and Christian Faith*. In it, different scientists had each written a chapter about the evidence in his or her field that pointed toward God.[2]

"It blew our minds!" Olsen said. "For the first time we began to see there were reasons behind Christianity."

They devoured that book and eventually came to the conclusion that, yes, a personal Creator-God does exist. And they continued to explore until all they had learned "came together into a wonderful, magnificent, glowing, fabulous picture of Jesus."

They gave their lives to him. Soon they felt called to serve in a place devoid of both Christians and medical care, and they ended up spending thirty-three years in the poverty-wracked nation of Bangladesh.

Viggo also wrote several books, including a great little piece about his spiritual journey called *The Agnostic Who Dared to Search*.[3]

Truth for Today

Two truths for today: First, science, properly understood and applied, reinforces our Christian faith. Second, nobody is beyond the reach of God's truth and grace.

THE BURDEN OF PROOF

"Will the one who contends with the Almighty correct him?
Let him who accuses God answer him!"

JOB 40:2

ATHEIST RICHARD DAWKINS, THE AUTHOR OF *THE GOD DELUSION*, likes to tell Christians that "the onus is on you to say why you believe in something."[1] His argument is that since we're the ones claiming God exists, it is up to *us* to explain why that claim is true.

I love Mark's Mittelberg's response to this challenge in his book *The Questions Christians Hope No One Will Ask (With Answers):*[2] "It would be easy to get fretful about this and say, 'Oh no, the onus is on me. What am I going to do? The onus is on—wait a minute, what's an *onus*? Anyway, whatever it is, it's on *me!*'

"Now, that's partly true. We do need to give a good defense. But we need to get on the offense too. For example, you could reply, 'You say the onus is on me because I believe in something? Well, what about you? Do you believe in the Holocaust? So do I. But who is the onus on regarding *that*? The people who believe it or the people who deny it?'

"Obviously, it's on those who deny it. When it comes to well-known facts of history such as the Holocaust, it is the small minority denying common knowledge who bear the burden of proof. Similarly, in a world where the majority of people believe in God, and in which many strong arguments have been made for his existence and his activity in people's lives, it's the people who deny this common knowledge who should bear the burden of proof.

"Honestly, I'd be willing to split the onus right down the middle because—and this is important—nobody is neutral; everybody is making a claim to something. The atheist is making the claim that there is no God, those in other religions are making their particular claims about God's existence and nature, and we Christians are doing this as well. So all of us should be willing to give a defense for what we believe."

I couldn't agree more. The Bible teaches that as Christians we need to have a good defense ("Be prepared to give an answer" [1 Peter 3:15]) as well as a good offense ("We demolish arguments and every pretension that sets itself up against the knowledge of God" [2 Corinthians 10:5]).

Both are vital in our task to present Christ to a world that is dying without him.

Truth for Today

You don't have to be intimidated by the bold claims of the God-deniers. Truth is on our side, and "If God is for us, who can be against us?" (Romans 8:31).

GOD AND SLAVERY

There is neither Jew nor Gentile, neither slave nor free, nor is there male and female, for you are all one in Christ Jesus.

GALATIANS 3:28

"HOW CAN YOU BE A CHRISTIAN," PEOPLE ASK, "WHEN THE Bible condones slavery—and Jesus never condemned it?"

Here are some thoughts on this sensitive issue from my interview with theologian D. A. Carson.[1]

"In his book *Race and Culture*, African-American scholar Thomas Sowell points out that every major world culture until the modern period, without exception, has had slavery," Carson explained.[2] "While it could be tied to military conquests, usually slavery served an economic function. They didn't have bankruptcy laws, so if you got yourself into terrible hock, you sold yourself and/or your family into slavery. As it was discharging a debt, slavery was also providing work.

"In Roman times there were menial laborers who were slaves, and there were also others who were the equivalent of distinguished PhDs who were teaching families. And there was no association of a particular race with slavery.

"In American slavery, though, all blacks and only blacks were slaves. That was one of the peculiar horrors of it, and it generated an unfair sense of black inferiority that many of us continue to fight to this day.

"Now let's look at the Bible. In Jewish society, under the Law everyone was to be freed every Jubilee. In other words, there was a slavery liberation every seventh year, . . . and this was the framework in which Jesus was brought up.

"But you have to keep your eye on Jesus' mission. Essentially, he did not come to overturn the Roman economic system, which included slavery. He came to free men and women from their sins. And here's my point: what his message does is transform people so they begin to love God with all their heart, soul, mind, and strength and to love their neighbor as themselves. Naturally, that has an impact on the idea of slavery.

"Look at what the apostle Paul says in his letter to Philemon concerning a runaway slave named Onesimus. . . . [H]e tells Philemon he'd better treat Onesimus as a brother in Christ, just as he would treat Paul himself. And then, to make matters perfectly clear, Paul emphasizes, 'Remember, you owe your whole life to me because of the gospel.'"

It's worth adding that the modern slave trade was abolished largely through the efforts of Christians. This included the former slave ship owner John Newton, who found God's grace for his own life (and subsequently wrote the song "Amazing Grace"), and his friend William Wilberforce.

Truth for Today

The Bible upholds the dignity and worth of every human being—people created in the image of God. We must do the same.

GOD AND RACISM

I now realize how true it is that God does not show favoritism but accepts from every nation the one who fears him and does what is right.

ACTS 10:34–35

PETER GREW UP IN A CULTURE SHAPED BY GOD'S COMMANDS that Jewish people be separate from the nations around them. This was largely to keep their lineage distinct until the coming of the Messiah through them. But in spite of this separation, God made clear to them his intention that ultimately "all peoples on earth will be blessed through you" (Genesis 12:3).

After Jesus had come, God needed to help his people adjust their way of thinking, including the fact that their days of separation were over. Also, they had to accept that they should wholeheartedly follow their Messiah, Jesus, and take his gospel to every nation in the world (Matthew 28:18–20). He brought this message to Peter in a poignant way, giving him the vision in Acts 10 that told him to no longer consider things unclean that God now called clean—including foods as well as people. Peter got the point.

This is a message for every Christian. Years ago I knew a businessman who was a rabid racist with a superior and condescending attitude toward anyone of another color. He hardly made any effort to conceal his contempt for African-Americans, frequently letting his bigoted bile spill out in crude jokes and caustic remarks. No amount of argument could dissuade him from his disgusting opinions.

Then he became a follower of Jesus. As I watched in amazement, his attitudes, his perspective, and his values changed over time as God renewed his heart. He came to realize that he could no longer harbor ill will toward any person, since the Bible teaches that all people are made in the image of God. Today I can honestly say that he's genuinely caring and accepting of others, including those who are different from him.

Legislation didn't change this man. *Reason* didn't change him. *Emotional appeals* didn't change him. He'll tell you that *God* changed him from the inside out—decisively, completely, permanently. That's one of many examples I've seen of the gospel's power to transform vengeful haters into humanitarians, hard-hearted hoarders into soft-hearted givers, powermongers into selfless servants, and people who exploit others into those who embrace all.

Truth for Today

In spite of the powerful lesson that "God does not show favoritism," Peter did not change completely overnight. He had to relearn his views over time with God's help. No matter how mature we are, all of us need to keep learning and applying these lessons to our own lives as well.

LIFE WITHOUT GOD

If the dead are not raised, "Let us eat and drink, for tomorrow we die."

1 CORINTHIANS 15:32

I LIVED MY EARLY ADULT YEARS AS AN ATHEIST. WHILE I WON'T deny there were some exciting moments during that era, there were certainly some things missing from my life as well. Let me mention three in this reading and one more in the next.

1. PURPOSE. Sure, I had goals and was very driven in my career. But I didn't have a purpose that transcended my self-serving narcissistic desires. So I lived for pleasure and personal gain, and I was willing to run over anyone who got in my way.

2. MORAL COMPASS. Because of my lack of purpose, and because I didn't believe in a God who gave us moral principles to live by, I decided for myself what was good or bad, right or wrong. And I often chose the wrong things—things that hurt me, Leslie, and later our kids. I'm not saying I never did anything good, or that atheists can't live moral lives. It's just that without God there was no compelling reason to do so. More than that, there was no objective standard of right and wrong by which to make moral decisions, and as a result I often made a mess of things.

3. MEANING. When, as an atheist, I would honestly assess whether there was any greater meaning in my life, I'd come up empty. Not that I couldn't enjoy isolated moments and relationships, but I knew that in the grand scheme of things, it would all fade away. Nothing would last; nothing would outlive us. Renowned atheist Bertrand Russell summed up well what I knew in my

heart about mankind apart from God: "His origin, his growth, his hopes and fears, his loves and his beliefs, are but the outcome of accidental collocations of atoms. . . . No fire, no heroism, no intensity of thought and feeling, can preserve an individual life beyond the grave. . . . All the labours of the ages, all the devotion, all the inspiration, all the noonday brightness of human genius, are destined to extinction in the vast death of the solar system. . . . The whole temple of Man's achievement must inevitably be buried beneath the debris of a universe in ruins."[1]

Not a very exciting outlook, but from the atheistic perspective, an honest one. And we haven't even considered *death* apart from God, which we'll discuss in the next reading. Fortunately, atheism is not a point of view anyone is stuck with. God is patiently waiting for people to turn to him (see 2 Peter 3:9).

Truth for Today

Contrasted to these missing elements in my life, we as Christians can thank God that he has given us (1) compelling purpose, (2) a moral compass, and (3) true meaning in our lives.

DEATH WITHOUT GOD

Why, you do not even know what will happen tomorrow.
What is your life? You are a mist that appears for a little
while and then vanishes.

JAMES 4:14

IN THE PREVIOUS READING I DISCUSSED THREE AREAS THAT were lacking in my life when I was an atheist. Here is one more: having hope in the face of death.

Mark Mittelberg recently met an atheist who was outspoken about his belief that there is no God. Soon after they met, a relative of this man died and he was asked to say a few words at the funeral, which was to be held in a church.

All the man could say to the gathered group was that everyone ends up where animals go when they die—to deterioration and decay—and that we can never rely on the false comfort of ever seeing our loved ones again. It was a morose response, but the only one that his spiritual skepticism would allow.

I would have had the same response when I was an atheist. His perspective poignantly described the sadness, despair, and seeming finality of death for those who don't know Christ.

It doesn't have to be that way. Jesus promised that those who honestly seek him will find him. Further, for those who follow him, this life is only the beginning of a much greater reality—one that stretches throughout eternity. These promises are not poetic platitudes. They're true, and we can be confident in them because we serve the One who conquered the grave and triumphed over death. And it was Jesus who said: "I am the resurrection and the life. The one who believes in me will live, even though they die" (John 11:25).

Because of the words and the works of Jesus, we can be confident of life beyond what we're experiencing now. Death is not the end. We were made to live on in God's presence, in a new and greater world.

As I wrote in my book *The Case for Hope*, "When you reach out to Jesus in prayer and wholeheartedly receive the grace he offers you, then you too can have full confidence that when your eyes close in death, they will reopen immediately in God's presence. You can live with the confident expectation, assurance, and joy that you'll spend eternity in heaven with Jesus and countless fellow believers, your brothers and sisters in Christ."[1]

Truth for Today

Paul reminded us that Jesus died and rose again, so as his followers we don't have to "grieve like the rest of mankind, who have no hope" (1 Thessalonians 4:13).

HISTORY SPEAKS

Christ Jesus . . . in very nature God, . . . found in appearance as a man, . . . humbled himself by becoming obedient to death—even death on a cross! Therefore God exalted him to the highest place.

PHILIPPIANS 2:5–6, 8–9

MARK MITTELBERG HAD NEVER BEEN INSIDE A MOSQUE BEFORE, and neither had those taking the tour with him. They were welcomed, shown around, ushered into a large room, and asked to sit on the floor.

Soon the imam, dressed in white, spoke to them. He passionately explained the teachings of Islam and then grew more intense. "It is important for you to know that Allah is the one and only God, and that Muhammad—peace be upon him—was his true prophet. God is not divided, and he does not have a son," he declared emphatically. "Jesus—peace be upon him—was *not* the Son of God. He was a true prophet, like Muhammad, and we are to honor him—but we must never worship him. We worship Allah and Allah alone."

He also explained that Jesus did not die on the cross—Allah would never allow his prophet to die in such a shameful way. Then he wrapped up his comments and invited questions. As Mark listened, he wrestled with some matters at the heart of what he'd heard.

"I'm curious about something," Mark finally said. "Jesus' followers walked and talked with him for several years. They also reported that he repeatedly claimed to be the Son of God, that they watched him die on the cross, and that three days later they saw, talked, and ate with him after his resurrection. We have detailed accounts of what they heard and saw. These have been preserved in literally thousands of manuscript documents that attest to these realities.

"Now, correct me if I'm wrong," Mark continued. "But what Islam teaches us about Jesus seems to be based on the words of one man, Muhammad, who, six hundred years after the time of Christ, was sitting in a cave when—he claimed—an angel spoke to him and told him these things weren't so.

"I'm curious whether you have any historical or logical reasons for why we should accept that viewpoint over and against the actual historical record?"

The imam looked at Mark intently and declared, *"I choose to believe the prophet!"*

It was a telling clash of teachings. But *history* is clear: Jesus was the Son of God, he died on the cross, and he rose from the dead that first Easter morning.

Truth for Today

We can disagree with people without disrespecting them. We are called to know the truth and to stand firmly for it. I hope this story emboldens you in your faith today.

HOW WOULD JESUS VIEW ISLAM?

Jesus said, "If you hold to my teaching, you are really my disciples. Then you will know the truth, and the truth will set you free."

JOHN 8:31–32

HOW WOULD JESUS VIEW ISLAM? IT'S AN INTERESTING QUESTION, especially since Muhammad wasn't born until almost six hundred years after the time of Christ. To respond, I'll quote from an article Mark Mittelberg wrote for the academic journal *The City*.[1] Also, be aware that this is a very different question from asking how Jesus would view Muslims. *Islam* is a religion; *Muslims* are people. We'll address both questions in this reading and the next.

> I believe, based on Jesus' own words as well as the broader teachings of Scripture, that Jesus would strongly oppose the core teachings of Islam. Take, for example, the assertion that Jesus never claimed to be the Son of God.
>
> Jesus once asked his disciples: "'Who do you say I am?' Simon Peter answered, 'You are the Messiah, *the Son of the living God.*' Jesus replied, 'Blessed are you, Simon son of Jonah, for this was not revealed to you by flesh and blood, but *by my Father in heaven*'" (Matthew 16:15–17 emphases mine).
>
> So, for Jesus, belief in his deity was not an act of *shirk* (sin punishable by death in Islam); it was the doorway to *salvation*!
>
> And what would Jesus make of the claim that he didn't really die on the cross—that God would never allow his prophet

to suffer such shame? Besides pointing out that God often *did* allow his prophets to experience persecution and suffering (Matthew 5:12; this point is also made in the Qur'an. See, for example, 2:61, 2:91, 3:21, 3:112, 3:181, 3:183, and 4:155, and the list goes on), Jesus explicitly taught that "the Son of Man must suffer many things and be rejected by the elders, the chief priests and the teachers of the law, and that he must be killed and after three days rise again" (Mark 8:31). Moreover, he summed up his very purpose as that of coming "to serve, and to give his life as a ransom for many" (Mark 10:45).

In light of all of this, I believe Jesus would have rebuked the leaders of Islam for denying his death and resurrection, just as he chided some of the Jewish people after he had risen from the dead: "How foolish you are, and how slow to believe all that the prophets have spoken! Did not the Messiah have to suffer these things and then enter his glory?" (Luke 24:25–26). Further, Jesus "opened their minds so they could understand the Scriptures. He told them, 'This is what is written: The Messiah will suffer and rise from the dead on the third day, and repentance for the forgiveness of sins will be preached in his name to all nations'" (vv. 45–47).

So when the teachers of Islam—including Muhammad—deny Jesus' central claims about himself, about his redemptive mission, and about his atoning work on the cross and through his resurrection, Jesus would be forced to condemn their false teachings.

Truth for Today

Jesus was incarnate love, but he was also incarnate truth (John 14:6). While he was always ready to forgive those who were humble and repentant, he did not hesitate to challenge and correct teachings that went against God's revelation, the Bible.

HOW WOULD JESUS
VIEW MUSLIMS?

"I tell you, love your enemies and pray for those who persecute you, that you may be children of your Father in heaven."

MATTHEW 5:44–45

HOW WOULD JESUS VIEW MUSLIM PEOPLE? IN LIGHT OF THE long and tumultuous conflict between Islam and Christianity, some assume Jesus would view Muslims as his enemies.

Would he? Let's look at more of what Mark Mittelberg wrote about this in *The City*.[1]

I am confident Jesus would view Muslims not as enemies, but as *victims of the enemy*—the spiritual thief who "comes only to steal and kill and destroy" (John 10:10). Jesus, filled with love for those he came to reach, contrasted himself to that enemy by adding, "I have come that they may have life, and have it to the full" (John 10:10).

Abraham Lincoln reportedly said, "The best way to destroy an enemy is to make him a friend." And that is exactly what Jesus did. He treated every person, regardless of his or her spiritual background or past sins, as someone who was created in the image of God. They were individuals who mattered to the Father and who were worth laying down his life to save. No wonder people called Jesus "a friend of . . . sinners" (Luke 7:34).

So what would Jesus say to Muslims who have been living under the demands of Islam—seeking faithfully to make their confessions, pray in the right manner five times a day, give their alms, fast for a month every year, and do their pilgrimage to Mecca—all in the hopes of pleasing a deity who might never accept them?

I believe that Jesus would say to them, as he said in Matthew 11:28–30, "Come to me, all you who are weary and burdened, and I will give you rest. Take my yoke upon you and learn from me, for I am gentle and humble in heart, and you will find rest for your souls. For my yoke is easy and my burden is light."

Following Jesus' gracious example, I believe that we, as Christians, should also approach Muslims as friends and as potential brothers or sisters in Christ. In spite of the violence sometimes practiced in the name of Islam, most Muslims want to live in peace, enjoying the love of their families and friends. It is our privilege to introduce them to *the Prince of Peace,* and to bring them to *the God who is love.*

I think Mark is right—and I've met a number of Muslims who have put their trust in Christ after being loved, encouraged, and instructed by a Christian who modeled the caring attitudes of the Savior.[2]

Truth for Today

During Jesus' time on earth, the Jewish leaders viewed the Samaritans as foreigners and even enemies—people to steer clear of. Jesus, by contrast, went out of his way to talk to the "Woman at the Well," a Samaritan (see John 4:1–42). In the process, he not only reached her and her community with the message of grace; he also set an example of how we should approach anyone who believes differently than we do, including Muslims.

CHRISTIANS MEET A MUSLIM

"Suppose one of you has a hundred sheep and loses one of them. Doesn't he leave the ninety-nine in the open country and go after the lost sheep until he finds it?"

LUKE 15:4

HERE'S AN EXAMPLE OF WHAT CAN HAPPEN WHEN WE REACH out to share truth, love, and hospitality with someone who doesn't know Christ. This is also from Mark Mittelberg's piece in *The City*.[1]

I walked into an ice cream parlor in Texas with my friend Karl, a straight-shooting, hard-hitting business leader who loves God.

"Based on your appearance and accent," Karl said abruptly to the man behind the counter, "I'm guessing you're from the Middle East."

That caught the man's attention, and mine. "So that makes me curious: Are you a Muslim or a Christian?" I was fascinated to see how he'd respond.

"That's an interesting question," the man replied. "I grew up in the Islamic faith, but I don't know what to think—I guess I'm somewhere in the middle."

Gulp. Forget the ice cream!

Karl introduced himself to the man and then motioned me closer.

"Mark, I'd like you to meet my new friend, Fayz [pronounced "Fize"]. And Fayz, this is Mark." As we shook hands, Karl turned to me and added, "Fayz wants to know more about Jesus."

He does? I thought—while Fayz was probably thinking, *I do?*

"All right," I said, and launched into a short and somewhat awkward conversation about Jesus and the Bible. Later, we brought Fayz a copy of Lee Strobel's book *The Case for Christ*. Then Karl went back later with his wife, Barbara, who invited Fayz and his wife to their home for dinner and helped establish a friendship.

Around that time Karl and Barbara asked their adult Sunday school class to pray for their new Muslim friends. The class said they'd be happy to pray—but they wanted in on this evangelistic ice cream adventure themselves. Suddenly, God had unleashed a hundred hungry Baptists on this unsuspecting Muslim!

Soon there were many more Christians meeting Fayz, building friendships with him and his wife, inviting them to various events, sharing testimonies, and answering their spiritual questions. When the group discovered that Fayz was a medical student who was just selling ice cream to pay his way through medical school, some of them introduced him to other friends in the medical community, aiding him in his career.

In short, they were being the evangelistic church that Christ intended—loving, serving, and reaching out to this man and his family in a variety of ways.

In the process something amazing happened. Fayz started opening up to Jesus. Almost a year after that original conversation, Fayz, his wife, and their six-year-old daughter attended a Sunday service at Karl and Barbara's church—and before it was over, they had all given their lives to Christ.

Some people think of Muslims as enemies. I am pleased to call Fayz not only a *friend*, but also *my brother in Christ*.

Truth for Today

Remember: God loves all kinds of people from all kinds of backgrounds, and he does not want "anyone to perish, but everyone to come to repentance" (2 Peter 3:9). We need to love as God loves.

FINDING YOUR VOICE, PART 1

There are different kinds of gifts, but the same Spirit distributes them. There are different kinds of service, but the same Lord.

1 CORINTHIANS 12:4–5

THE PREVIOUS READING ILLUSTRATES GOD'S LOVE FOR PEOPLE of all backgrounds. More than that, it shows how God uses a variety of Christians in ways that are natural to them. Mark Mittelberg and Bill Hybels wrote about this in the book *Becoming a Contagious Christian*,[1] and then Mark and I turned that into the *Becoming a Contagious Christian* training course.[2]

God gave everyone unique personalities, and he wants to use us to share him in ways that fit us. Let's look at six styles, identify examples from Scripture, and identify who used each of these approaches in reaching out to Fayz. As you go through these, think about which style or styles might fit you.

1. **DIRECT STYLE.** Peter exemplified this approach, especially in Acts 2 where he boldly challenged his listeners with the gospel. Similarly, Karl was very direct in how he brought up and discussed spiritual matters with Fayz. It may have initially taken Fayz aback, but God used it to open up the conversation and to jump-start Fayz on his journey toward Christ.

2. **INTELLECTUAL STYLE.** Paul is an example of this approach. He was a logical thinker who naturally defended and debated God's truth in Athens in Acts 17. Likewise, in spite of the awkwardness of talking over an ice cream counter, Mark was a good example of the intellectual style as he gave helpful

information and answers to Fayz, and I've seen God use him in similar ways countless times.

3. **TESTIMONIAL STYLE.** We see this third style in the blind man Jesus healed in John 9 by miraculously giving him his sight. Before the man had a chance to blink, he was defending himself before the religious court, saying (in so many words), "I used to be blind, and now I can see—*deal with it!*" This is my main style as well—using my testimony to encourage others. Even though I wasn't there in person, my testimony made a difference in Fayz's life through *The Case for Christ*, where I combine my story with logic and evidence (since my other natural approach is the intellectual style).

Have I touched on your style yet? If not, I probably will tomorrow when we'll cover three other approaches. Either way, I hope you're feeling encouraged, knowing God wants to use you in ways that come naturally.

Truth for Today

God knew what he was doing when he made you. Your personality was constructed on purpose, and God wants to use you in natural ways to reach others who need him.

FINDING YOUR VOICE, PART 2

There are different kinds of working, but in all of them and in everyone it is the same God at work.

1 CORINTHIANS 12:6

WE'VE LOOKED AT THREE APPROACHES TO SHARING OUR FAITH. Today we'll look at three more, identify biblical examples, and identify who played these roles in reaching out to Fayz. My goal is to help you find a style or combination of styles that will fit you.

4. INTERPERSONAL STYLE. We see this approach in the former tax collector Matthew, who reached out to his previous coworkers by hosting a party for them. He also invited Jesus and the other disciples to come mix it up with them as a way to foster relationships between his older and newer friends (Luke 5:29). Barbara played a similar role by inviting Fayz and his wife into their home. This allowed her and Karl to form a real friendship with them and also to deepen their conversations about spiritual matters.

5. INVITATIONAL STYLE. The woman at the well was thrilled to meet Jesus, the Messiah. So she ran to her town in Samaria and invited her friends to come to the well to hear Jesus for themselves (John 4). They did, and as a result, some of them ended up putting their faith in Christ. Similarly, Karl and Barbara, along with friends from the Sunday school class, invited Fayz and his family to visit their church. Believe me, an invitation to a well-designed service or event can have a huge impact. It's part of how God reached me!

6. SERVING STYLE. A woman named Tabitha served needy people by making clothing for them (Acts 9). She was like a

first-century Mother Teresa. She served people in ways that made them realize there must be a God. Similarly, some people from the class served Fayz by introducing him to key members of the medical community, opening doors for his future career. God can use this kind of loving service to open people up to him in amazing ways.

You may not yet be active in sharing your faith, but I'll bet you can relate to at least one of these approaches in other areas of your life: *direct, intellectual, testimonial, interpersonal, invitational,* or *serving.* Or maybe you have a style that we haven't thought of yet. Regardless, let me urge you to let God use you by trying at least one of these methods to reach out to friends and family for Christ.

Truth for Today

As a Christian you are a member of the church to which Jesus gave the Great Commission (Matthew 28:18–20). So "go into all the world" while trying approaches that fit the way God made you.

TAKING THE BIBLE LITERALLY

*"I have come down to rescue them from the hand of the
Egyptians and to bring them up out of that land into a good
and spacious land, a land flowing with milk and honey."*

EXODUS 3:8

STUART BRISCOE, THE BRITISH BIBLE TEACHER WHO FOR MANY
years served as the pastor of Elmbrook Church in Wisconsin, once
told a story in a sermon about a spiritual conversation he had with
a man on an airplane.

"So, are you one of those people who takes the Bible *literally*?"
the man asked after realizing Briscoe was a pastor.

Knowing the guy had already sized him up as an out-of-date
fundamentalist, Briscoe's British wit kicked in. "Yes, I am," he said
with a twinkle in his eye. "And maybe you can help me figure out
what a certain Bible verse means."

"Well, I don't know that much about the Bible," the man
replied. "What are you trying to figure out?"

"The Bible says God led the Israelites into a land that was 'flowing with milk and honey,'" Briscoe began. "But how were they able
to walk around in all of that gooey mess? Milk and honey everywhere, flowing down the hillsides—it must have been awful!"

The man's smile acknowledged that Briscoe had gotten the
best of him.

Briscoe's point was clear: you can take the message of the Bible
literally without interpreting its various literary devices in a wood-
enly literal way.

Theologian R. C. Sproul explains, "Interpretation according
to the literal sense will take account of all figures of speech and

literary forms found in the text."[1] He continues, "We distinguish between lyric poetry and legal briefs, between newspaper accounts of current events and epic poems. We distinguish between the style of historical narratives and sermons, between realistic graphic description and hyperbole. Failure to make these distinctions when dealing with the Bible can lead to a host of problems with interpretation."[2]

So when the Bible says God is the Lion of Judah (Hosea 5:14; Revelation 5:5), we don't have to imagine him with a mane and big teeth. Or when it calls Jesus "the Lamb of God" (John 1:29), we don't need to see him as a woolly animal that bleats, and when he says he is a gate (John 10:7–10), we need not ascribe to him rusty hinges or a latch.

On the other hand, we must not write off these passages as mere metaphors. *They are literally true in what their authors intended to communicate*: God is a fierce defender; Jesus lays down his life for his friends; and he is the gateway to heaven for all who trust in him.

Truth for Today

The Bible is true in all that it teaches, so we should study it carefully.

UNTRUTHS IN THE BIBLE?

Now the serpent was more crafty than any of the wild animals the LORD God had made. . . . "You will not certainly die," the serpent said to the woman.

GENESIS 3:1, 4

AT FIRST GLANCE, EVEN THE SUGGESTION THAT THE BIBLE MIGHT contain anything untrue seems sacrilegious. But let's take a deeper look. Understanding this issue will help us better understand the Bible.

Theologians Norman Geisler and William Nix explain this about the Bible: "Inspiration necessitates the truthfulness of only what the Bible teaches."[1] They elaborate:

> The Bible teaches only *truth* (John 17:17), but it contains some lies, for example, Satan's lie (Genesis 3:4; cf. John 8:44) and Rahab's lie (Joshua 2:4). Inspiration covers the Bible fully and completely in the sense that it records accurately and truthfully even the lies and errors of sinful beings. The truth of Scripture is to be found in what the Bible *reveals*, not in everything it *records*. Unless this distinction is held, it may be incorrectly concluded that the Bible teaches immorality because it narrates David's sin (2 Samuel 11:4), that it promotes polygamy because it records Solomon's (1 Kings 11:3), or that it asserts atheism because it quotes the fool as saying "there is no God" (Psalm 14:1). In each case the interpreter of Scripture must seek the *commitment of the writer* of the particular passage in question. The important thing for the interpreter to keep in mind is not what the writer *seems* to say, not what he refers to, nor even whom he quotes, but what he *really affirms* in the text."[2]

In other words, the Bible is always true in what it *teaches*, but it doesn't endorse all that it *reports*. So, as Mark Mittelberg often points out, it records the religious ramblings of Job's friends, along with Job's reactions to them, after he entered into his time of testing described at the beginning of Job. This exchange goes on for the bulk of Job 4–37.

Finally Job 38:1–2 tells us, "Then the LORD spoke to Job out of the storm. He said: 'Who is this that obscures my plans with words without knowledge?'"

In other words, the Bible reports what Job and his friends said back and forth—*endlessly!*—but it doesn't endorse their statements. Yet people will often quote from those chapters as if it's what God wants us to know, without understanding that this section is just a record of what was said by Job's misguided companions, not something the Bible presents as a message from the Lord.

Bottom-line message: *reader, beware!* We need to study carefully and seek wisdom so we'll discern the real message the biblical writer— and, behind the writer, the Holy Spirit—intended us to understand.

Truth for Today

One of the keys to determining what the Bible teaches (versus what it merely records) is to read carefully the context of the passage. Often only then will you get the big picture of what is really being taught versus merely reported.

THE NATURE OF PROVERBS

Choose my instruction instead of silver, knowledge rather
than choice gold, for wisdom is more precious than rubies,
and nothing you desire can compare with her.

PROVERBS 8:10–11

AS I'VE EXPLAINED IN PRIOR READINGS, THE BIBLE IS ENTIRELY
true in everything it teaches. But sometimes we get confused about
or overestimate what the biblical author was actually trying to
say. And one of the most common places where such mistakes are
made is in the book of Proverbs.

What is a proverb? It is a wise saying that presents a general
truth. It is not, however, a universally guaranteed promise about
how life always works. Here's an example Mark Mittelberg uses:
"A gentle answer turns away wrath, but a harsh word stirs up
anger" (Proverbs 15:1). Now, how are we supposed to understand
this? Does a gentle answer (or, as some translations say, "a kind
answer") *always* turn away wrath? What about when Jesus was on
trial before his crucifixion? He didn't say a lot, but the little he did
say seemed to have been said gently. It obviously didn't turn away
his enemies' wrath.

Or what about Jewish people during the Holocaust, or black
people during slavery, or all kinds of other situations where injus-
tice has been the norm? Gentle answers may have helped ward off
immediate calamity, but they didn't turn away most of the ensuing
wrath.

As Paul said in 1 Corinthians 4:12–13, "When we are cursed,
we bless; when we are persecuted, we endure it; when we are slan-
dered, we answer kindly. We have become the scum of the earth,

the garbage of the world—right up to this moment." So Paul and his companions were answering kindly, but he said they were still being treated poorly, even at the time he was writing that report.

Now, don't misunderstand what I'm saying. The Proverbs are full of great wisdom from God. They will help us lead wise lives—lives that sidestep much of the pain and grief we otherwise would have experienced. But they aren't ironclad promises, nor were they intended to be. That's not the nature of a proverb—biblical or otherwise.

Understanding this helps prevent us from claiming promises from God that he didn't necessarily make. I hope it also encourages us to dive into the book of Proverbs so that we'll gain every bit of wisdom God offers through it. The benefits will be immeasurable.

Truth for Today

"Does not wisdom call out? Does not understanding raise her voice?" (Proverbs 8:1). Read and heed what God wants to say to you through his wisdom today!

TRUE RELIGION

*Religion that God our Father accepts as pure and faultless
is this: to look after orphans and widows in their distress
and to keep oneself from being polluted by the world.*

JAMES 1:27

FRIEDRICH NIETZSCHE, THE GERMAN NIHILIST PHILOSOPHER
who famously declared that God is dead, wrote a book called
The Anti-Christ in which he attacked Christianity as a blight on
humanity. Why? Because of our empathy and concern for the weak
and suffering.

"What is good?—whatever augments the feeling of power, the
will to power, power itself, in man," Nietzsche declared. "What
is evil?—whatever springs from weakness. . . . The weak and the
botched shall perish: first principle of our charity. And one should
help them to it. What is more harmful than any vice?—practical
sympathy for the botched and the weak—Christianity."[1]

Reflect on those words for a moment. It won't surprise you that
a young Bavarian housepainter reportedly gave out copies of one of
Nietzsche's books as Christmas presents to his friends. The housepainter's name? Adolf Hitler.[2]

Well, if Nietzsche was anti-Christ, Christ was anti-
Nietzsche—at least in terms of their teachings. Jesus said, "Come,
you who are blessed by my Father; take your inheritance, the kingdom prepared for you since the creation of the world. For I was
hungry and you gave me something to eat, I was thirsty and you
gave me something to drink, I was a stranger and you invited me
in, I needed clothes and you clothed me, I was sick and you looked
after me, I was in prison and you came to visit me. . . . Truly I tell

you, *whatever you did for one of the least of these brothers and sisters of mine, you did for me*" (Matthew 25:34–36, 40, emphasis mine).

Rather than promoting "the will to power," Jesus let go of his power in order to make "himself nothing by taking the very nature of a servant, being made in human likeness. And being found in appearance as a man, he humbled himself by becoming obedient to death—even death on a cross!" (Philippians 2:7–8). Why? Because he, with the Father, "so loved the world" that he was willing to "lay down [his] life for [his] friends (John 3:16; 15:13).

Oswald Chambers summed it up well: "Jesus Christ looks out for the weak ones whom the world shoves to the wall. He puts His back to the wall and receives them into His arms."[3]

Truth for Today

John admonished us, "This is how we know what love is: Jesus Christ laid down his life for us. And we ought to lay down our lives for our brothers and sisters" (1 John 3:16).

THE INSPIRATION
OF THE BIBLE

*All Scripture is God-breathed and is useful for teaching,
rebuking, correcting and training in righteousness, so that
the servant of God may be thoroughly equipped for every
good work.*

2 TIMOTHY 3:16–17

"THE BIBLE SAYS THAT ALL SCRIPTURE IS 'GOD-BREATHED,'" I
said to New Testament scholar Daniel B. Wallace. "Exactly what do
Christians believe was the process by which God created the New
Testament?"

"We aren't given a lot regarding the process of inspiration, but
we know the Bible wasn't dictated by God," the Dallas Theological
Seminary professor replied. "Look at the Old Testament: Isaiah has
a huge vocabulary and is often considered the Shakespeare of the
Hebrew prophets, while Amos was a simple farmer with a much
more modest vocabulary. Yet both books were inspired. Obviously,
this doesn't mean verbal dictation. God wasn't looking for stenog-
raphers but holy men to write his book."

"Then how does inspiration work?" I asked.

"We get some clues from where Matthew quotes the Old
Testament, saying that this 'was spoken by the Lord through the
prophet' [Matthew 1:22; 2:15 NKJV]. 'By the Lord' suggests God is
the ultimate agent of that prophecy. 'Through the prophet' suggests an intermediate agent who also uses his personality. That
means this prophet was not taking dictation from God; instead,
God was communicating through visions, dreams, and so forth,

and the prophet was putting it in his own words. So the process doesn't coerce the human personality, yet ultimately the result is exactly what God wanted to produce."

Seeking a crisp summary, I said, "Complete this sentence: when Christians say the Bible is *inspired*, they mean that—"

"It's both the word of God and the words of men. Lewis Sperry Chafer put it well: 'Without violating the authors' personalities, they wrote with their own feelings, literary abilities, and concerns. But in the end, God could say, *That's exactly what I wanted to have written.*'"[1]

Reflecting back on that discussion, I think Wallace explained well what the apostle Peter urged us to understand: "Above all, you must understand that no prophecy of Scripture came about by the prophet's own interpretation of things. For prophecy never had its origin in the human will, but prophets, though human, spoke from God as they were carried along by the Holy Spirit" (2 Peter 1:20–21).

Truth for Today

It's one thing to understand inspiration, but another actually to benefit from it. Peter said, "We also have the prophetic message as something completely reliable, and you will do well to pay attention to it" (2 Peter 1:19). We need to keep reading God's inspired revelation, the Bible, day after day in order to learn all that God wants to teach us.

JOTS AND TITTLES

"Verily I say unto you, Till heaven and earth pass, one jot or one tittle shall in no wise pass from the law, till all be fulfilled."

MATTHEW 5:18 KJV

MANY PEOPLE GREW UP FEELING CONFUSED ABOUT THE MEANING of "one jot or one tittle" in this verse from the Sermon on the Mount. Newer translations make it more understandable. Here's the NIV rendering: "Truly I tell you, until heaven and earth disappear, not *the smallest letter*, not *the least stroke of a pen*, will by any means disappear from the Law until everything is accomplished" (emphases mine).

Once you know the meaning of Jesus' words, his message is profound. He was saying that the "Law"—in other words, the revelation of God in the Old Testament—would be completely fulfilled. That means every promise, every warning, and every prediction, right down to "the smallest letter" and "the least stroke of a pen." And this was not some novel idea that Jesus suddenly came up with. He was rewording a promise God had made some seven hundred years earlier through the prophet Isaiah: "The grass withers and the flowers fall, but the word of our God endures forever" (Isaiah 40:8).

And remember after his resurrection when Jesus walked along the path with the two disciples on the road to Emmaus? They didn't realize who he was as they were pondering the meaning of the events on that first Easter Sunday. Jesus finally spoke up and said, "How foolish you are, and how slow to believe all that the prophets have spoken! Did not the Messiah have to suffer these things and then enter his glory?" (Luke 24:25–26).

Think about that. Jesus chastised them for failing to understand and believe "all that the prophets have spoken." Specifically, if God's spokespeople said the Messiah would suffer horribly before being glorified, then they should have known what was coming—because God's word can never fail.

So, to apply this to our lives, we need to study to make sure we know what the Bible is really teaching. Once we understand its message, we can take that message to the bank.

How do we come to understand the Bible? In three simple steps:

1. Read the Bible regularly to see what it says.
2. Study what you've read to make sure you understand the real message. Consult reliable Christian commentaries and notes in study Bibles, and check your interpretations with proven teachers.
3. Act on what you now understand God to be saying, knowing that he will fulfill every jot and tittle.

Truth for Today

Paul said, "No matter how many promises God has made, they are 'Yes' in Christ" (2 Corinthians 1:20). God's Word is true; let's base our lives on it!

THE ALL-TIME BESTSELLER

The word of God is alive and active. Sharper than any
double-edged sword, it penetrates even to dividing soul
and spirit, joints and marrow; it judges the thoughts and
attitudes of the heart. Nothing in all creation is hidden
from God's sight.

HEBREWS 4:12–13

"THE BIBLE IS THE BESTSELLING BOOK OF ALL TIME," WROTE
Mark Mittelberg in his book *The Reason Why: Faith Makes Sense*.[1]
"A staggering 100 million copies are printed every year, and it is
estimated that worldwide there are nearly 8 billion in print. The
text of the Bible has been published in 450 different languages, the
New Testament portion in 1,400 languages, and the gospel of Mark
in 2,370 languages. And these figures do not include the many
digital versions of the Bible that millions of people view online."[2]
Clearly this is a book that people are interested in, and their fasci-
nation only seems to keep growing.

"The Bible is also a book that makes big claims and promises,"
Mark continued. "It says it is a message from God—a revelation . . .
telling us of himself and his purposes for us. And it declares that
it has enduring value and relevance, as explained in Isaiah 40:8
[NLT]: 'The grass withers and the flowers fade, but the word of our
God stands forever.'

"It has been called an owner's manual for people—a book written through the inspiration of our Maker as a guide to help us live
in a way that honors him and that works out for our own good as
well. Second Timothy 3:16 [NLT] explains, 'All Scripture is . . . useful to teach us what is true and to make us realize what is wrong in

our lives. It corrects us when we are wrong and teaches us to do what is right.'

"What sets the Bible apart, giving us confidence that it really is what it claims to be—God's revelation—and that it alone best 'corrects us when we are wrong and teaches us to do what is right'?"

Much can be said in answer to that question. In the readings that follow, I'll discuss the Bible's *consistency, early dates, living line, textual superiority,* and *archaeological verification.*

But let me say this: From my experience, the Bible is a book like none other. It truly is, as today's verse says, "alive and active." I'm often surprised how passages in this book, which was written so long ago, can leap off the page and hit me afresh with truth, assurance, encouragement, and occasionally a much-needed challenge.

Truth for Today

"Taste and see that the LORD is good," says Psalm 34:8. I would say the same about his Word, the Bible—but you need to read it regularly to move beyond tasting and enjoy a full meal.

THE BIBLE'S CONSISTENCY

Concerning this salvation, the prophets, who spoke of the grace that was to come to you, searched intently and with the greatest care, trying to find out the time and circumstances to which the Spirit of Christ in them was pointing when he predicted the sufferings of the Messiah and the glories that would follow.

1 PETER 1:10–11

IF YOU THINK OF THE BIBLE AS JUST A SINGLE BOOK, THEN YOU won't sense the power of the following example. But when you realize the Bible is actually a collection of many books—sixty-six, to be exact—then the power of this argument becomes clear. Here's how Christian apologists Norman Geisler and William Nix explain the evidence concerning the consistency of God's Word.

"The Bible is composed of sixty-six books, written over a period of some fifteen hundred years by nearly forty authors in several languages containing hundreds of topics, yet the Bible possesses an amazing unity of theme—Jesus Christ. One problem—sin—and one solution—the Savior—unify its pages from Genesis to Revelation.

"It is only later reflection, both by the prophets themselves (e.g., 1 Peter 1:10–11) and later generations, which has discovered that the Bible is really one book whose 'chapters' were written by men who had no explicit knowledge of the overall structure. Their role could be compared to that of different men writing chapters of a novel for which none of them have even an overall outline. Whatever unity the book has must come from beyond them."[1]

In *Confident Faith*, Mark Mittelberg adds, "This degree of consistency would be difficult enough to achieve within a single book by a solo author—but when you add the complexity of multiple writers, from multiple countries, in multiple languages, over multiple centuries, dealing with multiple problems and situations, the Bible's incredible cohesion and unified message are nothing short of miraculous.

"The best way to get a sense of this is to spend some time reading the Bible for yourself. As you read, I think you'll notice the logical integrity, the consistent relevance, the real-world accuracy, and the subjective-but-real 'ring of truth' that countless people have affirmed over the years."[2]

I would affirm that "ring of truth." I'm sometimes left breathless when I sense that what I just read, though it is traced back to Paul, John, or David, had its source in the mind of God. He spoke through them straight into my heart and life.

Truth for Today

The Bible contains many books from many authors, but the more you read it, the more you'll recognize the voice of just one Author, speaking to you as no one else could.

EARLY DATES

*Since I myself have carefully investigated everything from
the beginning, I too decided to write an orderly account . . .
so that you may know the certainty of the things you have
been taught.*

LUKE 1:3–4

"SCHOLARLY THEOLOGIANS HAVE MADE AN OVERWHELMING
case," claims Richard Dawkins, "that the gospels are not reliable
accounts of what happened in the history of the real world. All
were written long after the death of Jesus."[1]

This is a common claim, but one that has been thoroughly
refuted. Although the standard scholarly dating of the Gospels is
in the AD 70s, 80s, and 90s, Dr. Craig Blomberg explains that earlier dates can be supported by looking at the book of Acts, which
was written by Luke, a physician, historian, and close companion
of the apostle Paul.

"Acts ends apparently unfinished—Paul is a central figure of
the book, and he's under house arrest in Rome. With that the book
abruptly halts," said Blomberg, author of *The Historical Reliability
of the Gospels*. "What happens to Paul? We don't find out from
Acts, probably because the book was written before Paul was put
to death.

"That means Acts cannot be dated any later than AD 62.
Having established that, we can then move backward from there.
Since Acts is the second of a two-part work, we know the first
part—the gospel of Luke—must have been written earlier than
that. And since Luke incorporates parts of the gospel of Mark, this
means Mark is even earlier.

"If you allow maybe a year for each of those, you end up with Mark written no later than about AD 60, maybe even the late 50s. If Jesus was put to death in AD 30 or 33, we're talking about a maximum gap of thirty years or so.

"Historically speaking," Blomberg concluded, "that's like a news flash!"[2]

"To put this into our own context," Mark Mittelberg explains, "most of the New Testament would have been completed within a span of years similar to the time that has elapsed between now and the year when the first *Star Wars* movie came out, Apple released the Apple II computer, Jimmy Carter became president, and Elvis Presley died—all of which happened in 1977—and those events are vividly remembered by many of us today."[3]

I would add that if somebody today tried to rewrite history about any of these modern events, it would be quickly detected and refuted. Yet there is no record of any contemporaries challenging the details in the gospel record.

Truth for Today

The New Testament has repeatedly shown itself to be a trustworthy record of Jesus' ministry, death, and resurrection. This is another reason we can have a confident faith in him.

THE LIVING LINE

"Blessed are those who have not seen and yet have believed."

JOHN 20:29

"EARLY DATES, LIVING LINE, ERICK NELSON'S DOING FINE." IT was a memorable quote from a debate between Nelson, a Christian, and a skeptical opponent, held in a small Southern California college classroom.

It was the first debate Mark Mittelberg had ever witnessed. He never forgot Nelson's point that the authenticity of the New Testament is strongly supported by these two arguments (among others): *early dates*, which we just looked at, and *living line*, which points to the apostolic fathers who were trained and commissioned by some of the apostles themselves.

"Consider Clement, for example," said historian Michael Licona in an interview I had with him. "The early church father Irenaeus reports that Clement had conversed with the apostles. In fact, Irenaeus commented that he 'might be said to have the preaching of the apostles still echoing, and their traditions before his eyes.' Tertullian, the African church father, said Clement was ordained by Peter himself.

"In his letter to the Corinthian church, written in the first century, [Clement wrote]: 'Therefore, having received orders and complete certainty caused by the resurrection of our Lord Jesus Christ and believing in the Word of God, [the disciples] went with the Holy Spirit's certainty, preaching the good news that the kingdom of God is about to come.'

"Then we have Polycarp. Irenaeus says that Polycarp was

'instructed by the apostles, and conversed with many who had seen Christ,' including John; that he 'recalled their very words'; and that he 'always taught the things which he had learned from the apostles.' Tertullian confirms that John appointed Polycarp as bishop of the church in Smyrna.

"Around AD 110," Licona added, "Polycarp wrote a letter to the Philippian church in which he mentions the resurrection of Jesus no fewer than five times. He was referring to Paul and the other apostles when he said: 'For they did not love the present age, but him who died for our benefit and for our sake was raised by God.'"[1]

These "apostolic fathers" authored the Epistle of Clement of Rome, the Epistles of Ignatius, the Epistle of Polycarp, the Epistle of Barnabas, and others. In many places these writings attest to the basic facts about Jesus, particularly his teachings, his crucifixion, his resurrection, and his divine nature.

"What is significant about Ignatius," historian Edwin Yamauchi told me, "is that he emphasized both the deity of Jesus and the humanity of Jesus. He also stressed the historical underpinnings of Christianity; he wrote in one letter, on his way to being executed, that Jesus was truly persecuted under Pilate, was truly crucified, was truly raised from the dead, and that those who believe in him would be raised too."[2]

Truth for Today

Early dates, living line . . . the New Testament is doing fine!

"AN EMBARRASSMENT OF RICHES"

"Heaven and earth will pass away, but my words will never pass away."

—MARK 13:31

"YOU CAN'T TRUST THE BIBLE," SAYS THE POPULAR BELIEF. "IT'S been translated and retranslated so many times. Besides, it's thousands of years old. *Who knows* what the original writings really said?"

Mark Mittelberg gives a good answer to this challenge in his book *Confident Faith*: "The Bible we have today is not the end of some long chain of translations from one language to the next—say, from Greek to Latin, then Latin to German, then German to English, and so on. Rather, it is a direct translation from the historical manuscripts in the original languages—Hebrew for the Old Testament and Greek for the New Testament. Every good version goes back to the earliest documents and, based on many years of linguistic and cultural studies, puts what was written there into accurate contemporary language. The result is that we can easily read and understand what was originally recorded in Hebrew and Greek by the biblical writers.

"Also, for the New Testament, we have more than 5,800 copies of early Greek manuscripts or partial manuscripts[1]—and about 20,000 more in other languages.[2] As is the case with all ancient writings, we don't have the original handwritten documents themselves (called the *autographs*), but we do have an astounding number of reliable copies.

"What makes the New Testament really stand out is that we have so many *more* copies of it than we have of any other ancient work, and they are so much *earlier* (in other words, dating closer to the time of the original writing)."[3]

According to New Testament scholar Daniel B. Wallace, we have

an embarrassment of riches compared to the data the classical Greek and Latin scholars have to contend with. The average classical author's literary remains number no more than twenty copies. We have more than 1,000 times the manuscript data for the New Testament than we do for the average Greco-Roman author. Not only this, but the extant manuscripts of the average classical author are no earlier than 500 years after the time he wrote. For the New Testament, we are waiting mere decades for surviving copies.[4]

These other historical works are still considered reliable. That being the case, when you consider the thousands of New Testament manuscripts and a time gap that is so amazingly small, there really is no question that the New Testament is historically reliable.

Truth for Today

If *any* ancient writings can be trusted as authentic, then the Bible so much more. God has seen to it that we have a highly accurate replica of the original writings of Scripture. Count on it!

ARCHAEOLOGY AND THE BIBLE, PART 1

"I have spoken to you of earthly things and you do not believe; how then will you believe if I speak of heavenly things?"

JOHN 3:12

ANYONE CAN MAKE UP A STORY. BUT AS A JOURNALIST WITH legal training—and a skeptic by nature—I have always needed hard evidence to back up accounts that make claims to the supernatural. In other words, the kinds of claims we see throughout the Bible. So I asked biblical scholar Norman Geisler about what the findings of archaeology can establish for us.[1]

"There have been thousands of archaeological finds in the Middle East that support the picture presented in the biblical record," Geisler said.

"There was a discovery not long ago confirming [details about] King David. The patriarchs—the narratives about Abraham, Isaac, and Jacob—were once considered legendary, but as more has become known, these stories are increasingly corroborated. The destruction of Sodom and Gomorrah was thought to be mythological until evidence was uncovered that all five of the cities mentioned in Genesis were, in fact, situated just as the Old Testament says. As far as their destruction goes, archaeologist Clifford Wilson said there is 'permanent evidence of the great conflagration that took place in the long-distant past.'[2]

"Furthermore," Geisler added, "various aspects of the Jewish captivity have been confirmed. Also, every reference in the Old

Testament to an Assyrian king has been proven correct; an excavation during the 1960s confirmed that the Israelites could, indeed, have entered Jerusalem by way of a tunnel during David's reign; there is evidence the world did have a single language at one time, as the Bible says; the site of Solomon's temple is now being excavated; and on and on. Many times, archaeologists have been skeptical of the Old Testament, only to have new discoveries corroborate the biblical account."

"For example?" I asked Geisler.

"The Bible makes about three dozen references to the Hittites, but critics used to charge that there was no evidence that such people ever existed. Now archaeologists digging in modern Turkey have discovered the records of the Hittites. As the great archaeologist William F. Albright declared, 'There can be no doubt that archaeology has confirmed the substantial historicity of Old Testament tradition.'"[3]

While not everything in the Bible can be tested by archaeology, discoveries have repeatedly confirmed claims made in the Old Testament Scriptures.

Truth for Today

It's easy to doubt extraordinary claims, especially when they surround a civilization that existed so long ago. But be encouraged that time and again archaeological discoveries have confirmed the truth of those claims, sometimes in very broad ways, and other times more specifically. We have great reasons to trust the Bible!

ARCHAEOLOGY AND
THE BIBLE, PART 2

"This is what I told you while I was still with you:
Everything must be fulfilled that is written about me in the
Law of Moses, the Prophets and the Psalms."

Luke 24:44

IN MY INTERVIEW WITH DR. NORMAN GEISLER, HE GAVE GREAT
examples of ways archaeology has supported the Old Testament, as
we saw in the previous reading. So I asked him to summarize any
similar evidence for the New Testament.[1]

"The noted Roman historian Colin J. Hemer, in *The Book of*
Acts in the Setting of Hellenistic History, shows how archaeology
has confirmed not dozens, but hundreds and hundreds of details
from the biblical account of the early church," Geisler began.[2]
"Even small details have been corroborated, like which way the
wind blows, how deep the water is a certain distance from the
shore, what kind of disease a particular island had, the names of
local officials, and so forth.

"Now, Acts was authored by the historian Luke. Hemer gives
more than a dozen reasons why Acts had to have been written
before AD 62, or about thirty years after Jesus' crucifixion. Even
earlier, Luke wrote the gospel of Luke, which is substantially the
same as the other biblical accounts of Jesus' life.

"So here you have an impeccable historian, who has been
proven right in hundreds of details and never proven wrong, writing the whole history of Jesus and the early church. And it's written
within one generation while eyewitnesses were still alive and could

have disputed it if it were exaggerated or false. You don't have anything like that from any other religious book from the ancient world."

"Is Hemer a lone voice on that?" I asked Geisler.

"Hardly," he replied. "Prominent historian Sir William Ramsay started out as a skeptic, but after studying Acts he concluded that 'in various details the narrative showed marvelous truth.'[3] The great Oxford University classical historian A. N. Sherwin-White said, 'For Acts the confirmation of historicity is overwhelming,' and 'any attempt to reject its basic historicity must now appear absurd.'"[4]

I would add that for anyone who doubts the degree to which archaeological research supports the claims of the Bible, there is a bimonthly publication called the *Biblical Archaeological Review* that covers the latest finds.[5] Also, Zondervan's *Archaeological Study Bible* is an excellent study resource that is overflowing with examples and pictures of these kinds of discoveries. Such publications illustrate the strength of the evidence that supports Scripture.

Truth for Today

Throughout these readings I've stressed the importance of loving truth. Be encouraged that the weight of archaeological research overwhelmingly supports the truth claims of the Old and New Testaments.

ARCHAEOLOGY AND THE BOOK OF MORMON

"At that time if anyone says to you, 'Look, here is the Messiah!' or, 'There he is!' do not believe it. For false messiahs and false prophets will appear and perform great signs and wonders to deceive, if possible, even the elect. See, I have told you ahead of time."

MATTHEW 24:23–25

AS WE'VE SEEN IN THE PREVIOUS TWO READINGS, ARCHAEOLOGY'S repeated affirmations of the biblical account—both the Old Testament and New Testament—provide important corroboration for its reliability.

John McRay, who was a professor of archaeology and is the author of *Archaeology and the New Testament*, said there's no question that archaeological findings have enhanced the New Testament's credibility. And he assured me, "Archaeology has not produced anything that is unequivocally a contradiction to the Bible."[1]

This, however, is in stark contrast to how archaeology has proved to be devastating for Mormonism. Although Joseph Smith, the founder of the Mormon Church, claimed that his Book of Mormon is "the most correct of any book upon the earth,"[2] archaeology has repeatedly failed to substantiate its claims about events that supposedly occurred long ago in the Americas, including Jesus' alleged appearances there.

In fact, I wrote to the Smithsonian Institute to inquire whether there is any evidence supporting the claims of Mormonism, only to be told that they see "no direct connection between the archaeology of the New World and the subject matter of the book."

Authors John Ankerberg and John Weldon concluded, "No Book of Mormon cities have ever been located, no Book of Mormon person, place, nation, or name has ever been found, no Book of Mormon artifacts, no Book of Mormon scriptures, no Book of Mormon inscriptions, ... nothing which demonstrates the Book of Mormon is anything other than myth or invention has *ever* been found."[3]

Said Bill McKeever and Eric Johnson in their book *Mormonism 101*: "Many biblical archaeological discoveries are made every year; if not for the lack of funding and laborers, there is so much more waiting to be discovered. . . . When the Book of Mormon is considered, however, there is nothing that can be positively identified to support the names, places, and events written by ancient Americans. . . . Until Book of Mormon evidence moves beyond the realm of faith, it can be rightly classified as a myth, legend, or story without any basis in historical fact."[4]

I understand that there are many sincere Mormons for whom this information is hard to hear. They need to consider it, though, because so much of what the Mormon church teaches contradicts Scripture and the teachings of Christ.

Truth for Today

It's encouraging to know that we don't have to take the Bible on blind faith; it has been confirmed, time and again, by a bedrock of archaeological facts—and in ways that other religions' "holy books" have not.

A COPYCAT RELIGION?

We did not follow cleverly devised stories when we told you about the coming of our Lord Jesus Christ in power, but we were eyewitnesses of his majesty.

2 PETER 1:16

"NOTHING IN CHRISTIANITY IS ORIGINAL," CLAIMED THE NOVEL *The Da Vinci Code,* adding that everything of importance in Christianity —from communion to Jesus' birthday to Sunday worship—was "taken directly from earlier pagan mystery religions."[1]

The argument is simple: a whole bevy of mythological characters were born of virgins, died violently, and were resurrected from the dead in antiquity, but nobody takes them seriously. So why should anyone trust similar claims about Jesus that were obviously copied from these earlier pagan mystery religions?

This critique, popularized a century ago by European historians, has returned with a vengeance, becoming one of the most ubiquitous objections to the historical understanding of Jesus. It has spread around the Internet like a computer virus and been forcefully presented in numerous bestselling books.

The "parallels" appear stunning. According to proponents of this "copycat" theory, the pre-Christian god Mithras, for example, was born of a virgin in a cave on December 25, was considered a great traveling teacher, had twelve disciples, sacrificed himself for world peace, was buried in a tomb, and rose again three days later.[2] How could Christians possibly explain away such obvious plagiarism?

Were the supernatural qualities of Jesus merely ideas borrowed from ancient mythology and attached to the story of the Nazarene by his overzealous followers after his death? Is Jesus no more divine than

Zeus? Are the reports of his resurrection no more credible than the fantastical tales of Osiris or Baal?

The highly respected author and professor Ronald H. Nash explained in *The Gospel and the Greeks* that these theories were prevalent from about 1890 to 1940 but were largely answered and disproven by scholars. He lamented, however, the revival of these discredited theories. He said popular publications were "repeating claims and arguments that should have been laid to rest decades ago," circulating "one-sided and misinformed arguments," and ignoring "the weighty scholarly opinion" that has already been published to refute their assertions.[3] He later added, "Efforts to undermine the uniqueness of the Christian revelation via claims of a pagan religious influence collapse quickly once a full account of the information is available."[4]

To illustrate Nash's point, we'll unpack the example of Mithras in the next reading. For now let me remind you of an old saying: "A lie can travel halfway around the world while the truth is putting on its shoes."

Truth for Today

In light of such attacks on our faith, keep Peter's words in mind: "We did not follow cleverly devised stories. . . . [We] were eyewitnesses of his majesty" (2 Peter 1:16).

MYTHS ABOUT MITHRAS

*We also have the prophetic message as something
completely reliable, and you will do well to pay attention to
it, as to a light shining in a dark place.*

2 PETER 1:19

IN THE PREVIOUS READING WE SAW THAT CRITICS ACCUSE
New Testament writers of copying many of their claims about Jesus
from earlier religions. One of their favorite examples is the mythological god named Mithras, whose story originated long before
Jesus. They claim that Mithras was born of a virgin in a cave on
December 25, was a great traveling teacher, had twelve disciples,
sacrificed himself for world peace, was buried in a tomb, and rose
again three days later.

This appears to prove that Christianity stole its ideas about
Jesus from the mystery religion of Mithraism. But what happens
when we look deeper? I sat down with a historian who has given
his life to studying—and answering—these kinds of challenges,
Dr. Edwin Yamauchi. Here's a summary of our conversation about
the claims of Mithraism[1]:

Mithras was born of a virgin in a cave.

Historians agree that the myth actually says that Mithras
emerged fully grown out of a rock! No virgins and no caves. Also,
nowhere does the Bible say Jesus was born in a cave.

Mithras was born on December 25.

And? The Bible doesn't say when Jesus was born. Some think
it was in the spring, others in January. It wasn't until centuries
later that Christians chose December 25 to celebrate his birth—
probably, at least in part, to claim a pagan holiday for Christ.

Mithras was a traveling teacher with twelve disciples.

No, he was supposedly a god, not a teacher. In one version of the story he had only one follower, while in another version he had two—but never twelve.

Mithras sacrificed himself for world peace.

Actually he was known for killing a bull. He didn't sacrifice himself for anything.

Mithras was buried in a tomb and resurrected after three days.

There are no records of beliefs about Mithras's death, so no resurrection either.

As you can see, the alleged parallels between Mithras and Jesus dissolve under scrutiny. I asked Yamauchi about those making such claims. He replied that generally, "They don't have the languages, they don't study the original sources, they don't pay attention to the dates, and they frequently quote ideas that were popular in the nineteenth and twentieth centuries but have already been refuted."[2]

And yet they want us to believe them!

Truth for Today

The apostle Paul warned us to test truth claims and to "hold on to what is good" (1 Thessalonians 5:21). The claims that Christianity is a copycat religion have been tested and debunked, so we can confidently hold on to what is good: Christ.

THE BIBLE'S LITERARY DEVICES

Jesus spoke all these things to the crowd in parables; he did not say anything to them without using a parable.

MATTHEW 13:34

WE HAVE ALREADY SEEN HOW THE USE OF ONE TYPE OF LITER-ary genre in Proverbs, a poetic style that presents wise sayings and truths, affected how we should understand and apply it in the real world (see "The Nature of Proverbs"). But there are many other literary devices and genres in the Bible. Norman Geisler and William Nix explain:

> There is no reason to suppose that God can utilize only one style or literary genre in His communication to man. The Bible reveals a number of literary devices. Several whole books are written in *poetic style* (e.g., Job, Psalms, Proverbs). The synoptic gospels [Matthew, Mark, and Luke] are filled with *parables*. In Galatians 4, Paul uses an example of an *allegory*. The New Testament abounds with *metaphors* (e.g., 2 Cor. 3:2–3; James 3:6) and *similes* (cf. Matt. 20:1; James 1:6); *hyperboles* may also be found (e.g., Col. 1:23; John 21:25; 2 Cor. 3:2). And Jesus Himself used the device of *satire* (Matt. 19:24 with 23:24). . . . "Inspiration" must not be viewed as a mechanical or wooden process. It is, rather, a dynamic and personal process that results in a divinely authoritative and inerrant product—the written Word of God.[1]

In today's verse, Matthew 13:34, we are told that Jesus used parables to speak to the crowds. Parables are stories used to draw lessons out of various life situations. But it would be a mistake to force literalism onto these parables by demanding, for example, that Jesus give the name and address of the real prodigal son before we are willing to learn lessons from the story. Instead we need to accept parables for what they are and accept the truth Jesus was conveying through them.

Or when Mark reported, "The whole Judean countryside and all the people of Jerusalem went out to [John the Baptist]" (Mark 1:5), we need to recognize this as an intentional use of hyperbole (overstatement designed to make a point). So we are not required to believe that literally every human being in the entire city—including infants, the infirm, blind and lame beggars, and every scribe and Pharisee—went to hear John. Rather, we need to understand that Mark was using overstatement to help us understand that overwhelming numbers of people heard John.

The challenge is to study in order to interpret properly each literary genre in the way the author intended.[2] Then we can best recognize and benefit from the points the writer was trying to make.

Truth for Today

Here's the challenge: move beyond being a casual Bible reader, and become a serious student of God's Word. Also, consult reputable study Bibles and Bible commentaries to learn how various evangelical scholars interpret the passages you're investigating.

DISTORTING THE SCRIPTURES

*[Paul's] letters contain some things that are hard to
understand, which ignorant and unstable people distort, as
they do the other Scriptures, to their own destruction.*

2 PETER 3:16

BELIEVE IT OR NOT, MARK MITTELBERG AND I USED TO PERFORM
a drama in churches. We did it first at Willow Creek Community
Church in Chicago, but later at other churches around the United
States and Europe. We called it "A Café Encounter," and I played
a spiritual skeptic (which was easy for me), while Mark played a
Christian (also easy for him).

We didn't win any acting awards, but we did make some solid
points. After we had gone back and forth a few times on some
of my objections about the Bible—with Mark giving some great
answers—I would pull out this one, which you may have heard in
some of your own conversations:

LEE: Well, Mark, even if the Bible *can* be defended, it doesn't
really matter, because that's just your interpretation—and you can
make the Bible say whatever you want it to.

MARK: Really, Lee? The words don't have any meaning in
themselves—but can mean whatever the reader decides to make
of them?

LEE: Sure, people do that all the time!

MARK: [*Pauses.*] Lee, that's great!

LEE: *What's* great?

MARK: I'm thrilled to hear that you finally understand what
I've been saying, that you agree with me, and that you want to
become a Christian right now. It's fantastic!

LEE: What are you talking about? I didn't say that!

MARK: Well, maybe not with those exact words, but that's the way I'm *interpreting* what you've been saying.

LEE: Wait—*what?*—you can't do that! I'm *not* a Christian and *don't* agree with you! You need to listen more carefully so you understand what I'm really saying.

MARK: You know, Lee, you're right. And all *I'm* really saying is that what you want me to do for *you*, you need to do for *the Bible*.

LEE: Okay . . .

MARK: Just like any good teacher, the writers of Scripture had specific ideas they wanted to get across, and they effectively communicated those thoughts with words that any fair-minded person can understand. The fact that some people try to twist the Bible to make it say things it really doesn't say does not detract from the fact that the main message of the Bible is abundantly clear. We just need to read it carefully and, as with any good literature, seek to understand what the authors intended to convey. If you'll do that, I'm confident you'll see that its message is not hard to understand—and that it is powerful.

In keeping with Mark's message, let me offer a quote that is often attributed to a different Mark—this one with the last name Twain: "It ain't those parts of the Bible that I can't understand that bother me, it's the parts that I do understand."

Truth for Today

The apostle Paul wrote, "Faith comes from hearing the message, and the message is heard through the word about Christ" (Romans 10:17). If we drop our defenses and read that Word, it will inform and guide our lives.

INTERPRETING SCRIPTURE

Do your best to present yourself to God as one approved,
a worker who does not need to be ashamed and who
correctly handles the word of truth.

2 TIMOTHY 2:15

"AREN'T MANY OF JESUS' TEACHINGS OPEN TO DIFFERING interpretations?" I asked Christian philosopher Paul Copan.[1]

"The golden rule of interpretation is that you treat someone's teachings as you would want your own to be interpreted," Copan replied. "We can't read whatever we want into what Jesus said; we have to seek to understand accurately what he was communicating. This involves a certain amount of study in order to comprehend what he was saying. But picking and choosing verses out of context, spinning them to say what we want them to say—that's not responsible scholarship.

"The question is, are we willing to take Jesus seriously—even if his teachings may not sit comfortably with us? They may challenge us, they may force us to overturn a lot of our cherished beliefs about ourselves, but are we willing to confront what he taught without distorting it?"

"Still," I pointed out, "some people are very sincere in interpreting Jesus differently than the church traditionally has."

"I'll grant that they're sincere," Copan conceded. "Paul talks about the importance of sincerity and simplicity in urging a pure devotion to Christ. Sincerity is important, but, Lee, we can't overlook this: *sincerity is not sufficient.*

"Weren't Hitler and Stalin sincerely committed to their beliefs? I'm sure they were. The idea that God would applaud their sincerity is absurd. Sometimes people can be very committed and seemingly sincere, but it's at the expense of suppressing their conscience. They've rejected and resisted the truth or suppressed their moral impulses.

"Sincerity doesn't make a person right. Sincerity doesn't make something true. I could believe with all the sincerity in the world that the earth is flat, but that doesn't make it so. I can sincerely believe that I'm every bit as divine as Jesus, but that doesn't change the fact that I'm a creature, not the Creator."

The upshot is that we need to approach Jesus' words—and the Bible in general—with a spirit of humility and an attitude of teachability. We need to let God's revelation change *us*, and make sure we're never trying to change *it*. As Jesus replied when the devil was trying to bend and misuse Scripture, "It is written: 'Man shall not live on bread alone, but on every word that comes from the mouth of God'" (Matthew 4:4, quoting Deuteronomy 8:3).

Truth for Today
Humility and teachability are two traits we should cultivate as we approach God's Word, the Bible. Only with these will we be able to hear and apply all he wants to tell us.

"BORN-AGAINERS"

You have been born again, not of perishable seed, but of imperishable, through the living and enduring word of God.

1 PETER 1:23

"WE AREN'T ONE OF THOSE 'BORN-AGAINER' CHURCHES, ARE we?" asked a visitor to our church on the phone to Mark Mittelberg.

Proceeding cautiously, Mark asked, "Well, what do you mean by 'born-againer' churches?"

"You know," the man replied, "those fanatical, cultlike places that try to force everyone to join them and then immediately start to brainwash them."

"Oh!" Mark responded. "No, we're not one of *those* places!" The man was relieved to hear this, and he expressed how much he had enjoyed the couple of services he had visited so far. Mark said he was glad about that and asked him a few questions to try to better understand where he was spiritually. He seemed to be a newer Christian—one with definite misunderstandings about what it means to be "born again"!

"I'd like to loop back to your original question," Mark continued, "by explaining that in spite of all the abuses and misconceptions of the idea, Jesus did tell us in John 3 that although we've all been born *physically*, we need to come alive *spiritually* as well. He described this as a spiritual birth—and it's from *him* we get the term *born again*. When we understand what Jesus meant, we begin to see that this is a really important concept. In fact, every one of us needs to come alive spiritually as Jesus explained."

The man listened carefully and agreed with what Mark was

saying, but he was also relieved to know that his new church wasn't one of those manipulative places he'd been warned about.

That conversation reminded Mark of something we have seen in our culture for a long time: mass confusion about the term *born again*. As I've talked to people about this, I've realized some of them think being born again means having an ecstatic experience in which your head spins, you foam at the mouth, and your body levitates—like a scene from some horror movie.

So our challenge is to do what Mark did: help them sort out fact from fiction about what it means to be born again. People need to know the real meaning of Jesus' words when he said in John 3:3, "Very truly I tell you, no one can see the kingdom of God unless they are born again."

Truth for Today

Two truths are important today: First, if we're not sure we've come alive spiritually in the way Jesus said we must, we need to pray earnestly for that to happen. Second, as born-again followers of Christ, we need to tell others how they too can come alive in him.

LOST GOSPELS?

*If anybody is preaching to you a gospel other than what
you accepted, let them be under God's curse!*

GALATIANS 1:9

"THE BIBLE DID NOT ARRIVE BY FAX FROM HEAVEN."
So argues the fictional Dr. Teabing:

> The Bible is a product of *man*, my dear. Not of God. The Bible
> did not fall magically from the clouds. Man created it as a his-
> torical record of tumultuous times, and it has evolved through
> countless translations, additions, and revisions. History has
> never had a definitive version of the book. . . . More than *eighty*
> gospels were considered for the New Testament, and yet only a
> relative few were chosen for inclusion—Matthew, Mark, Luke,
> and John among them.[1]

Some commentators claim that other writings should have
been included in the New Testament, including the "gnostic gospels." The theologically liberal Jesus Seminar published a work
called *The Complete Gospels*, presenting sixteen other so-called
gospels and implying they are equally valid to the biblical ones.

But are these claims valid? Eminent scholar Bruce Metzger
countered that those were "written later than the four gospels,
in the second, third, fourth, fifth, even sixth century, long after
Jesus, and they're generally quite banal. They carry names—like
the Gospel of Peter and the Gospel of Mary—that are unrelated to
their real authorship."[2]

Even the gospels of Thomas and Judas—probably the earliest
examples—were penned between AD 175 and 200. That's more

than 140 years after the life of Jesus. Which account of the Civil War would you trust: one from a historian who lived during the war, or from someone today who relies on stories and rumors passed down for one and a half centuries? I know which I'd bet on.

Also, consider the teachings of these "gospels." N. T. Wright says the gnostics held to four main ideas: "a wicked world; a wicked god who made it; salvation consisting of rescue from it; and rescue coming through the imparting of secret knowledge, especially knowledge that one has the divine spark within one's own self."[3] A quick scan of the biblical Gospels shows these ideas are foreign to Jesus' teachings. The real Gospels say, for example, that God is good (Luke 18:19), that we're to be an influence in the world, not be plucked out of it (John 17:15), and that salvation comes from knowing the true God, not secret knowledge (John 17:3).

We can trust the writings of Matthew, Mark, Luke, and John because they were written close to the time when Jesus lived, are rooted in eyewitness testimony, are corroborated by history and archaeology, and square with other biblical teachings. None of this is true of the later impersonators.

Truth for Today

Psalm 119:160 assures us concerning God's revelation: "All your words are true." I'll stick with what has proven to be God's true Word: the Bible.

DOUBTING (THE GOSPEL OF) THOMAS

*Then he said to Thomas, "Put your finger here; see my hands.
Reach out your hand and put it into my side. Stop doubting
and believe." Thomas said to him, "My Lord and my God!"*

JOHN 20:27–28

THOMAS WAS A DISCIPLE OF JESUS WHO SUFFERED A BOUT
with doubt. But then Jesus himself convinced Thomas that he had
returned from the dead. This led to Thomas's strong affirmation
of faith in the risen Savior and his subsequent ministry of sharing
the good news about Christ. Church tradition tells us Thomas later
took the gospel all the way to India.

The "Gospel of Thomas," however, is a gnostic gospel that was
written, at the earliest, in the late second century—about a hundred years after the authentic biblical Gospels of Matthew, Mark,
Luke, and John. Therefore it was unrelated to the real Thomas and
far removed from Jesus' life.

Worse, its teachings range from unbiblical to utterly illogical.
It claims, for example, that salvation comes from understanding
oneself authentically—a message diametrically opposed to the
biblical message. It also claims Jesus said, "If you fast, you will
bring sin upon yourselves, and if you pray, you will be condemned,
and if you give to charity, you will harm your spirits."[1]

It gets worse. It also quotes Jesus as saying, "Lucky is the lion
that the human will eat, so that the lion becomes human. And foul
is the human that the lion will eat, and the lion still will become
human."[2]

Say what?

Also, the Gospel of Thomas portrays Jesus as being against women. At one point Simon Peter said to Jesus, "Make Mary leave us, for females don't deserve life." Jesus purportedly responded, "Look, I will guide her to make her male, so she too may become a living spirit resembling you males. For every female who makes herself male will enter the domain of Heaven."[3]

This is an affront to the teachings of the real Jesus, who elevated women in a very countercultural way.

For these reasons and more, I have huge doubts about the gospel of Thomas. When I asked Bible scholar Craig Evans what value Thomas has for us, he didn't mince words: "I don't know that Thomas has any value for everyday Christians. If you're looking for the real Jesus, there are far, far better places to go—like the canonical Gospels."[4]

In other words, Matthew, Mark, Luke, and John.

Truth for Today

Why are some people so enamored of Thomas and the other gnostic gospels? Perhaps because they offer a sense of spirituality but without the strong moral and spiritual claims of the real Jesus and the real Gospels. True Christ-followers want to know and follow the true Christ of the Bible.

PEOPLE WHO HAVE NEVER HEARD, PART 1

"Ask and it will be given to you; seek and you will find;
knock and the door will be opened to you."

MATTHEW 7:7

IT'S A COMMON QUESTION: "WHAT ABOUT PEOPLE WHO'VE grown up in places where they don't have the opportunity to hear about Jesus? How is God going to judge them?" You've probably heard this concern, and maybe you have even voiced it yourself.

In *The Questions Christians Hope No One Will Ask (With Answers)*, Mark Mittelberg offers five thoughts about this, which I'll summarize in this reading and the next.[1]

First, the idea that the "Christian West" is trying to reach the rest of the world is way out of date. In many ways, the opposite is true. Look at this startling missions report:

> One of every eight people on the planet is a practicing Christian who is active in his/her faith. The number of believers in what used to be "mission fields" now surpasses the number of believers in the countries from which missionaries were originally sent. In fact, more missionaries are now sent from non-Western churches than from the traditional mission-sending bases in the West.[2]

This means many of the people we thought had little chance of hearing the gospel are already Christians, and some of them are mobilizing to come and reach us in the increasingly secular West!

Second, Jesus addressed this issue when he promised, "Ask and it will be given to you; seek and you will find; knock and the door will be opened to you" (Matthew 7:7). Notice he did not limit this to any certain groups or time frames. Anyone who genuinely seeks God will be led to him.

How? In a variety of ways. For example, many Muslims who once seemed unreachable are having dreams and visions of Jesus and are putting their faith in him. There is also the example of a former Hindu man, the late Mahendra Singhal, whom I met years ago. Mahendra was raised in a Hindu home in India, grew up offering food to the idols in the Hindu temple, and was later tutored by gurus his parents hired to teach him about their religion.

The only problem was that Mahendra asked too many questions and gradually realized his religion wasn't providing real answers. So he kept on seeking the truth until one day he saw an ad in the local newspaper about a Bible correspondence course, which led him to begin studying the Bible. Not long after that he met some Christians, heard the gospel, and gave his life to Christ.[3]

Truth for Today

These examples are reminders that the Holy Spirit is moving throughout the world to convict people "about sin and righteousness and judgment" (John 16:8), and he is drawing them to Christ.

PEOPLE WHO HAVE NEVER HEARD, PART 2

*"Everyone who asks receives; the one who seeks finds; and
to the one who knocks, the door will be opened."*

MATTHEW 7:8

IN THIS READING WE'LL COMPLETE OUR FIVE THOUGHTS ABOUT
the question of how God will judge those who haven't heard the
gospel.[1]

*Third, though not everyone has equal access to the gospel, people
are still responsible to follow whatever light God has given them.*
For Mahendra, the man I mentioned in the previous reading,
that meant asking more and more questions when things didn't
make sense and actively seeking truth wherever he could find it—
including an ad for a Bible course.

For others it might be discovering God through his works in
nature. Romans 1:20 says, "Since the creation of the world God's
invisible qualities—his eternal power and divine nature—have been
clearly seen, being understood from what has been made, so that
people are without excuse." But if people will seek the God who had
enough knowledge, power, and creativity to produce a universe like
this, they will have the chance to encounter him. He can lead them
into his broader truths and to salvation through Christ.

Fourth, God will be fair in how he judges. He will deal with
people who reject him according to how much light they were
given and what they did with it. So the person who has minimal
information and little opportunity (and rejects it) will be judged
less severely than the person who was given more (and rejects

that)—though everybody has some measure of light and therefore some responsibility. (We'll discuss this in the next reading.)

Finally, those who ask this question have *heard the message— probably many times.* So after sharing some of these thoughts, you can gently remind them that they *have* received the information as well as the opportunity and are therefore more responsible for what they do with it than any of the people they're concerned about.

This provides you the chance to then ask them, if they're not a Christian already, what's stopping them from receiving the grace of God that has so clearly and freely been offered to them.

Truth for Today

This is obviously more than an academic question. Jesus sent us into the world to share his good news, but some two thousand years later many still have not heard it. We should let this prompt us to pray for, support, and participate in efforts to reach as many people as possible for him.

ARE ALL SINS THE SAME?

*"From everyone who has been given much, much will be
demanded; and from the one who has been entrusted with
much, much more will be asked."*

LUKE 12:48

AS A BOY, MARK MITTELBERG WAS BOTHERED WHEN HE WOULD
hear Sunday school teachers say that all sins are equally evil, so
God views them all the same. In fact, he remembers being told that
the sweet little old lady next door, if she rejects Jesus, will be judged
by God in the same exact way as people like Adolf Hitler. Even in
his young mind this didn't seem right. The teachings of Jesus later
affirmed that to him.[1]

Jesus said in Luke 12:47–48, "The servant who knows the master's will and does not get ready or does not do what the master
wants will be beaten with many blows. But the one who does not
know and does things deserving punishment will be beaten with
few blows." Then Jesus added what has become a well-known verse,
"From everyone who has been given much, much will be demanded;
and from the one who has been entrusted with much, much more
will be asked" (v. 48). This is often paraphrased, "to whom much is
given, much is required"—and obviously the inverse would be true.

Also, Jesus repeatedly said there would be greater judgment for
those who heard and rejected him than there would be for earlier
groups who had ignored less obvious revelations from God (see,
for example, Matthew 10:15; 11:21–24; 12:41–42; and correspond-
ing passages in the other Gospels).

Why is this important? Because it assures us and our spiritually curious friends that God is logical and fair in how he judges.

Mark not only found this information liberating when he first discovered it, but he has also found it freeing to spiritual seekers he has shared it with over the years. This includes the father of a friend, for whom this had become a spiritual sticking point. After Mark showed him this biblical rationale concerning God's judgment, the last barrier was gone, and he was ready to receive Christ. So Mark led him in a prayer of commitment.

It is important to add, though, that Mark and I are careful to make sure people understand that everyone has received at least *some* information, or spiritual light (Romans 1:18–20), and thus everyone—including the proverbial little old lady next door—has at least some degree of responsibility before God. Therefore, *every* person still needs to hear and respond to the gospel message.

Truth for Today

Jesus' teachings about God's judgment assure us of what Abraham affirmed in Genesis 18:25: "Will not the Judge of all the earth do right?"

IS JUDGING ALWAYS WRONG?

"Do not judge, or you too will be judged."

MATTHEW 7:1

FEW THINGS ARE AS POLITICALLY INCORRECT THESE DAYS AS saying that other people are wrong about their religious beliefs. Such a claim smacks of *judgmentalism*, which should be avoided at all costs.

"Aren't you judging other people when you say they're wrong? And didn't Jesus say in Matthew 7:1, 'Do not judge, or you too will be judged'?" I asked Christian author and apologist Paul Copan.[1]

He was undaunted by my challenge. In fact, the mere mention of that verse brought a smile to his face. "That passage has replaced John 3:16 as the favorite verse that people like to quote," he said. "Unfortunately, though, many of them misinterpret what Jesus was saying. Jesus wasn't implying that we should never make judgments about people."

"How do you know?" I asked.

"Because in John 7:24, Jesus said, 'Do not judge by appearances, but judge with right judgment' [RSV]. He was clarifying that it's all right—in fact, it's a good thing—to make *proper* judgments about people. What Jesus condemned is a critical and judgmental attitude or unholy sense of moral superiority.

"The Bible says in Galatians 6:1 [RSV] that if a fellow Christian is caught in a sin, then those who are spiritual should seek to restore him or her 'in a spirit of gentleness. Look to yourself, lest you too be tempted.' God wants us to examine ourselves first for the problems we so readily detect in other people. Only then should we seek to remove the speck in the other person's eye [Matthew 7:1–5].

So judgmentalism is the ugly refusal to acknowledge that 'there but for the grace of God go I.'"

"So the key issue is our *attitude*?" I asked.

"Yes, that's right. We can hold our convictions firmly and yet treat people with dignity and respect even though they disagree with us. We can have a spirit of humility while at the same time explaining why we believe someone is wrong. Ephesians 4:15 talks about 'speaking the truth in love' [RSV]. That should be our goal."

Reflecting on this, I also realized Jesus said, "Watch out for false prophets" (Matthew 7:15). Unfortunately these people don't wear False Prophet labels! So how will we know who they are? Jesus continued, "They come to you in sheep's clothing, but inwardly they are ferocious wolves. *By their fruit you will recognize them*" (Matthew 7:15–16, emphasis mine). So, without using the actual word, Jesus was telling us to *judge* prophets by their fruit.

Truth for Today

As Christians, we must judge with the wisdom and discernment God provides us. But we must always avoid a critical, judgmental spirit.

LOVING THOSE WHO DISAGREE

"I tell you, love your enemies. . . . If you love those who love you, what reward will you get? Are not even the tax collectors doing that?"

MATTHEW 5:44, 46

I HAVE HAD THE PRIVILEGE, ALONG WITH MARK MITTELBERG, of befriending a well-known Muslim who was open to discussing Christianity while remaining firm in his Islamic beliefs. He came over to my house, where he and his girlfriend, along with Mark and me and our wives, enjoyed an evening grilling steaks together and discussing theology and history. We disagreed on fundamental spiritual issues, but none of us became belligerent or were offended along the way. Instead, we were civil and respectful toward one another without pretending to agree on everything.

I shared the story of that friendship and interaction with Christian philosopher Paul Copan. "That's exactly what true tolerance is about," he said. "Dialogue shouldn't begin by assuming the equality of all truth claims, which is a ridiculous position. Instead, dialogue should begin with assuming the equality of all *persons*.

"Each of us is made in the image of God and therefore has dignity and value as an individual. You can say, 'I accept you as a person, but that doesn't mean I embrace the beliefs that you hold.' You can have a discussion with your Muslim friend and thoroughly respect him even though you believe on rational grounds that he's mistaken."[1]

These were great thoughts, but let me take it a step further. Mark and I don't just respect or tolerate our friend. We've developed a real love for him, and we ache for him to know and experience Christ in the way we have.

Closer to home, I have a relative who's an atheist. Over decades of following Christ I've made countless attempts to share my faith with him. I've talked to him over holiday meals. I've gotten into arguments that were well intentioned but probably counterproductive. I've sent letters urging him to reconsider his stance and books to challenge his thinking. Every evangelistic sermon I've ever written has been composed with him in mind.

But he has never shown a hint of interest in hearing more. In spite of that, I don't just respect or tolerate him. I love him with everything I've got, and I can't imagine heaven without him.

Truth for Today

We need to love truth, but truth alone won't move us to reach others. We must also love *people*. Whom does God want you to love and reach out to for him?

SPEAKING THE TRUTH IN LOVE

Brothers and sisters, if someone is caught in a sin, you who live by the Spirit should restore that person gently.

GALATIANS 6:1

THE FOLLOWING IS FROM A RECENT LETTER BY A GODLY FRIEND of Mark's and mine, written to a younger believer.

I pray you'll take a deep breath and find a quiet, private place before reading this. . . . Ready?

I've heard about your recent announcement—of a lifestyle you know is against God's will. This news has grieved me to the core. How can I even begin to respond? What can I possibly say that won't sound too harsh, too emotional, or too "Christian"?

You're a bright person. But over the years I've seen changes that have caused me concern—influences drawing you away from Christ. Now I wish I had spoken up at those times.

I love you so much, but I need to speak the truth to you. Please hear me, my friend.

The enemy of your soul has weakened you over time—lying to you, pulling you down, convincing you to compromise, desensitizing you to the conviction of the Holy Spirit. This enemy is allowing you the pleasures of sin for a season, getting you to fall for counterfeit beliefs, and, finally, gaining victory over you. And all this has come with the applause of the world. No surprise, is it, that those who mock Christianity are over-joyed when you become more like them?

You are in a dangerous place. You are quite literally in Satan's grip right now. "Do not be deceived: God cannot be mocked. A man reaps what he sows. Whoever sows to please their flesh, from the flesh will reap destruction; whoever sows to please the Spirit, from the Spirit will reap eternal life" (Galatians 6:7–8).

You know the Bible verses. God says what you are doing is wrong and that it will ultimately damage you. He says, "Repent, then, and turn to God, so that your sins may be wiped out" (Acts 3:19). And he says, "Seek the Lord while he may be found; call on him while he is near. Let the wicked forsake their ways and the unrighteous their thoughts. Let them turn to the Lord, and he will have mercy on them, and to our God, for he will freely pardon" (Isaiah 55:6–7).

Escaping this will take a radical step. There's a raging battle for your soul. You need to forsake the ungodly influences and the environment you have entrenched yourself in. No job, career, fame, friendship, lover, wealth, or anything else this fallen world has to offer is worth losing Jesus!

"'Come now, and let us reason together,' says the Lord, 'Though your sins are like scarlet, they shall be as white as snow'" (Isaiah 1:18 NKJV).

I am here to help you in any way I can, at any time you are ready.

May your heart receive this, in Jesus' name.

It doesn't matter what the young believer's sins were; our friend was determined to speak the truth in love. This is a powerful example of the kind of directness that can change a life and guide someone back from a potentially deadly path.

Truth for Today

Paul, like our friend, was known for "speaking the truth in love" (Ephesians 4:15). Make it your goal to speak real truth with an attitude of real love. God will use you!

DOES ANYONE REALLY SEEK GOD?

There is no one righteous, not even one; there is no one who understands; there is no one who seeks God.

ROMANS 3:10–11

SOME PEOPLE SEE THAT THE APOSTLE PAUL SAID, "THERE IS no one who seeks God" and view it as an open-and-shut case: *there are no spiritual seekers.*

But maybe we should open the case again and see what *else* Paul said. When speaking to the philosophers in Athens, for example, he explained that God created people *"so that they would seek him and perhaps reach out for him and find him*, though he is not far from any one of us" (Acts 17:27, emphasis mine).

And of course Jesus said, "Ask and it will be given to you; *seek and you will find*; knock and the door will be opened to you. For everyone who asks receives; *the one who seeks finds*; and to the one who knocks, the door will be opened" (Matthew 7:7–8, emphases mine).

So how can we put these ideas together? Mark Mittelberg wrote:

Let's be clear about this: in our own power and volition, no one seeks after God. Romans 3:11 removes any ambiguity about this. Anyone who is really seeking God is doing so because the Holy Spirit is already working in his or her life (see John 16:8). All genuine seeking is a response to God's activity.

This often leads to the question of how broadly God's Spirit is drawing people. Is the invitation genuinely open to every person, with some accepting it and some rejecting it, or is it effectively open only to those of God's choosing? Well, I respect those on both sides of that debate, but to me it seems Scripture is clear that "God so loved *the world* that he gave his one and only Son, that *whoever* believes in him shall not perish but have eternal life" (John 3:16, emphases mine) and that the invitation Jesus gave in Matthew 7:7–8 was open to *anyone* who would seek, knock, or ask.

The key issue is that we all need to do *our* part in making the message clear and accessible to everyone we possibly can, trusting God to do *his* part in drawing people and changing hearts. Whenever that happens, the Calvinist and the Arminian can sit at the table together and have a friendly chat about their theories while they join in joyful celebration, along with the angels in heaven (Luke 15:10), over this new brother or sister in Christ![1]

I would simply add that for me this is not a theoretical issue. I was a spiritual seeker for almost two years before I, by God's grace and through the enabling power of the Holy Spirit, gave my life to Christ.

Truth for Today

Here's a great reminder for you or anyone you know who is searching for God: "You will seek me and find me when you seek me with all your heart" (Jeremiah 29:13).

RESPONDING TO REINCARNATION, PART 1

Just as people are destined to die once, and after that to face judgment, so Christ was sacrificed once to take away the sins of many.

HEBREWS 9:27–28

REINCARNATION IS AN IDEA THAT IS BECOMING INCREASINGLY popular in the West, but it's actually quite Eastern. This teaching is found in both Hinduism and Buddhism; it purports that we live many lives, each one allowing us to try to do things better and to work off the bad karma we accumulated by doing bad things in former lives.

The Bible, however, does not support this idea. Quite the opposite. The writer of Hebrews, for example, taught that we are "destined to die once, and after that to face judgment." No do-overs or second tries. Also, when Jesus told the story of the rich man and Lazarus in Luke 16:19–31, he said when they died, their fate was sealed based on what they'd done during their one and only life.

I asked Christian philosopher Paul Copan about the increasing popularity of reincarnation.

"Some people in the West see reincarnation as another crack at life in order to get things right," Copan said, "sort of like the movie *Groundhog Day*. There's an attraction to saying we have many opportunities and not just one lifetime. Actually, the reality is quite different." He gestured toward me. "You've been to India, right?"

"I've spent some time there, yes," I said.

"I have too. And I'm sure you've noticed that reincarnation is a very oppressive burden in that Hindu culture, as it is in the Buddhist world," he said. "For example, if you're a low caste or no caste Hindu, then you're stuck at that low level because that's what you deserve from your previous life. And people shouldn't reach out to help you, because they might jeopardize their own karma by interfering with your living out the miserable existence that you deserve."[1]

I knew he was right. What sounds on the surface like a magnanimous belief that gives people multiple opportunities to live a better life turns out to create a devastating situation for millions of people who are mired in hopeless poverty day to day.

So the Bible refutes the idea of reincarnation, and the realities of the world prove the fruit of reincarnation to be destructive. So what's the good news? Jesus already died for our sins so we wouldn't have to try to pay them off ourselves.

Truth for Today

"When the kindness and love of God our Savior appeared, he saved us, not because of righteous things we had done, but because of his mercy" (Titus 3:4–5). That's a promise to embrace both today and forever.

RESPONDING TO REINCARNATION, PART 2

Nothing in all creation is hidden from God's sight. Everything is uncovered and laid bare before the eyes of him to whom we must give account.

HEBREWS 4:13

IN ADDITION TO THE BIBLICAL PROBLEMS WITH REINCARNA-tion, there are serious logical problems as well. Mark Mittelberg had a chance to share some of those with a woman on an airplane:

I was on a long flight, sitting next to a soft-spoken Asian woman. We chatted a bit, and then religion came up. She was a Buddhist, and I mentioned that I'm a Christian.

"I'm curious about a couple things related to the Buddhist faith," I said. "Would you mind if I run them by you?" She seemed pleasantly surprised to be asked.

"First, am I understanding correctly that you don't believe in a personal God—one with a mind and personality, who we could talk to like a friend?" She acknowledged this, saying that in her understanding "god" is an impersonal force, and everything that exists is part of it.

"And," I proceeded, "you believe in reincarnation—that we go through many lifetimes, striving to work off the bad karma we've earned through wrong deeds done in previous lives?" Again, she affirmed this was right.

"But you don't remember your wrong deeds that earned you the bad karma, or anything else from previous lifetimes, correct?" She nodded.

"Then here are my two questions," I continued. "First, if you don't remember what you've done in past lives, and if there's no personal God to keep track of it, *then who's the karma keeper?*"

She looked at me quizzically and asked me to explain.

"Who keeps track of how much bad karma you have in your karma account, and who tabulates how well you're doing in paying off that debt so someday you can achieve nirvana?"

"I don't know," she admitted. "I've never really thought about it."

"While you're thinking about it," I continued while breathing a silent prayer, "here's my second question. Where is the *justice* in our having to pay for sins we don't remember and aren't even sure we ever committed? Is that really fair?"

My new friend acknowledged she had no idea how to answer my questions and had never really contemplated concerns like these.

As gently as I knew how, I explained that I had been contemplating these questions for a long time, and I was pretty sure Buddhism didn't have good answers.

Then I suggested that the concepts of sin, forgiveness, and salvation found in Christian teachings were much more cohesive and satisfying—and urged her to read the New Testament gospels—Matthew, Mark, Luke, and John—to see firsthand what Jesus taught about these things.

I hope this dialogue helps you to see that the mathematics of reincarnation just don't add up. By contrast, the logic of the gospel is both compelling and attractive.

Truth for Today

Here's that gospel: "For it is by grace you have been saved, through faith—and this is not from yourselves, it is the gift of God—not by works, so that no one can boast" (Ephesians 2:8–9). *That* is truth worth celebrating—and sharing!

ANGRY ATHEISTS

Although they knew God, they neither glorified him as God
nor gave thanks to him, but their thinking became futile
and their foolish hearts were darkened.

ROMANS 1:21

"I DON'T BELIEVE IN UNICORNS," MARK MITTELBERG TELLS audiences, "but I'm not *mad* at them!"

He goes on to explain that while not every atheist is angry, anger seems to be a common trait among many skeptics. "Such passion from atheists," he says, "seems strange when aimed at something that, according to them, does not exist."[1]

Why such passion? Perhaps because "belief in God forces a person to face the fact that he or she is accountable to him. Many people are unwilling to accept accountability to anyone, let alone God. Romans 1:18–19 [NLT] says that they 'know the truth about God because he has made it obvious to them,' but that they 'suppress the truth.' That's why I think many take refuge in atheism or agnosticism—because it is a convenient escape from the challenging reality that they are accountable to their Creator. What is presented as 'I cannot believe' is more usually in reality 'I do not want to believe.'"[2]

Atheistic philosopher Thomas Nagel acknowledged in *The Last Word*, "I want atheism to be true and am made uneasy by the fact that some of the most intelligent and well-informed people I know are religious believers. It isn't just that I don't believe in God and, naturally, hope that I'm right in my belief. It's that I hope there is no God! I don't want there to be a God; I don't want the universe to be like that."[3]

Perhaps this helps explain why the late Christopher Hitchens, author of *God Is Not Great: How Religion Poisons Everything*, once described himself not as an atheist, but as an "antitheist" in an article titled "Nothing Sacred: Journalist and Provocateur Christopher Hitchens Picks a Fight with God."[4]

I too often felt that way as an atheist. I didn't *want* God to be real or Christianity to be true. That's why I tried so hard to find a scandal at Leslie's church—to poke holes not just in it, but in her faith as a whole. That way, I figured, I could get her out of this cult she'd joined, and we could get back to living our lives the way we wanted to, according to our own self-centered desires. When that plan didn't work for me, I became angry.

I am thankful God helped that anger subside just enough for me to crack open the door to the truth.

Truth for Today

Disbelief is often not an intellectual issue, but a problem of the will. That's why humility is often the prerequisite to spiritual discovery.

DRIFTING AWAY FROM GOD

"When the Son of Man comes, will he find faith on the earth?"

LUKE 18:8

"PEOPLE ARE BASICALLY GOOD," WE'VE BEEN TOLD. "THEIR intentions are noble, but sometimes they fall short of their lofty aspirations. Still, there's a spark of the divine within each of us."

Seriously? Don't the people who say these things ever turn on the news?

And there are those who tell us, "Deep down I'm really a good person; God will accept me on the merits of what I've done." Don't they ever look in the mirror? Have they lost all touch with their God-given consciences and of the Holy Spirit's convictions of sin?

Don't take these questions as condescension. I was just as lost as they were—probably *more* lost. I lived with a spiritual blindness that fooled me into thinking that if there were a God, he'd probably be pretty impressed with me. Yet now, living on the other side of redemption, it's hard for me to comprehend the delusion I once lived under. It's the same delusion that plagues our broader culture.

But rather than trying to explain this further, I'll let the Bible address us directly. Read these words carefully, thinking about what's happening all around us every day:

> There will be terrible times in the last days. People will be lovers of themselves, lovers of money, boastful, proud, abusive, disobedient to their parents, ungrateful, unholy, without love, unforgiving, slanderous, without self-control, brutal, not lovers of the good, treacherous, rash, conceited, lovers of pleasure rather than lovers of God—having a form of godliness but denying its power. (2 Timothy 3:1–5)

I don't know if we're in "the last days" Paul referred to—though we're certainly two thousand years closer than he was. Either way, what an eye-opening description of the world we live in. Like a good doctor, Paul diagnosed the disease and accurately pointed out a revealing list of the symptoms our society is exhibiting.

How should we respond to such a sobering prognosis? By running to the One with the cure! And by taking God's remedy and sharing it with as many other people as possible, as quickly as possible.

The gospel message is not only good news—it's a matter of life and death for a world that is plagued by the deadly disease of sin.

Truth for Today

"What can wash away my sins?" the old hymn asks. "Nothing but the blood of Jesus!" This sin-sick world is growing increasingly unhealthy. However, "It is not the healthy who need a doctor, but the sick," Jesus told us. "I have not come to call the righteous, but sinners to repentance" (Luke 5:31–32).

NEVER ALONE

"The Advocate, the Holy Spirit, whom the Father will send in my name, will teach you all things and will remind you of everything I have said to you."

JOHN 14:26

MARK AND I HAD LED A CONFERENCE ON HOW EVERY CHRISTIAN can get in on the "unexpected adventure" of sharing our faith with others. It was a successful but exhausting event, and we were finally on the airplane to fly home to our families.

We were relationally fatigued. As we buckled in, it was good to know we'd be able to relax and get a little rest.

Our friend Andy, however, found himself in the row in front of us seated next to a stranger who turned out to be very talkative. The man, an atheist, was raising objections to the Christian faith, and Andy patiently responded to each of them.

Way to go, Andy! Mark and I were proud of him for finding the energy to engage the guy—energy we obviously lacked!

Throughout their conversation, Andy later told us, he assured himself he wasn't alone. *I've got Lee Strobel and Mark Mittelberg backing me up*, he told himself. *If this guy comes up with an objection I've never heard, these guys, who are probably listening with rapt attention, will lean forward and provide any information I need.*

I'm not sure whether Andy glanced over his shoulder in the hope of getting an approving nod or just heard one of us snoring, but at some point he realized his spiritual comrades were sleeping like babies.

A lot of help these guys are, Andy thought. *They can't even stay awake long enough to give a buddy a little support.*

But then he realized he'd answered the guy's questions and presented the gospel on his own. It was probably not the way Lee or Mark would have, but who cares? Maybe he'd done it better!

And maybe the evangelistic "backup" he was hoping for had been provided by God, but in a more direct and powerful way. Perhaps Andy didn't need the assistance of friends, but rather the guidance and affirmation of the One who knew the heart and mind of that atheist and who loved him more than we ever could.

I'm glad Andy was there for him when Mark and I weren't—and that we all have the promise of the Holy Spirit's power, guidance, and wisdom to help us "make the most of every opportunity" (Colossians 4:5).

Truth for Today

"Surely I am with you always," Jesus said, "to the very end of the age" (Matthew 28:20). So when you seek to do God's work, you're never doing it alone. His presence and power are always with you.

BIBLICAL MARRIAGE

A man leaves his father and mother and is united to his wife, and they become one flesh.

GENESIS 2:24

"LET'S START AT THE BEGINNING. *THIS IS A FOOTBALL.*"

These were the words of one of the most successful coaches in history, Vince Lombardi.[1] His team, the Green Bay Packers, had been through a long series of losses, and as their new coach he brought them back to the basics of the game and ultimately to success. At the end of that season, the Packers beat the New York Giants 37–0 to win the NFL Championship.

For those of us who watch what is happening in the culture in relation to marriage, family, and morality, we've been through a tough season and experienced a long series of losses. Many are fighting societal changes in a piecemeal fashion, winning here and there but losing more often. Maybe it's time to get back to the basics.

"Let's start at the beginning," God seems to say in Genesis 2:24. "*This is a marriage.*"

It really isn't complicated. According to the verse, a man leaves his parents, and a woman does the same—and she becomes his wife. The two "become one flesh." The formula is: One Man + One Woman = One Flesh.

That's the biblical sexual ethic. Anything outside of that—sex before marriage, sex between nonspouses, sex between two men or two women or in a group—is strictly out of bounds and considered a serious sin.

"Yes, but that's the Old Testament," some protest. "That's when there were lots of laws, and a harsher God, and severe punishment for small infractions. Surely the kinder, gentler God of the New Testament eased off such strict rulings!"

"Let's go back to the beginning," Jesus seemed to say in Matthew 19. *This is* still *a marriage.*"

"Haven't you read," Jesus said, "that at the beginning the Creator 'made them male and female,' and said, 'For this reason a man will leave his father and mother and be united to his wife, and the two will become one flesh'? So they are no longer two, but one flesh. Therefore what God has joined together, let no one separate" (Matthew 19:4–6).

Call me old-fashioned, but I think the Creator knew what he was doing when he made us male and female and when he instituted biblical marriage. He loves us and wants us to have success as individuals, as couples and families, and as a society. We depart from his blueprint at our peril.

Truth for Today

Jesus was clear about God-ordained marriage and the sinfulness of relations outside the permanent union between a man and a woman. Let's have the courage to uphold and live out this biblical understanding and to gently point others to it.

ALLEGED CONTRADICTIONS, PART 1

The law of the Lord is perfect, refreshing the soul. The statutes of the Lord are trustworthy, making wise the simple.

Psalm 19:7

AS AN ATHEIST I PEPPERED ILL-PREPARED CHRISTIANS WITH A flurry of apparent biblical contradictions and discrepancies. They'd usually get flustered because they couldn't answer them, and I'd walk away feeling smug and self-satisfied.

Then, during my spiritual search, I had to go back and try to resolve the very issues I'd raised with others. I'm thankful that I found answers that satisfied my heart and mind. Years later, when working on *The Case for Faith*, I had the chance to raise some of those concerns with Bible scholar Norman Geisler.[1]

"I've made a hobby of collecting alleged discrepancies, inaccuracies, and conflicting statements in the Bible," Geisler said with a smile. "I have a list of about eight hundred of them. A few years ago I coauthored a book called *When Critics Ask*, which devotes nearly six hundred pages to setting the record straight.[2] All I can tell you is that in my experience when critics raise these objections, they invariably violate one of seventeen principles for interpreting Scripture."

"What are those?" I asked.

"For example, assuming the unexplained is unexplainable. I'm sure some sharp critic could say to me, 'What about this issue?' and even though I've done a forty-year study of these things, I wouldn't be able to answer him. What does that prove—that the Bible has an error, or Geisler is ignorant? I'd give the benefit of the doubt to the Bible because, of the eight hundred allegations I've studied, I haven't found one single error in the Bible, but I've found a lot of errors by the critics."

"Is that really reasonable," I asked Geisler, "to give the Bible the benefit of the doubt?"

"Yes, it is," he insisted. "When a scientist comes upon an anomaly in nature, does he give up science? When our space probe found braided rings around Jupiter, this was contrary to all scientific explanations. So do you remember when all the NASA scientists resigned because they couldn't explain it?"

I laughed. "Of course not."

"Exactly. They didn't give up. They said, 'Ah, there must be an explanation,' and they continued to study. I approach the Bible the same way. It has proven over and over to be accurate, even when I initially thought it wasn't. Why shouldn't I give it the benefit of the doubt now? We need to approach the Bible the way an American is treated in court: presumed innocent until proven guilty."

Truth for Today

For Christians the Bible is a faithful guide through thick and thin. As we would with any close friend, we should trust it unless and until it's proven untrustworthy.

ALLEGED CONTRADICTIONS, PART 2

The precepts of the LORD are right, giving joy to the heart.
The commands of the LORD are radiant, giving light to the
eyes.

PSALM 19:8

WE HAVE LEARNED FROM NORMAN GEISLER THAT WE SHOULD treat the Bible like a friend: give it the benefit of the doubt when questions arise.

"Critics do the opposite," Geisler explained. "They denied the Hittites of the Old Testament ever existed. Now archaeologists have found the Hittite library. Critics say, 'Well, I guess the Bible was right in that verse, but I don't accept the rest.' Wait a minute! When it has been proven to be accurate over and over again in hundreds of details, the burden of proof is on the critic, not on the Bible."

I asked Geisler to describe other principles for resolving apparent conflicts.

"Failing to understand the context of the passage," he said. "This is the most common mistake critics make. Taking words out of context, you can even cause the Bible to prove there's no God. After all, Psalm 14:1 comes right out and says it: 'There is no God.' But, of course, in context it says, *'The fool says in his heart, "There is no God."'* Therefore, context is critically important, and most often critics are guilty of wrenching verses out of context to create an alleged discrepancy when there isn't one.

"Another mistake is assuming a partial report is a false report. Matthew reported that Peter said to Jesus, 'You are the Christ, the

Son of the living God.' Mark said, 'You are the Christ.' Luke said, 'The Christ of God' [Matthew 16:16 ESV; Mark 8:29 ESV; Luke 9:20 ESV]. Critics say, 'See? Error!' I say, 'Where's the error?' Matthew didn't say, 'You *aren't* the Christ' and Mark said, 'You are.' Matthew gave more. That's not an error; those are complementary.

"Other mistakes include neglecting to interpret difficult passages in light of clear ones; basing a teaching on an obscure passage; forgetting that the Bible uses nontechnical, everyday language; failing to remember the Bible uses different literary devices; and forgetting that the Bible is a human book with human characteristics."

"If it's a human book," I said, "aren't errors inevitable?"

"Except for, say, the Ten Commandments, the Bible wasn't dictated," Geisler replied. "The writers weren't secretaries to the Holy Spirit. Sometimes they used human sources or used different literary styles or wrote from different perspectives or emphasized different interests or revealed human thought patterns and emotions. There's no problem with that. But like Christ, the Bible is totally human, yet without error."[1]

Truth for Today

The Bible is a wonder—God is communicating his message through the colorful personalities of human authors. We learn perfect truth from him, through imperfect vessels like us.

ALLEGED CONTRADICTIONS, PART 3

The fear of the LORD is pure, enduring forever. The decrees of the LORD are firm, and all of them are righteous.

PSALM 19:9

NORMAN GEISLER HAD MADE A STRONG DEFENSE OF THE trustworthiness of the Bible, but there was so much more we could discuss. In my limited time remaining with him, I decided to raise a couple of specific concerns.[1]

"However," I interjected, "people bring up alleged contradictions all the time."

"Like what, for example?" he asked calmly, but hinting at a hunger to be challenged. "What are the most common you hear?"

I thought for a moment. "Matthew said there was one angel at Jesus' tomb; John said there were two. The Gospels say Judas hung himself; Acts says his bowels gushed out."

"You're right; those are frequently cited," he replied. "But they're easily reconciled. Concerning the angels, have you ever noticed that whenever you have two of anything, you also have one? It never fails. Matthew didn't say there was *only* one. John was providing more detail by saying there were two.

"As for Judas' suicide, you hang yourself in a tree or over the edge of a cliff. It was against the law to touch a dead body in those days. So somebody came along later, found his body, cut the rope, and the bloated body fell onto the rocks. What happened? The bowels gushed out, just as the Bible says. The accounts are not contradictory; they're complementary."

The ease with which that answer rolled off his tongue amazed me. So many people have been deeply troubled over the years by just that one question—and Geisler had answered it nonchalantly between sips of soda. Frankly, it was a bit of a faith-booster for me, and I hope it is for you too.

Not that every alleged contradiction is easily answered. In fact, as Geisler had explained, at times you don't know an answer and need to choose to trust the book anyway in light of all the other answers you *have* found.

Still, nothing seemed to intimidate the man. And I was comforted by the fact that *The Big Book of Bible Difficulties* he and Howe had written addresses more than eight hundred similar issues.[2]

I left that interview with an enhanced sense of confidence that, in spite of the frequent questions and objections that come my way, the Bible can *still* be trusted.

In fact, I've staked my life on it.

Truth for Today

The Bible has proven itself to be a book we can stake our lives on. And think about this: If we ignore it, then we're staking our lives on it not being true. As I've said before, I'd recommend betting on the Bible.

HOPELESSLY CORRUPTED?

This is the disciple who testifies to these things and who
wrote them down. We know that his testimony is true.

JOHN 21:24

"YOU DO REALIZE THAT THE BIBLE HAS BEEN CORRUPTED, RIGHT?"
Nabeel asked his new friend, David, who was reading the Scriptures.

"Oh yeah?"

"Yeah," Nabeel continued. "It's been changed over time.
Everyone knows that." David, unconvinced, wanted to talk about
it. Thus began a multiyear dialogue between this devout Muslim,
Nabeel Qureshi, and a recent convert to Christianity, David Wood.[1]

The beliefs Nabeel expressed that day are standard Islamic
thought. Muslims view Jesus as a prophet of Allah, and their
original gospel writings about him in what they call the Holy Injil
as inspired by God. The problem, they'll tell you, is that the Injil
has been hopelessly corrupted and is therefore no longer a reliable
source of information.

This viewpoint itself, however, is fraught with problems—even
from an Islamic perspective. For example, the Muslim holy book,
the Qur'an, explicitly *endorses* the Injil, as well as the broader Bible,
as revelation from Allah: "He has revealed to you the Book with
truth, verifying that which is before it, and He revealed the Torah
and the Gospel aforetime, a guidance for the people, and He sent
the Qur'an" (Qur'an 3:3–4).[2]

Muslims claim those are the writings that have now been corrupted and therefore cannot be trusted. But this is disproven by
the fact that the Bible of the seventh century (which the Qur'an

endorsed as being revealed by Allah) is the same as the Bible of the twenty-first century. It has *not* changed.

Furthermore, the charge that the Bible has been corrupted contradicts the clear teaching of the Qur'an when it says, "And recite what has been revealed to you of the Book of your Lord, there is none who can alter His words; and you shall not find any refuge besides Him" (Qur'an 18:27;[3] also see Qur'an 6:114–115). In other words, Allah promises to protect his written revelations, including the Bible; and "there is none who can alter His word."

Therefore our biblical account of Jesus (1) was endorsed by the Qur'an; (2) is unchanged since the time of Muhammad; and (3) can't be changed because nobody has the power to corrupt or alter God's words (according to the Qur'an).[4]

Bottom line: the Holy Injil, the gospel account about Jesus, is true—for Christians, for Muslims, and for anyone with the courage to read it for themselves. This is part of the reason that, after years of dialogue with David and study on his own, Nabeel ended up becoming a follower of Jesus.[5]

Truth for Today

God really has preserved the Bible from corruption, and we can confidently share its truths with others—including our Muslim friends.

A POSITIVE CASE
FOR THE BIBLE

*"The Advocate, the Holy Spirit, whom the Father will send
in my name, will teach you all things and will remind you
of everything I have said to you."*

JOHN 14:26

WE HAVE ADDRESSED A NUMBER OF OBJECTIONS TO THE BIBLE.
Today we'll present a three-part case *for* the Bible.[1]

*The New Testament is, at minimum,
a reliable historical record.*

I believe it is much more than that; I'm convinced it's the
inspired and authoritative Word of God. But people don't have to
start there. We just need to help them see that it is, at the very least,
a trustworthy account of the life and ministry of Jesus Christ.

How? As we've seen, it was written early, was based on eyewitness accounts, and has been preserved in a great number of
historical manuscripts. Also, secular history and archaeology have
confirmed many of its details.

Noted scholar Craig Evans summed it up well, especially concerning the biographies of Jesus: "There's every reason to conclude
that the Gospels have fairly and accurately reported the essential
elements of Jesus' teachings, life, death, and resurrection. They're
early enough, they're rooted into the right streams that go back to
Jesus and the original people, there's continuity, there's proxim-
ity, there's verification of certain distinct points with archaeology
and other documents, and then there's the inner logic. That's what
pulls it all together."[2]

The historical record presents Jesus as the unique Son of God.

Jesus was clear about his divine identity, and he demonstrated it through his sinless life, supernatural insights, fulfillment of ancient prophecies, amazing miracles, and especially rising from the dead. He had credentials like no other spiritual leader—credentials that demonstrate he was who he claimed to be: the unique Son of God.

Jesus, the Son of God, taught that the Bible is the inspired Word of God.

Jesus had a lot to say about the Bible of his day, the Old Testament. He quoted from it often, and in every case he upheld its accuracy and divine authority. If there had been parts that needed to be corrected, surely he, the Son of God, would have done so. But Jesus based his ministry and teachings on its sure foundation. He treated the historic parts as history, the prophetic books as prophecy, and the teaching sections as truth to be obeyed. He also empowered his disciples, under the guidance of the Holy Spirit, to remember and write what would become the New Testament (John 14:26).

We can trust the Bible because Jesus did.

Truth for Today

Jesus said, "The Scripture cannot be broken" (John 10:35 NKJV), and, "Heaven and earth will pass away, but my words will never pass away" (Matthew 24:35). If you're a follower of Jesus, you can trust whatever Jesus trusts.

A GOD PROJECTION?

Sing to God, sing in praise of his name. . . . His name is the
LORD. A father to the fatherless, a defender of widows, is
God in his holy dwelling.

PSALM 68:4–5

"GOD DID NOT, AS THE BIBLE SAYS, MAKE MAN IN HIS IMAGE; on the contrary, man, as I have shown in *The Essence of Christianity*, made God in his image," said German philosopher Ludwig Feuerbach. He argued that people unconsciously project their best qualities onto an imaginary being they call God.[1]

Much of what we see in the world's religions consists of what Feuerbach described—people projecting into the sky the attributes they've observed in humanity, creating a "God" who looks much like them. Consider, for example, the Greek gods and goddesses.

Sigmund Freud took this argument a step further. "In fact," explains theologian Alister McGrath, "it is probably fair to say that the 'projection' or 'wish-fulfillment' theory is best known today in its Freudian variant, rather than in Feuerbach's original version. . . . Freud explored the origins of this projection of an ideal father figure. . . . 'My father will protect me; he is in control.' . . . Belief in a personal God is thus little more than an infantile delusion. Religion is wishful thinking."[2]

This claim, however, does nothing to prove anything about the existence of the real God. Its proponents generally ignore the overwhelming evidence for a Creator who made humans in his image.

Also, their argument can cut both ways. Maybe it's actually *a rejection of their human fathers* that motivates people to project that rejection into the sky, resulting in their denial of the God who made them. That, I believe, is what happened to me after a series of relational fallouts with my dad.

I wasn't aware that many well-known atheists throughout history—Friedrich Nietzsche, David Hume, Bertrand Russell, John-Paul Sartre, Albert Camus, Arthur Schopenhauer, Ludwig Feuerbach, Voltaire, H. G. Wells, Madalyn Murray O'Hair, and others—had felt abandoned or deeply disappointed with their own fathers, making it less likely they'd be open to a heavenly Father.[3]

When I was growing up, doubts festered in me as my teachers insisted science had eclipsed the need for God, and I was increasingly pulled toward skepticism. Something was missing—in my family and in my soul—that created a gnawing need I couldn't even describe at the time. I'm thankful that God eventually broke through with his truth to convince me and with his love to soften and draw me.[4]

Truth for Today

God is the Father many of us never had. He loves us enough to tell us the truth, to correct us when we go astray, and to forgive us when we come home to him—and, best yet, he loves us through the entire process.

THE NEW TESTAMENT CANON

*Every word of God is flawless; he is a shield to those who
take refuge in him. Do not add to his words, or he will
rebuke you and prove you a liar.*

PROVERBS 30:5–6

"FOR A LONG TIME," WROTE ATHEISTIC AUTHOR CHRISTOPHER
Hitchens, "there was an incandescent debate over which of the
'Gospels' should be regarded as divinely inspired. Some argued for
these and some for others, and many a life was horribly lost on the
proposition."[1]

In spite of Hitchens's characteristically cynical slant, it is true
that there was much discussion and some debate about what should
be included in the New Testament *canon*—a term that describes the
collection of books and epistles that have officially been accepted
as part of the Bible. I talked about this issue with eminent New
Testament scholar Bruce Metzger.[2]

"How did the early church leaders determine which books
would be considered authoritative and which would be discarded?"
I asked. "And what criteria did they use in determining which
documents would be included in the New Testament?"

"Basically, the early church had three criteria," he explained.
"First, the books must have *apostolic authority*. That is, they must
have been written either by apostles themselves, who were eyewitnesses to what they wrote about, or by followers of apostles.

"Second, there was the criterion of *conformity to what was called
the rule of faith*. That is, was the document congruent with the basic
Christian tradition that the church recognized as normative?

"And, third, there was the criterion of whether a document had
had *continuous acceptance and usage by the church at large.*

"What's remarkable," Metzger continued, "is that even though the fringes of the canon remained unsettled for a while, there was actually a high degree of unanimity concerning the greater part of the New Testament within the first two centuries. And this was true among very diverse congregations scattered over a wide area."

F. F. Bruce, another highly respected scholar and author of *The New Testament Documents: Are They Reliable?*, added this: "The historic Christian belief is that the Holy Spirit, who controlled the writing of the individual books, also controlled their selection and collection, thus continuing to fulfill our Lord's promise that He would guide His disciples 'into all the truth' (John 16:13)."[3]

So, as you can see, there was human as well as divine care in collecting the canon of books we now know as the New Testament.

Truth for Today

Paul assured us that "All Scripture is God-breathed and is useful for teaching, rebuking, correcting and training in righteousness, so that the servant of God may be thoroughly equipped for every good work" (2 Timothy 3:16–17). So let's submit to the authority of *all* of the Bible.

THE REAL JESUS

The Word became flesh and made his dwelling among us.
We have seen his glory, the glory of the one and only Son,
who came from the Father, full of grace and truth.

JOHN 1:14

"IS THERE A TREND TOWARD PEOPLE SAYING JESUS WAS ONLY a make-believe character?" asked Natalie on my online newsletter. "My nephew, who's a college freshman, said he doubts whether Jesus ever existed."

My answer to Natalie is this: if it's a trend, it's only because the Internet is so efficient at propagating silly and baseless theories. The vast majority of scholars scoff at the claims of these so-called mythicists, who assert that Jesus never really existed but was created out of legend and mythology.

According to Bart Ehrman, the religious studies professor who is critical of many of the teachings of Christianity, skeptics started making these accusations in the nineteenth century, and the mythicist view is now widely found in agnostic and atheist circles in the United States.

But even Ehrman—himself an agnostic—believes "Jesus did exist, whether we like it or not."[1] Ehrman wrote his book *Did Jesus Exist?* because he wanted to establish that the mythicists are wrong in what they think. And he charged in a recent interview: "Rather than succeeding in debunking religion they just make themselves look foolish."[2]

In the book *Jesus and His World: The Archaeological Evidence*, New Testament professor Craig Evans sets the record straight. He critiques writings by author Tom Harpur, who says there's not even a "shred" of evidence Jesus lived, and Jesus Seminar participant Robert Price, who "rejects almost every argument or proffered piece of evidence that there was a Jesus of history."[3]

"Not surprisingly, the radical skepticism of Harpur and Price has gained no scholarly following. Harpur's strange theory . . . has been thoroughly refuted and is not followed by any reputable historian or Egyptologist. No major historian or New Testament scholar follows Price either," concludes Evans.[4]

Eminent scholar James D. G. Dunn of the University of Durham expressed astonishment that anyone still holds Price's opinion that "it is quite likely that there never was any historical Jesus." Responding to an essay by Price, Dunn used such descriptors as "sad, really," "disappointing," "ludicrous," "smacks of some desperation," "scraping the barrel," and "really quite unbalanced" in analyzing Price's ill-supported assertions.[5]

Unfortunately, though, the Internet can function as a virtual life-support system, continuing to keep these sorts of wacky theories alive despite the avalanche of evidence on the other side.

Truth for Today

The denial of Jesus' existence is another reminder that we need to be cautious whenever we consume information from the Internet. We must carefully weigh whether the propagators of wild theories offer any real support for their claims.

NEW TESTAMENT FORGERIES

*Paul, a servant of Christ Jesus, called to be an apostle and
set apart for the gospel of God. . . . I, Tertius, who wrote
down this letter, greet you in the Lord.*

ROMANS 1:1; 16:22

IN HIS BOOK *FORGED*, AGNOSTIC PROFESSOR BART EHRMAN
says approximately 70 percent of New Testament writings were not
written by those to whom they are attributed. That's quite a claim!
Here's an excerpt of what New Testament scholar Michael Licona,
who has debated Ehrman twice, told me in response:[1]

> Most, though not all, of the arguments against traditional
> authorship fall into two categories: style and content. However,
> if an author employed a secretary to write what he dictated as
> well as provide varying degrees of editing, this would explain
> why some letters in the New Testament whose authorship is
> questionable have vocabulary, grammar, some content, and an
> overall writing style that differs, even significantly, from the
> undisputed letters. Ehrman recognizes this: "Virtually all of the
> problems with what I've been calling forgeries can be solved if
> secretaries were heavily involved in the composition of the early
> Christian writings."[2]
>
> Did Paul use a secretary at least occasionally? We may
> answer with an unequivocal yes. Ehrman concedes: "There is
> no doubt that the apostle Paul used a secretary on occasion."[3]
> But he contends that there's no evidence that Paul used them
> for any other services such as editing to correct grammar and
> improve style, coauthor to contribute to content, or compose the
> letter with the named author giving his final approval.[4]

Ehrman said there is no evidence of the heavy reliance on a secretary for editing by anyone outside of the ultra-wealthy.[5] But Paul tells us he had churches that supported him, and we know he had coworkers whom he mentions in his letters. They would naturally have been the couriers and could even have served as his secretaries. So, he would have incurred little to no labor costs.

Licona concludes that for these and other reasons, "Ehrman's argument fails since Paul may not have incurred any costs for his extensive use of a secretary, the important occasions for writing the letters would have motivated Paul's extensive use of a secretary, and Paul clearly states that others were involved in the actual writing of the letters. . . . As an old friend of mine would say, Ehrman is left with a firm grasp on an empty sack."[6]

Truth for Today

Critics have employed a variety of arguments to try to discredit the Bible. But the deeper you look, the more reasons you'll find to trust "the Holy Scriptures, which are able to make you wise for salvation" (2 Timothy 3:15).

VARIATIONS IN BIBLICAL MANUSCRIPTS

"Blessed is the one who keeps the words of the prophecy written in this scroll."

REVELATION 22:7

A COMMON CHALLENGE TO THE RELIABILITY OF THE BIBLE IS to point out the variations between the manuscripts of the New Testament. This is not a new argument, but it is enjoying new popularity thanks to agnostic scholar Bart Ehrman in his bestselling book *Misquoting Jesus*.

Ehrman points out that we don't have the original copies of the New Testament.[1] That's true—though we don't have the originals of *any* ancient writings, sacred or secular. What we have instead are handwritten copies.

Ehrman also states correctly that there are between two hundred thousand and four hundred thousand variants, or differences, between the copies that we have.[2] So the implication is clear: How can we trust the Bible if it's pockmarked with errors? How do we really know what the original documents said if we don't actually possess them?

This has shaken the faith of some people, but it need not. We have good reasons to believe the New Testament has been reliably preserved.

First, the more copies you have of any document, the more variations you'll have. So, for example, if you only have a handful of manuscript copies—as is the case of most ancient literature—then there won't be very many differences either. But when you have more than 5,800 manuscript copies of the New Testament, then you'll also have many more variations between them. The high number of variants is actually a by-product of the overwhelming quantity of copies that we have and is a mark of strength.

Second, the more copies you have, the easier it is to determine what the original said; there's so much more to compare in order to weed out mistakes.

I should also point out that as much as 80 percent of the variants in the New Testament documents are minor spelling errors. Only 1 percent has the potential of affecting the meaning in some way. And even those variants are largely about insignificant issues, with not a single cardinal doctrine of the church in jeopardy.[3]

Years ago I interviewed eminent scholar Bruce M. Metzger, who was Ehrman's mentor at Princeton. I asked how his many decades of studying the New Testament's text had affected his faith.

"Oh," he said, "it has increased the basis of my personal faith to see the firmness with which these materials have come down to us, with a multiplicity of copies, some of which are very ancient. . . . I know with confidence that my trust in Jesus has been well placed."[4]

Truth for Today

The evidence is strong: the Bible you read today is a reliable version of the original writings of Scripture.

JESUS' IMPACT ON THE WORLD

Jesus did many other things as well. If every one of them were written down, I suppose that even the whole world would not have room for the books that would be written.

JOHN 21:25

MUCH HAS BEEN WRITTEN ABOUT JESUS' SPIRITUAL IMPACT on people. My friend and former colleague pastor John Ortberg summarized some ways Jesus influenced the world.[1]

Children

In the ancient world children were routinely left to die of exposure or sold into slavery. Jesus' treatment of and teachings about children led to the forbidding of such practices as well as to the establishment of orphanages and godparents.

Education

Love of learning led to monasteries, which became the cradle of academic guilds. Universities such as Cambridge, Oxford, and Harvard all began as Jesus-inspired efforts to love God with all one's mind. The ancient world loved education but tended to reserve it for the elite; the notion that every child bore God's image helped fuel the move for universal literacy.

Compassion

Jesus had a universal concern for the suffering that transcended the rules of the ancient world. His compassion for the poor and the sick led to institutions for lepers, the beginning of modern-day hospitals. They were the world's first charitable, volunteer-run institutions.

Humility

The ancient world honored many virtues such as courage and wisdom, but not humility. "Rank must be preserved," said Cicero. Jesus' life as a foot-washing servant would eventually lead to the adoption of humility as a widely admired virtue. Historian John Dickson writes, "It is unlikely that any of us would aspire to this virtue were it not for the historical impact of his crucifixion."[2]

Forgiveness

In the ancient world, virtue meant rewarding your friends and punishing your enemies. Conan the Barbarian was paraphrasing Genghis Khan in his answer to the question "What is best in life?" Conan said, "To crush your enemies, see them driven before you, and hear the lamentation of their women." An alternative idea came from Galilee: what is best in life is to love your enemies and see them reconciled to you.

Humanitarian Reform

Jesus' inclusion of women led to a community to which women flocked in disproportionate numbers. Slaves—up to a third of ancient populations—might wander into a church and have a slave owner wash their feet. One ancient text instructed bishops not to interrupt worship to greet a wealthy attender, but to sit on the floor to welcome the poor. Paul said, "There is neither Jew nor Gentile, neither slave nor free, nor is there male and female, for you are all one in Christ Jesus" (Galatians 3:28). Thomas Cahill wrote that this was the first statement of egalitarianism in human literature.

The unpredictable influence of an unelected carpenter continues to endure and spread across the world.

Truth for Today

Jesus has influenced our culture in ways that few people grasp or appreciate. This gives us even more reasons to trust and follow him.

SPECULATIONS ABOUT A MULTIVERSE

Oh, the depth of the riches of the wisdom and knowledge of God! How unsearchable his judgments, and his paths beyond tracing out!

ROMANS 11:33

"WHAT IF THERE ARE AN INFINITE NUMBER OF OTHER UNIVERSES existing apart from ours?" I asked apologist William Lane Craig, raising a common naturalistic theory.[1]

"Then the odds would be that one of them would have the right conditions for sustaining life," he answered. "And that's the one in which we happen to find ourselves."

Craig had heard this theory before. "It's called the Many Worlds Hypothesis," he said. "Here's the problem: these other theoretical universes are inaccessible to us, and therefore there's no possible way to provide any evidence that this might be true. It's purely a concept, an idea, without scientific proof. The prominent British scientist and theologian John Polkinghorne has called it 'pseudo-science' and 'a metaphysical guess.'[2]

"And think about it: if this were true, it would make rational conduct of life impossible because you could explain away anything—no matter how improbable—by postulating an infinite number of other universes."

"What do you mean?" I asked.

"For example, if you were dealing cards in a poker game and each time you dealt yourself four aces, you couldn't be accused of cheating, no matter how improbable the situation. You could merely point out that in an infinite ensemble of universes, there will occur a universe in which every time a person deals, he deals four aces to himself and therefore—*lucky me!*—I just happen to be in that universe!

"This is pure metaphysics. There's no real reason to believe such parallel worlds exist. The very fact that skeptics have to come up with such an outlandish theory is because the fine-tuning of the universe points powerfully toward an Intelligent Designer, and some people will hypothesize anything to avoid reaching that conclusion."

I knew that this astonishingly precise balance of the universe was one of the main factors that led Harvard-educated Patrick Glynn to abandon atheism and become a Christian, as he details in his book *God: The Evidence.*[3]

Science philosopher Robin Collins added that for any multiverse theory to become reality, it would have required some kind of "many universes generator." He explained, "It's highly unlikely that such a universe-generating system would have all the right components and ingredients in place by random chance, just like random chance can't account for how a bread-maker produces loaves of bread. So if a many-universe generating system exists, it would be best explained by *design.*"[4]

Truth for Today

It's interesting that scientists would embrace such a speculative theory without scientific evidence in an apparent effort to avoid the fact that God lovingly fine-tuned the universe to support life!

THE ARGUMENT
FROM MORALITY

They show that the requirements of the law are written on their hearts, their consciences also bearing witness, and their thoughts sometimes accusing them and at other times even defending them.

ROMANS 2:15

IN MY DISCUSSION WITH SCHOLAR AND APOLOGIST WILLIAM Lane Craig, he explained that "Another factor pointing toward God is the existence of objective moral values in the universe. If God does not exist, then objective moral values do not exist.[1]

"Objective moral values are valid and binding independently of whether anyone believes in them or not," Craig elaborated. "For example, to label the Holocaust objectively wrong is to say it was wrong even though the Nazis thought that it was right. And it would still be wrong even if the Nazis had won World War II. Now, if God does not exist, then moral values are not objective in this way."

I asked Craig to explain why.

"Because if there is no God, then moral values are merely the products of socio-biological evolution. In fact, that's what many atheists think. According to philosopher Michael Ruse: 'Morality is a biological adaptation no less than are hands and feet and teeth,' and morality is 'just an aid to survival and reproduction. . . . Any deeper meaning is illusory.'[2]

"Or if there is no God, then morality is just a matter of personal taste, akin to statements like 'Broccoli tastes good.' Well, it tastes good to some people but bad to others. There isn't any objective truth about that; it's a subjective matter of taste. And to say that killing innocent children is wrong would just be an expression of taste, saying, 'I don't like the killing of innocent children.'

"Like Ruse and atheist Bertrand Russell, I don't see any reason to think that in the absence of God, the morality evolved by *homo sapiens* is objective. After all, if there is no God, then what's so special about human beings? They're just accidental by-products of nature that have only recently evolved on a tiny speck of dust lost somewhere in a mindless universe and are doomed to perish forever in a relatively short time.

"However, we all know deep down that, in fact, objective moral values *do* exist. All we have to do to see that is simply to ask ourselves: 'Is torturing a child for fun really a morally neutral act?' I'm persuaded you'd say, 'No, that's not morally neutral; it's really wrong to do that.'

"And since these objective moral values cannot exist without God and they unquestionably do exist, then it follows logically and inescapably that God exists."

Truth for Today

Scripture and our consciences point to the same facts: there is a real right and wrong, and our understanding of it flows from the nature of the holy God.

TALE OF TWO PRODIGALS

"So he got up and went to his father. But while he was still a long way off, his father saw him and was filled with compassion for him; he ran to his son, threw his arms around him and kissed him."

LUKE 15:20

"WHICH TEACHING OF JESUS BEST CRYSTALIZES GRACE FOR you?" I asked apologetics professor Craig Hazen.[1]

Hazen was quick to respond. "It's got to be the story of the prodigal son. It's over the top! It really does show how we're not just talking about mercy; we're talking about a God who's singularly focused on having a love relationship with us and is willing to do just about anything for that.

"In this parable, the son takes his inheritance and says, 'I'm going my own way.' The father probably took a deep breath and said, 'Oh, I hope one day he comes back!' And after a disastrous life that helps him realize the enormity of his sin, the son *does* come back—and scanning the horizon, the father sees him, and without a moment of hesitation, he runs to him with a ring, sandals, and a feast. The father doesn't just begrudgingly allow his son secondary status as a disfavored servant, but he orders a party in his honor and reinstates him as his child.

"What a story of undeserved favor!" Hazen exclaimed. "You don't find anything like that in the other religions of the world."[2]

"Are you sure?" I asked. "I thought there was a story in Buddhist literature that parallels the prodigal son parable."

"Well, they're similar to the degree that they both involve sons who rebelled and left home, then later saw the error of their way and came back. But the Buddhist story ends quite differently—the son has to work off his misdeeds."

"How?" I asked.

"He ends up toiling for twenty-five years, hauling dung. So that provides a stark contrast between the God of grace and a religion where people have to work their way to nirvana."

A feast with the fatted calf versus hauling piles of dung—yes, quite a difference, I mused.

"The prodigal son is a product of Christian theology, which is a wellspring of grace, forgiveness, and hope," Hazen concluded. "You find the prodigal son story coming from the lips of Jesus—and nobody else."

Truth for Today

"This son of mine was dead and is alive again; he was lost and is found," said the father in the parable. "So they began to celebrate" (Luke 15:24). What a stunning picture Jesus painted of God's love and grace toward any sinner, any of us, who is willing to come home to him.

GRACE FOR "GOOD" PEOPLE

For all have sinned and fall short of the glory of God, and all are justified freely by his grace through the redemption that came by Christ Jesus.

ROMANS 3:23–24

SOME PEOPLE ARE IN OBVIOUS NEED OF GOD'S FORGIVENESS, but then there are the Craig Hazens of the world—the sons who never were prodigals, the nice folks who seem morally superior. Hazen was "on the straight and narrow," but he was also a skeptic.[1]

"No Christian had ever offered me good reasons to believe," he explained, "so I was basically coming to the conclusion that the world is probably all about me. Then a girl invited me to church. I remember the message, based on the fourth chapter of John, where Jesus offers the Samaritan woman 'living water' that leads to eternal life. I figured, *What do I have to lose?* I walked forward at the altar call, but frankly it was just an experiment at the time."

"What happened?"

"They took me to a side room for counseling. I thought, *Uh-oh, this is where the brainwashing takes place.* Before long, all the counselors were clustered around me because I was peppering them with questions nobody could answer."

"So you walked out unconvinced?"

"Pretty much, but I had started a journey. They began giving me books and tapes and following up with phone calls. I studied the issues for several months, and finally God sealed it. I became convinced Christianity is true.

"A couple of years later evangelists came to the college I was attending and brought some guys who had very dramatic testimonies. I was thinking, *Man, I want to jump up there too, but I want to give a different testimony.* You see, I *wasn't* in the gutter, I *wasn't* one of the dregs of society, I had great promise, and I *still* desperately needed God!

"Here's what I came to understand: having good table manners, getting As in school, saying 'please' and 'thank you,' and being nice to people—that's all pretty trivial stuff. Actually, I was in rebellion against a holy God so powerful that he could speak billions of galaxies into existence. Now, that's *huge*! I was ignoring him, I was turning my back on him, and my sins—my pride, my smugness, my selfishness, and all of my secret deceit and illicit desires—had created an enormous gap between us.

"Romans 3:23 says, 'All have sinned and fall short of the glory of God.' Over time, I came to realize that includes me.

"I needed forgiveness, and I found grace through Jesus."

Truth for Today

Whether our sins are subtle or spectacular, we *all* need grace. Fortunately, it's available to each of us through Christ.

THE DIVINE ENCODER

*I praise you because I am fearfully and wonderfully made;
your works are wonderful, I know that full well.*

PSALM 139:14

A POWERFUL EXAMPLE OF DESIGN IN THE UNIVERSE COMES from the evidence of biological information, specifically the incredibly complex information encoded in DNA. The six feet of DNA coiled inside every one of our body's one hundred trillion cells contain a four-letter chemical alphabet that spells out precise assembly instructions for all the proteins from which our bodies are made.

Dr. Francis Collins, former head of the international Human Genome Project, which mapped the entire human DNA sequence, explains it like this:

> This newly revealed text was 3 billion letters long, and written in a strange and cryptographic four-letter code. Such is the amazing complexity of the information carried within each cell of the human body, that a live reading of that code at a rate of one letter per second would take thirty-one years, even if reading continued day and night. Printing these letters out in regular font size on normal bond paper and binding them all together would result in a tower the height of the Washington Monument.[1]

Cambridge-educated science philosopher Stephen Meyer, whom I interviewed for my book *The Case for a Creator,* demonstrated that no hypothesis has come close to explaining how information could have gotten into biological matter by naturalistic means.

On the contrary, he said that whenever we find a sequential arrangement that is complex and corresponds to an independent pattern or function, this kind of information is *always* the product of intelligence. "Books, computer codes, and DNA all have these two properties," he said. "We know books and computer codes are designed by intelligence, and the presence of this type of information in DNA also implies an intelligent source."[2]

In addition, Meyer said the dazzling array of new life-forms that suddenly appeared fully formed in the fossil record, with no prior transitions, would have required the infusion of massive amounts of new biological information. "Information is the hallmark of mind," said Meyer. "And purely from the evidence of genetics and biology, we can infer the existence of a mind that's far greater than our own—a conscious, purposeful, rational, intelligent designer who's amazingly creative."[3]

That sounds a lot like the mind that, according to Genesis 2:7, "formed a man from the dust of the ground and breathed into his nostrils the breath of life."

Truth for Today

We were "fearfully and wonderfully made" in ways that go beyond our comprehension. Let this prompt us to worship our incomprehensible God!

EVIDENCE FROM CONSCIOUSNESS

*We are confident, I say, and would prefer to be away from
the body and at home with the Lord.*

2 CORINTHIANS 5:8

FOR CENTURIES, THE HUMAN SOUL HAS ENCHANTED POETS,
intrigued theologians, challenged philosophers, and dumbfounded
scientists. Teresa of Ávila, a mystic in the sixteenth century,
described it eloquently: "I began to think of the soul as if it were a
castle made of a single diamond or of very clear crystal, in which
there are many rooms, just as in heaven there are many mansions."[1]

Today, many scientists are concluding that the laws of chemistry and physics cannot explain our experience of consciousness.
In my interview with Professor J. P. Moreland for *The Case for a
Creator*, he defined *consciousness* as our introspections, sensations,
thoughts, emotions, desires, beliefs, and free choices that make us
alive and aware. The soul contains this consciousness and ani-
mates our body.

"What makes you think the soul is real?" I asked Moreland.[2]

"First, we're aware that we're different than our consciousness
and our body. We know that we're beings who have consciousness
and a body, but we're not merely the same thing as our conscious
life or our physical life.

"I *am* a soul, and I *have* a body. We don't learn about people
by studying their bodies. We learn about people by finding out
how they feel, what they think, what they're passionate about, what
their worldview is, and so forth. Staring at their body might tell us

whether they like exercise, but that's not very helpful. That's why we want to get 'inside' people to learn about them."

According to a researcher who showed that consciousness can continue after a person's brain has stopped functioning, current scientific findings "would support the view that 'mind,' 'consciousness,' and the 'soul' are separate entities from the brain."[3]

Moreland adds, "You can't get something from nothing." If the universe began with dead matter having no consciousness, "how, then, do you get something totally different—consciousness, living, thinking, feeling, believing creatures—from materials that don't have that?" But if everything started with the mind of God, he said, "We don't have a problem with explaining the origin of our mind."

Darwinist philosopher Michael Ruse conceded, "No one, certainly not the Darwinian as such, seems to have any answer" to the consciousness issue.[4] Nobel Prize–winning neurophysiologist John C. Eccles concluded from the evidence "that there is what we might call a supernatural origin of my unique self-conscious mind or my unique selfhood or soul."[5]

At bottom, the evidence for the existence of our souls is strong, and that forms compelling evidence for the existence of God as well.

Truth for Today

As J. P. Moreland explained, you *are* a soul, and you *have* a body. And God lovingly created every part of you.

THE EVIDENCE OF DESIGN

Do you not know? Have you not heard? The LORD is the everlasting God, the Creator of the ends of the earth.

ISAIAH 40:28

"FEW PLACES ARE AS BEAUTIFUL AS MONTANA'S BEARTOOTH Mountains," wrote Mark Mittelberg in our book *The Unexpected Adventure*.[1] "The sky is clear, the air crisp, and the aroma of pine needles fragrant. Then there are the high-altitude flowers, with shapes, colors, and sizes you just don't see when you're hanging out in the lowlands."

Being the avid *indoorsman* that I am, I'll take his word for it!

"Heidi and I enjoyed a trip to the region," Mark continued, "when we met Dan, who had come up alone. We invited him to join us for a day hike up a mountain that overlooked the area. It was a beautiful morning. We walked along chatting and enjoying the alpine scenery, and the higher we climbed the more variations we noticed of the mountain flowers.

"'You know, God must have quite an imagination to create such beauty,' I ventured. 'We keep seeing all these incredible shapes and colors of flowers—the Creator must really be creative!'

"Dan glanced back at me and said, 'Well, I guess that would be true if you believed in God, but I don't.'

"End of discussion. Or so he thought.

"Dan didn't realize it, but I was thinking, *Finally, something really interesting to talk about. Enough about* floral *life; let's talk about* eternal *life.*

"I replied, 'Really? You don't believe in God? Why not?'

"All the rest of the way up the mountain, Dan laid out the

348

reasons we shouldn't believe in God, why he couldn't exist, and how we can live without some distant deity. We listened patiently, waiting until it seemed right to offer some of our own thoughts.

"That opportunity occurred during the hike back *down* the mountain. I tried to answer the objections Dan had raised and to present compelling evidence for God's existence. We talked about science, logic, philosophy, history, archeology, and I explained how all of this—and how knowing Christ in a personal way—had impacted our own lives.

"Our discussion lasted all the way back to our base camp, where we started a campfire and talked until the fire burned out, about four or five hours in total. Dan heard some information he hadn't encountered before. And I trust God will use that conversation whenever Dan reflects back on our time together."

Truth for Today

Not only is the evidence from design powerful for us as Christians, but it's also compelling information to share with our friends and acquaintances. It can become, as the Holy Spirit works, a link in the chain of their coming to faith in Christ.

EVEN ON THE BAD DAYS

How long, LORD? Will you forget me forever? How long will you hide your face from me?

PSALM 13:1

I'M A STRONG OPTIMIST . . . EXCEPT WHEN I'M NOT. MOST OF the time I'm positive, and I'm sometimes over-the-top positive when I think I can do or conquer anything. My friend Mark jokingly calls those times my "manic stages."

Being manic can actually be fun, but I come down emotionally too. No, I'm not manic-depressive, thank goodness, but sometimes things gang up and get to me. Maybe that's why I relate to King David.

The guy could be exuberant. On one occasion, the Bible tells us, "Wearing a linen ephod, David was dancing before the LORD with all his might" (2 Samuel 6:14). That's a temptation I've never succumbed to (and never will, since I don't even own a linen ephod!).

On other days, David could say things like this:

How long, LORD? Will you forget me forever? How long will you hide your face from me? How long must I wrestle with my thoughts and day after day have sorrow in my heart? How long will my enemy triumph over me? Look on me and answer, LORD my God. Give light to my eyes, or I will sleep in death, and my enemy will say, "I have overcome him," and my foes will rejoice when I fall. (Psalm 13:1–4)

Can you relate to any of that? I can, unfortunately. There are days I feel like God has forgotten me or is hiding his face. I periodically "wrestle with my thoughts" or feel "sorrow in my heart."

I sometimes feel defeated by enemies and foes, mostly unseen and unnamed, and perhaps even imagined.

Fortunately there's good news. First, like David, we can be honest about how we feel. In fact, God wants us to come to him as we are, with our real feelings, fears, and frustrations, and to pour out our hearts to him about them. Second, again like David, we can choose to praise God even in the midst of our pain. Look at what he said at the end of this psalm:

> But I trust in your unfailing love; my heart rejoices in your salvation.
> I will sing the LORD's praise, for he has been good to me. (13:5–6)

Honestly, I'm still learning how to trust and to praise God in the midst of hard times. But I know that he is there waiting for me even on the bad days.

Truth for Today

God's love for us doesn't go up and down with our feelings or emotions. We can pour out our frustrations to him, but we are wise to follow David's example and end with affirmations of our trust and praise.

THE REALITY OF HEAVEN

*"My Father's house has many rooms; if that were not so,
would I have told you that I am going there to prepare a
place for you?"*

JOHN 14:2

"IF YOU ARE REALLY A PRODUCT OF A MATERIALISTIC UNIVERSE,
how is it that you don't feel at home there?" asked C. S. Lewis.
"Though I do not believe . . . that my desire for Paradise proves
that I shall enjoy it, I think it a pretty good indication that such a
thing exists and that some men will," he added elsewhere. "If I find
in myself a desire which no experience in this world can satisfy, the
most probable explanation is that I was made for another world."[1]

There are many reasons to believe in heaven. Mark Mittelberg
gives an overview of a number of them in his book *The Questions
Christians Hope No One Will Ask (With Answers)*, including the
awareness of eternity in our hearts (Ecclesiastes 3:11); the evidence
from near-death experiences;[2] our sense of ultimate justice; and
our intuitive knowledge of a home beyond the horizon.[3]

But I agree when Mark adds, "For all the reasons one might
believe in life after death—specifically that there is a heaven and
a hell—the most compelling argument is Jesus' direct and clear
teaching on the topic." That's because, "In all of history, no one
else had the credentials he had or, therefore, the ability to authori-
tatively tell us the truth about these realities."[4]

Jesus alone fulfilled the Old Testament prophecies of the coming Messiah. He alone lived a sinless life. He alone did a multitude
of miracles, died for our sins, and rose from the dead to prove it
was all true. And he alone could say, "You are from below; I am

from above. You are of this world; I am not of this world" (John 8:23). Therefore Jesus alone could tell us about the afterlife because he had already been there—not to mention that he had created it in the first place.

And Jesus, the unique Son of God, assured us that heaven and hell are real and that real people go to each of these places depending on their relationship with him. As he said in today's verse, he is preparing a place for us and "will come back to take you to be with [him]" (John 14:3).

Truth for Today

Heaven is real and you can really go there—if you trust and follow Christ. You can count on it, because you can count on him.

UNCLAIMED RICHES

Do you show contempt for the riches of his kindness,
forbearance and patience, not realizing that God's kindness
is intended to lead you to repentance?

ROMANS 2:4

"YOU MIGHT BE RICH" AND NOT EVEN KNOW IT. SO SCREAMED the headline of a 2009 *Dateline NBC* feature as well as countless websites and advertisements. According to reports, there are millions of dollars in unclaimed funds throughout the United States, with a total of $41.7 billion on hold.[1] And who knows how much more in the other nations of the world? Can you imagine? Untold wealth, just waiting for its rightful owners to step up and claim it![2]

As exciting as that might seem, it pales in comparison to the value of the unclaimed spiritual treasures that await those of us who step up to receive God's amazing gift of grace. The Bible describes it:

> Because of his great love for us, *God, who is rich in mercy*, made us alive with Christ even when we were dead in transgressions—it is by grace you have been saved. And God raised us up with Christ and seated us with him in the heavenly realms in Christ Jesus, in order that in the coming ages *he might show the incomparable riches of his grace*, expressed in his kindness to us in Christ Jesus. (Ephesians 2:4–7, emphases mine)

Just as in the case of the unclaimed money, however, people won't benefit from this wealth unless they know these resources are available to them and take the steps necessary to access those resources. That's why this idea is so important. Christ came to purchase our salvation on the cross; he came as our substitute. The price has been paid; God's forgiveness and eternal life have been made available. So what must we do to access them?

Our instinctive answer is that we're going to have to work for it. It is ingrained in our very nature: *If it's worth anything, it'll cost something. If we want to have it, we've got to earn it.*

We work hard to pay off our debts and to get ahead. Then we find out we owe a spiritual debt. As Romans 3:23 and 6:23 put it, "For all have sinned and fall short of the glory of God. . . . The wages of sin is death."

So how do we react? We futilely start trying to pay back those wages and earn our way back into God's good graces. And in the process we miss the point: *God is offering us the greatest gift ever given, through his Son, Jesus.*

Truth for Today

The second half of Romans 6:23 tells us what we need to know: "The gift of God is eternal life in Christ Jesus our Lord." But we, and our friends, must humbly receive that gift. Only then will the unclaimed spiritual riches be ours.

THE WEAPONS WE
FIGHT WITH, PART 1

*The weapons we fight with are not the weapons of the
world. On the contrary, they have divine power to demolish
strongholds.*

2 CORINTHIANS 10:4

"WHAT IS LIFE BUT A GREAT BATTLE," ASKED BRITISH PASTOR
Charles Spurgeon, "lasting from our earliest days until we sheathe
the sword in death?"[1]

If you have followed Christ for any length of time, then you
know Spurgeon was right: the Christian life is one of conflict. We
have a spiritual enemy who is real, and the culture increasingly
stands against what we believe. This is especially true when we are
attempting to defend biblical teachings and morality. As the saying
goes, "It's a war out there!"

So today's question is, how can we fight and win that war?
Paul told us, "The weapons we fight with . . . have divine power
to demolish strongholds" (2 Corinthians 10:4). But we have to go
to Ephesians 6:13–18 to discover what those weapons actually are.
Paul lists the following tools for battle:

- TRUTH (V. 14): It's a recurring theme: we must be lovers of
  truth (2 Thessalonians 2:10). But to love truth we must
  know the truth, and to know it we must diligently study
  it. This means we should study the Bible, yes—but we
  also need to read great books on Christian apologetics,
  philosophy, history, science, and similar topics, all with the

goal of developing a strong Christian worldview. Then we will "be prepared to give an answer" (1 Peter 3:15) and to "demolish arguments" and "take captive every thought to make it obedient to Christ" (2 Corinthians 10:5).

- RIGHTEOUSNESS (EPHESIANS 6:14): There are many people who are full of knowledge, but who disqualify themselves and their influence by how they live. Nothing repels people more than hypocrisy. That's why Paul emphasized his own example when writing to his apprentice Timothy: "You, however, know all about my teaching, my way of life, my purpose, faith, patience, love, endurance" (2 Timothy 3:10). It's also the reason he admonished fellow believers, "Whatever happens, conduct yourselves in a manner worthy of the gospel of Christ" (Philippians 1:27). He knew our message would have power only if it were backed up by a life of authenticity.

We will continue to look at "the weapons we fight with" in the readings ahead. But looking at the two we've discussed today, it's interesting that Paul admonished Timothy to "watch your *life* and *doctrine* closely" (1 Timothy 4:16, emphases mine).

Truth for Today

Here's the complete verse: "Watch your life and doctrine closely. Persevere in them, because if you do, you will save both yourself and your hearers." This shows how important truth and righteousness are—for us and for our friends.

THE WEAPONS WE FIGHT WITH, PART 2

*Stand firm then . . . with your feet fitted with the readiness
that comes from the gospel of peace.*

EPHESIANS 6:14–15

TODAY WE'LL CONTINUE LEARNING ABOUT THE WEAPONS GOD
has given us for fighting our ongoing spiritual battles, based on the
apostle Paul's teachings in Ephesians 6.

- THE GOSPEL OF PEACE (EPHESIANS 6:15): It's interesting
  that Paul referred to our message as the gospel of *peace*.
  Elsewhere he talked about the *power* of the gospel (Romans
  1:16), the *mystery* of the gospel (Ephesians 6:19), the
  exclusivity of the gospel (Galatians 1:6–9), and the *cause* of
  the gospel (Philippians 4:3).

  There are probably two reasons for his emphasis on peace
  in this passage. The first is that, though people are at war
  with God, they are desperate for peace in their lives. They
  don't know how or where to look for it, but they like the idea
  of it. So when they hear "the gospel of peace" telling them
  how they can know the Prince of Peace, something in their
  souls says, *"Yes!"* A second reason is that the best weapon for
  fighting a war is one that ultimately stops the fighting and
  brings lasting peace. That's the gospel.

- FAITH (EPHESIANS 6:16): "In addition to all this," Paul
  continued, "take up the shield of faith, with which you can
  extinguish all the flaming arrows of the evil one" (Ephesians
  6:16). He was not just talking about the initial step of

putting our faith in Christ, but a daily life of faith, or trust, in Christ. And that faith "comes from hearing the message, and the message is heard through the word about Christ" (Romans 10:17). This, again, includes studying the Bible directly as well as learning all we can about Christ through broader reading and reflection—just like you're doing now.

- SALVATION AND THE WORD OF GOD (EPHESIANS 6:17): Ephesians 6:17 says, "Take the helmet of salvation and the sword of the Spirit, which is the word of God." There are times when battles don't go well. Sometimes soldiers get backed into corners without reinforcements or heavy artillery to back them up. But even on the worst of days, we still have our salvation in Christ, which assures us that no matter what, we're still loved, still forgiven, and still assured of eternity in heaven. How do we know? The Word of God here guarantees it (see also Romans 8:37–39).

Truth for Today

"I write these things to you who believe in the name of the Son of God," said John, "so that you may *know* that you have eternal life" (1 John 5:13, emphasis mine). The gospel of peace, faith in Christ, salvation through him, and the assurance of God's Word—these are weapons to help you not just survive but to thrive as a messenger of God's truth.

THE WEAPONS WE FIGHT WITH, PART 3

*Pray in the Spirit on all occasions with all kinds of prayers
and requests. With this in mind, be alert and always keep
on praying for all the Lord's people.*

EPHESIANS 6:18

IT'S NO COINCIDENCE THAT SOME PEOPLE ARE KNOWN AS "PRAYER warriors." They understand prayer is not some sleepy activity Christians do to fulfill their "quiet time" requirements, or to pass time with a bunch of bored believers in some church basement.

Rather, they understand that prayer is a weapon—in some ways *the* weapon—for contending with the dark forces aligned against us as well as for drawing close to the Savior and gaining his protection, strength, wisdom, and guidance. This is the final weapon we'll discuss in the arsenal God has provided, as described in Ephesians 6.

- PRAYER (EPHESIANS 6:18): Author E. M. Bounds sums up well the power and potential of this spiritual weapon:

Prayer is the easiest and hardest of all things, the simplest and the sublimest, the weakest and the most powerful; its results lie outside the range of human possibilities—they are limited only by the omnipotence of God.

Few Christians have anything but a vague idea of the power of prayer; fewer still have any experience of that power. The church seems almost wholly unaware of the power God puts into her hand; this spiritual *carte blanche* on the infinite resources of God's wisdom and power is rarely, if ever, used—never used to the full measure of honoring God.

Prayer is our most formidable weapon, but the one in which we are the least skilled, the most averse to its use.[1]

That last line warrants repeating: "Prayer is *our most formidable weapon*, but the one in which we are *the least skilled, the most averse to its use*" (emphasis mine). As Christians who care deeply about truth and being "prepared to give an answer" (1 Peter 3:15), it's easy to operate almost exclusively in our heads—viewing every problem as an intellectual problem in need of a good answer.

Yes, answers are important. But if we want God's *power* in our lives and if we want to win our spiritual battles, then we must engage wholeheartedly using this most formidable of all the weapons God has given us: prayer.

Truth for Today

God's Word urges us: "Be strong in the Lord and in his mighty power. Put on the full armor of God, so that you can take your stand against the devil's schemes. For our struggle is not against flesh and blood, but against the rulers, against the authorities, against the powers of this dark world and against the spiritual forces of evil in the heavenly realms" (Ephesians 6:10–12).

ENDNOTES

Science Meets Scripture

1. Steven Weinberg, *The First Three Minutes*, updated ed. (New York: Basic Books, 1988), 5.
2. Ibid.
3. Ibid., 6.
4. Robert Jastrow, *God and the Astronomers*, 2nd ed. (New York: W. W. Norton, 1992), 13.
5. Ibid., 107.

The Origins of Life

1. Paul Davies, "Are We Alone in the Universe?" *New York Times*, November 18, 2013, http://www.nytimes.com/2013/11/19/opinion/are-we-alone-in-the-universe.html?_r=1.
2. Lee Strobel, *The Case for Faith* (Grand Rapids, MI: Zondervan, 2000), 87–112.
3. Gregg Easterbrook, "The New Convergence," *Wired,* December 1, 2001, http://www.wired.com/2002/12/convergence-3/.
4. Strobel, *The Case for Faith*, 108.
5. Francis Crick, *Life Itself* (New York: Simon and Schuster, 1981), 88.
6. Strobel, *The Case for Faith*, 108.

Made in God's Image

1. Ian Tattersall, *Becoming Human: Evolution and Human Uniqueness* (Orlando, FL: Harcourt Brace & Company, 1998), 188.

Can We Trust the Story of Jonah?

1. "Jesus often directly compared Old Testament events with important spiritual truths. He related his death and resurrection to Jonah and the great fish (Matthew 12:40), his second coming to Noah and the flood (Matthew 24:37–39). Both the occasion and the manner of comparison make it clear that Jesus was affirming the historicity of those Old Testament events. Jesus asserted to Nicodemus, 'If I told you earthly things and you do not believe, how shall you believe if I tell you heavenly things?' (John 3:12). The corollary to that statement is that, if the Bible does not speak truthfully about the physical world, it cannot be trusted when it speaks about the spiritual world. The two are intimately related." Norman L. Geisler, *Baker Encyclopedia of Christian Apologetics* (Grand Rapids, MI: Baker Books, 1999), 75.
2. There is a story about a fisherman in the late 1800s named James Bartley who allegedly was swallowed by a whale and later found alive in its belly. The story made the rounds and has often been repeated in Christian literature as an example of what happened to Jonah. The story, however, has been found to be false. See Edward B. Davis, "A Modern Jonah," *Perspectives*, December 1, 1991, on the *Reasons to Believe* website, http://www.reasons.org/articles/a-modern-jonah.

Seek God Wholeheartedly
1. Blaise Pascal, *Pensées*, trans. W. F. Trotter (1910; Mineola, NY: Dover Publications, 2003), 259.

A Scientist Discovers God
1. John Noble Wilford, "Sizing Up the Cosmos: An Astronomer's Quest," *New York Times*, March 12, 1991, http://www.nytimes.com/1991/03/12/science/sizing-up-the-cosmos-an-astronomer-s-quest.html?pagewanted=all.
2. Sharon Begley, "Science Finds God," *Newsweek*, July 20, 1998, http://www.washingtonpost.com/wp-srv/newsweek/science_of_god/scienceofgod.htm.
3. Ibid.

Divine Condescension
1. C. S. Lewis, *Mere Christianity* (1952; New York: HarperCollins, 2001), 179.
2. Bruce A. Ware, *Big Truths for Young Hearts* (Wheaton, IL: Crossway Books, 2009), 109.

The Heavens Declare
1. As quoted in Mark Mittelberg, *Confident Faith* (Carol Stream, IL: Tyndale, 2013), 162–164.
2. Robert Jastrow, *God and the Astronomers,* 2nd ed. (New York: W. W. Norton, 1992), 103.
3. Ibid., 14.

Who Designed the Designer?
1. Richard Dawkins, *The God Delusion* (New York: Houghton Mifflin, 2006), 158.
2. Ibid., 109.
3. Drawn from the discussion in Mark Mittelberg, *Confident Faith* (Carol Stream, IL: Tyndale, 2013), 162–164.
4. "Star Survey Reaches 70 Sextillion," CNN.com, July 23, 2003, http://www.cnn.com/2003/TECH/space/07/22/stars.survey.

People Matter
1. A. E. Samaan, *From a "Race of Masters" to a "Master Race": 1948 To 1848* (published through www.CreateSpace.com and A. E. Samaan: 2013), 754. Can be seen at: https://books.google.com/books?id=JkXJZtI9DQoC&q=Society%27s+needs+come+before+the+individual%27s+needs#v=snippet&q=Society's%20needs%20come%20before%20the%20individual's%20needs&f=false.

The Messiah Tribe
1. See the detailed explanation for this in Josh and Sean McDowell's *The Bible Handbook of Difficult Verses* (Eugene, OR: Harvest House Publishers, 2013), 182–183. Also, Norman Geisler and Thomas Howe, *The Big Book of Bible Difficulties* (Grand Rapids, MI: Baker Books, 1992), 385–386.

The Universe Offers Clues
1. Stephen Hawking and Roger Penrose, *The Nature of Space and Time* (Princeton, NJ: Princeton University Press, 1996), 20.

2. My interview with William Lane Craig can be found in *The Case for Faith* (Grand Rapids, MI: Zondervan, 2000), 75–84.

3. David Hume in John Stewart, February 1754, in *The Letters of David Hume*, vol. 1, ed., J. Y. T. Greig (Oxford: Clarendon Press, 1932), 187 [as cited in Strobel, *The Case for Faith*, 282].

Something from Nothing?

1. From Lee Strobel, *The Case for a Creator* (Grand Rapids, MI: Zondervan, 2004), 101.

2. Bob and Gretchen Passantino, "Atheism vs. Christianity, A Response to Unanswered Questions," Answers.org, 1993, http://answers.org/atheism/zindler.html.

God Is Eternal?

1. George H. Smith, *Atheism* (Amherst, NY: Prometheus Books, 1989), 239.

2. David M. Brooks, *The Necessity of Atheism* (New York: Freethought Press, 1935), 102–103.

3. From an interview with Dr. William Lane Craig in Lee Strobel, *The Case for Christ Study Bible* (Grand Rapids, MI: MI, Zondervan, 2009), 34.

4. Ibid.

5. James Oliver Buswell, Jr., *A Systematic Theology of the Christian Religion*, vol. 1 (Grand Rapids, MI: Zondervan, 1962), 42.

On a Razor's Edge

1. The full interview with Robin Collins is published in Lee Strobel, "The Evidence of Physics," in *The Case for a Creator* (Grand Rapids, MI: Zondervan, 2004), 128–151.

Design at the Molecular Level

1. My interview with Michael Behe is presented in Lee Strobel, "The Evidence of Physics," in *The Case for a Creator* (Grand Rapids, MI: Zondervan, 2004), 193.

If I Were Guessing . . .

1. Peter W. Stoner and Robert C. Newman, *Science Speaks: Scientific Proof of the Accuracy of Prophecy and the Bible*, online ed. (Chicago: Moody Press, revised in 2005 by Peter Stoner's grandson Don W. Stoner), 47. Posted online at: http://www.fbcduke.net/hp_wordpress/wp-content/uploads/2013/03 /ScienceSpeaks.pdf.

2. Ibid.

The Suffering Messiah

1. Text of full interview with Louis Lapides in Lee Strobel, "The Fingerprint Evidence," in *The Case for Christ* (Grand Rapids, MI: Zondervan, 1998), 172–185.

Prophetic Odds

1. Based on the original version of Peter W. Stoner, *Science Speaks* (Chicago: Moody Press, 1969), 109.

2. For complete interview with Louis Lapides, see Lee Strobel, "The Fingerprint Evidence," in *The Case for Christ* (Grand Rapids, MI: Zondervan, 1998), 172–185.

Pierced

1. *The Moody Bible Commentary* (Chicago: Moody Publishers, 2014), 1512.

2. Some have challenged this translation of the Hebrew term (*ka-aru*), but *The Moody Bible Commentary* lists five reasons to prefer this translation, including the fact that "it is supported by three of the four ancient translations (LXX, the Peshitta, and the Vulgate)." Also, this reading "is attested in the earliest manuscript of this psalm (5/6 HevPs) from the Dead Sea Scrolls, which predates the medieval manuscripts by approximately one thousand years." *Moody Bible Commentary*, 779–780.

3. According to the *Encyclopædia Britannica*, crucifixion was used as a form of execution "from about the 6th century BCE to the 4th century CE" (*Encylopædia Britannica Online*, s.v. "Crucifixion," accessed November 15, 2015, http://www.britannica.com /topic/crucifixion-capital-punishment). Other sources indicate that "the Phoenicians introduced [crucifixion] to Rome in the 3rd century BC" (F. P. Retief and L. Cilliers, "The history and pathology of crucifixion," abstract, *South African Medical Journal* 93 [December 2003], 12:938–941, indexed by PubMed.gov, http://www.ncbi.nlm.nih.gov /pubmed/14750495).

In Search of Nazareth

1. Craig A. Evans, *Jesus and His World: The Archaeological Evidence* (Louisville, KY: Westminster John Knox Press, 2012), 13.

2. Ken Dark, "Has Jesus' Nazareth House Been Found?" *Biblical Archaeology Review* 41.2 (March/April 2015).

3. Ken Dark, "Early Roman-Period Nazareth and the Sisters of Nazareth Convent," *The Antiquaries Journal* 92 (2012), 37–64.

4. Yardenna Alexandre, "Mary's Well, Nazareth: The Late Hellenistic to the Ottoman Periods," *Israel Antiquities Authority Report* 49 (2012).

Did Jesus Really Die?

1. From an article on Shabir Ally's website titled "A Rejoinder to James (Part 1)," October 19, 2007, http://www.shabirally.com/rejoinder_to_james.php.

2. This information was given by Dr. Alexander Metherell in my interview with him in Lee Strobel, "The Medical Evidence," in *The Case for Christ* (Grand Rapids, MI: Zondervan, 1998), 193–202.

3. William D. Edwards et al., "On the Physical Death of Jesus Christ," *Journal of the American Medical Association* (March 21, 1986), 1455–1463.

4. John Dominic Crossan, *Who Killed Jesus?* (San Francisco: HarperSanFrancisco, 1996), 4.

5. Gerd Lüdemann, *The Resurrection of Christ: A Historical Inquiry* (Amherst, NY: Prometheus Books, 2004), 50.

Was the Tomb Empty?

1. Bart D. Ehrman, *How Jesus Became God: The Exaltation of a Jewish Preacher from Galilee* (New York: HarperCollins, 2014), 153.

2. Craig A. Evans, *How God Became Jesus: The Real Origins of Belief in Jesus' Divine Nature* (Grand Rapids, MI: Zondervan, 2014), 73.
3. Ibid., 79.
4. Ibid., 66.
5. Ibid., 83.

Resurrection News Flash!
1. See the devotional on "Early Dates," page 260.
2. James D. G. Dunn, *Jesus Remembered* (Grand Rapids, MI: Eerdmans, 2003), 855, emphasis in original.

The Resurrected Jesus Appears
1. From my interview with Dr. Licona, see Lee Strobel, *The Case for the Real Jesus* (Grand Rapids, MI: Zondervan, 2007), 118.
2. Gerd Lüdemann, *What Really Happened to Jesus?* trans. John Bowden (Louisville, KY: Westminster John Knox, 1995), 80.

Dreaming Disciples?
1. Lee Strobel, *The Case for Christ* (Grand Rapids, MI: Zondervan, 1998), 239.
2. Ibid., 238–239.

The Jerusalem Factor
1. Lee Strobel, *The Case for the Real Jesus* (Grand Rapids, MI: Zondervan, 2008), 123.
2. Mark Mittelberg, *Confident Faith* (Carol Stream, IL: Tyndale, 2014), 208.

Evidence Beyond the Bible
1. Lee Strobel, *The Case for Christ* (Grand Rapids, MI: Zondervan, 1998), 114.
2. Gary R. Habermas, *The Historical Jesus* (Joplin, MO: College Press Publishing Company, 1996), 251.
3. Ibid., 224–225.

The Case for the Resurrection
1. These points about Jesus' resurrection have been strongly influenced by my friend Gary Habermas and his book *The Historical Jesus* (Joplin, MO: College Press Publishing Company, 1996).
2. Lee Strobel, *The Case for Christ* (Grand Rapids, MI: Zondervan, 1998), 90–91.
3. Habermas, *The Historical Jesus*, 251.

The Hope of Easter
1. Rick Warren, "The Answer Is Easter: Find Hope This Easter with Pastor Rick Warren," an excerpt of a promotional video sent out by Saddleback Church prior to their 2014 Easter services. Posted on YouTube by Saddleback Church, April 12, 2014, https://www.youtube.com/watch?v=SHcfq1Hf1hE.

They'll Know Us by Our . . . What?

1. Leland Ryken, *Words of Delight: A Literary Introduction to the Bible* (Grand Rapids, MI: Baker, 1992), 445.
2. Norman Geisler and Thomas Howe, *When Critics Ask* (Grand Rapids, MI: Baker, 1992), 340.
3. This answer was adapted from a 1993 article called "Atheism vs. Christianity, A Response to Unanswered Questions," by my late friends Bob and Gretchen Passantino. It can be viewed at Answers.org, http://answers.org/atheism/zindler.html.

How Many Gods?

1. Joseph Smith, in his April 7, 1844, King Follett funeral sermon, emphasis mine. The entire sermon can be read at the official website of The Church of Jesus Christ of Latter-Day Saints: Joseph Smith, Jr., "King Follett Sermon" (sermon, church conference in Nauvoo, IL, April 7, 1844), reproduced by the Church of Jesus Christ of Latter-Day Saints, https://www.lds.org/ensign/1971/04/the-king-follett-sermon?lang=eng.
2. Different Bible translations use a variety of terms, but this concept can be seen in passages such as Ephesians 5:22–23; 2 Corinthians 11:2–3; and Revelation 19:7.

Jesus Is God?

1. Dan Brown, *The Da Vinci Code* (New York: Doubleday, 2003), 233, emphasis his.

Is the Holy Spirit a Force?

1. This definition can be viewed at the official website of the Jehovah's Witnesses: "What Is the Holy Spirit?" JW.org, accessed November 15, 2015, http://www.jw.org/en/bible
-teachings/questions/what-is-the-holy-spirit/#?insight[search_id]=ba604074-f3cc-4489
-9bd1-26e355efce4d&insight[search_result_index]=0.

Tri-Unity

1. "[The Greek] is neuter, not masculine, so the assertion is not that Jesus and the Father are one person, but one 'thing.' Identity of the two persons is not what is asserted, but essential unity (unity of essence)." *NET Bible* (Richardson, TX: Biblical Studies Press, 2005), 2060. Also, the context makes this clear: if Jesus were claiming mere oneness of purpose with God, his listeners would have agreed and claimed the same thing. Instead, understanding his claim of deity (and not accepting it), they picked up stones to stone him.

The Implications of God's Nature

1. Abdu H. Murray, *Grand Central Question* (Downers Grove, IL: InterVarsity Press, 2014), 208.

What If Scientists Created Life?

1. James Oliver Buswell, Jr., *A Systematic Theology of the Christian Religion*, vol. 1 (Grand Rapids, MI: Zondervan, 1962), 324.
2. To read a creative presentation of this information, see Dr. A. E. Wilder-Smith's little book *He Who Thinks Has to Believe* (Ada, MI: Bethany House Publishers, 1981), 34.

Faith Is . . .
1. Sam Harris, "Letter to a Christian Nation: Afterword," from his website http://www
.samharris.org/afterword-to-the-vintage-books-edition.
2. From the mouth of one of Mark Twain's characters in *Pudd'nhead Wilson*. Mark
Twain, *Following the Equator: A Journey Around the World* (1897, Mineola, NY:
Dover, 1989), 132.

Belief That vs. Belief In
1. W. E. Vine, *An Expository Dictionary of New Testament Words* (Old Tappan, NJ:
Fleming H. Revell Company, 1966), 116.

Biblical Prophets vs. Muhammad
1. This information was adapted from my interview with Dr. Norman Geisler in
Lee Strobel, "Objection #4: God Isn't Worthy of Worship If He Kills Innocent
Children," in *The Case for Faith* (Grand Rapids, MI: Zondervan, 2000), 115.

Universal Fatherhood?
1. This exchange with Ravi Zacharias is reported in Lee Strobel, *The Case for Faith*
(Grand Rapids, MI: 2000), 147.

Points of Light, Part 1
1. Cliffe Knechtle, *Give Me an Answer* (Downers Grove, IL: InterVarsity, 1986), 54.

The Ultimate Light
1. Corrie ten Boom, *The Hiding Place* (1971, Grand Rapids, MI: Baker Books, 2006), 8.

The Denial of Evil
1. Jean-Paul Sartre, *Jean-Paul Sartre: Basic Writings*, ed. Stephen Priest (New York:
Routledge, 2001), 32.
2. Bertrand Russell, "Right and Wrong," in *The Elements of Ethics*, first published in
1910 in *Philosophical Essays*, public domain text online at http://fair-use.org
/bertrand-russell/the-elements-of-ethics/section-iii.
3. John D. Steinrucken, "Secularism's Ongoing Debt to Christianity," *American
Thinker*, March 25, 2010, www.americanthinker.com/articles/2010/03/secularisms
_ongoing_debt_to_ch.html.

The Deification of Evil
1. See article, "Devotion to Kali," Division of Religion and Philosophy, University of
Cumbria, accessed November 15, 2015, www.philtar.ac.uk/encyclopedia/hindu
/devot/kali.html.
2. Celebrity Faith Database, "George Lucas," Beliefnet.com, accessed November 15,
2015, http://www.beliefnet.com/Celebrity-Faith-Database/L/George-Lucas.aspx.

Evil as Evidence of God?
1. Adapted from Mark Mittelberg, *The Questions Christians Hope No One Will Ask (With Answers)* (Carol Stream, IL: Tyndale, 2010), 132–134.
2. C. S. Lewis, *Mere Christianity* (New York: Macmillan, 1960), 45–46, emphasis his.

Truth Prevails
1. This debate was held at Willow Creek Community Church in South Barrington, IL, on June 27, 1993. It can be viewed at http://www.youtube.com/watch?v=HuCA4rIX4cE. Here is a list of William Lane Craig's other debates: http://rfforum.websitetoolbox.com/post /show_single_post?pid=26017286&postcount=1.

What Is
1. Mark Mittelberg, *Confident Faith* (Carol Stream, IL: Tyndale, 2013), 29.

The Gospel Truth: God
1. Adapted from Mark Mittelberg, Lee Strobel, and Bill Hybels, "Session 5," in *Becoming a Contagious Christian: Leader's Guide*, updated ed. (Grand Rapids, MI: Zondervan, 2007), 212–214.

The Gospel Truth: People
1. Adapted from Mark Mittelberg, Lee Strobel, and Bill Hybels, "Session 5," in *Becoming a Contagious Christian: Leader's Guide*, updated ed. (Grand Rapids, MI: Zondervan, 2007), 214.
2. Bill Hybels and Mark Mittelberg, *Becoming a Contagious Christian* (Grand Rapids, MI: Zondervan 1994), 152.

The Gospel Truth: Christ, Part 1
1. Adapted from Mark Mittelberg, Lee Strobel, and Bill Hybels, "Session 5" in *Becoming a Contagious Christian: Leader's Guide*, updated ed. (Grand Rapids, MI: Zondervan, 2007), 214–216.

The Gospel Truth: Christ, Part 2
1. For a deeper discussion, see Mark Mittelberg, *The Reason Why: Faith Makes Sense* (Carol Stream, IL: Tyndale, 2011), especially the chapter "Is Divine Forgiveness Available?" starting on page 73.

The Gospel Truth: You
1. Adapted from Mark Mittelberg, Lee Strobel, and Bill Hybels, "Session 5," in *Becoming a Contagious Christian: Leader's Guide*, updated ed. (Grand Rapids, MI: Zondervan, 2007), 216–217.

Dying for Hope
1. "Pollster Gallup Feels Spirit Traveling All Over the World," *Chicago Tribune*, August 1, 1986, includes the first part of the quote. The quote in its entirety can be found in Lee Strobel, *What Jesus Would Say* (Grand Rapids, MI: Zondervan, 1994), 159.

Undesigned Coincidences

1. Jonathan McLatchie, "Undesigned Scriptural Coincidences: The Ring of Truth," CrossExamined.org, August 1, 2011, http://www.crossexamined.org/undesigned -scriptural-coincidences-the-ring-of-truth/.

Sweating Blood

1. My interview with Dr. Alexander Metherell is in Lee Strobel, "The Medical Evidence," in *The Case for Christ* (Grand Rapids, MI: Zondervan, 1998), 191.
2. J. E. Holoubek and A. E. Holoubek, "Blood, Sweat and Fear: 'A Classification of Hematidrosis,'" abstract, *Journal of Medicine* 27 (1996), (3–4): 115–33, indexed on PubMed, http://www.ncbi.nlm.nih.gov/pubmed/8982961.
3. Strobel, *The Case for Christ*, 203.

Jesus or No One

1. To read my complete interview with Dr. Brown, see Lee Strobel, "Challenge #5," in *The Case for the Real Jesus* (Grand Rapids, MI: Zondervan, 2007), 189.

Is It Wrong to Be Right?

1. A fuller discussion is published in Mark Mittelberg, *The Questions Christians Hope No One Will Ask (With Answers)* (Carol Stream, IL: Tyndale, 2010), 241.

Who Has Faith?

1. Adapted from Mark Mittelberg, *Confident Faith* (Carol Stream, IL: Tyndale, 2013), 2–3.

Faith Substitutes

1. Adapted from Mark Mittelberg, *Confident Faith* (Carol Stream, IL: Tyndale, 2013), 225–226.

Pathways to Belief, Part 1

1. Adapted from Mark Mittelberg, *Confident Faith* (Carol Stream, IL: Tyndale, 2013), chapters 2–8.

Pathways to Belief, Part 2

1. Adapted from Mark Mittelberg, *Confident Faith* (Carol Stream, IL: Tyndale, 2013), chapters 2–8.

Cool Christians

1. Adapted from Lee Strobel and Mark Mittelberg, *The Unexpected Adventure* (Grand Rapids, MI: Zondervan, 2009), 19–22.

Do vs. Done

1. Bill Hybels and Mark Mittelberg, *Becoming a Contagious Christian* (Grand Rapids, MI: Zondervan, 1994), 155–156.

God's Unique Love
1. From an article by David Wood, "Does Allah Love Unbelievers?" on the website *Answering Muslims*, October 31, 2012 (emphasis in the article), http://www.answeringmuslims.com /2012/10/does-allah-love-unbelievers.html.
2. From an interview with Shabir Ally, "Is Allah All-Loving?" on the website *On Islam*, April 14, 2013.

Impossibly Large Rocks
1. J. Warner Wallace, "Are There 'Limits' to God's Power?" *Cold-Case Christianity*, September 26, 2013, http://coldcasechristianity.com/2013/are-there-limits-to-gods-power/, emphasis his.

The Benefit of the Doubt
1. Mary Elizabeth Williams, "So What If Abortion Ends Life?" *Salon*, January 23, 2013, http://www.salon.com/2013/01/23/so_what_if_abortion_ends_life/.
2. This story is adapted from Mark Mittelberg, *The Questions Christians Hope No One Will Ask (With Answers)* (Carol Stream, IL: Tyndale, 2010), chapter 6, page 159, where you can read much more on the arguments against abortion.

Rest for the Weary
1. Augustine, *The Confessions* (Oxford: Oxford University Press, reissued 2008), 3.
2. Lamar Odom, quoted in Chris Palmer, "Finding Lamar Odom: Tracking Down the Elusive and Recently Embattled Former Star," *Bleacher Report*, October 20, 2015, http://www .bleacherreport.com/articles/2580319-finding-lamar-odom-tracking-down-the-elusive -and-recently-embattled-former-star.

An Exclusive Club?
1. D. T. Niles, quoted by Paul Little, *Know Why You Believe* (Downers Grove, IL: InterVarsity Press, 1988), 145.

An Avalanche of Scientific Information
1. Lee Strobel, *The Case for a Creator* (Grand Rapids, MI: Zondervan, 2004).

From Science to God
1. Adapted from my interview with Viggo Olsen in *The Case for a Creator* (Grand Rapids, MI: Zondervan, 2004), 287–291.
2. American Scientific Affiliation, *Modern Science and Christian Faith* (Wheaton, IL: Van Kampen, 1948).
3. Viggo Olsen, *The Agnostic Who Dared to Search* (Chicago: Moody Press, 1974). His other books are *Daktar* and *Daktar II*, both published by Moody Press.

The Burden of Proof
1. Richard Dawkins said this on the Fox News program *The O'Reilly Factor*, April 23, 2007.
2. Adapted from Mark Mittelberg, *The Questions Christians Hope No One Will Ask (With Answers)* (Carol Stream, IL: Tyndale, 2010), 291–292.

God and Slavery

1. My full interview with D. A. Carson can be read in Lee Strobel, "Did Jesus Fulfill the Attributes of God?" in *The Case for Christ* (Grand Rapids, MI: Zondervan, 1998), 166–169.
2. Thomas Sowell, *Race and Culture* (New York: Basic, 1994).

Life Without God

1. Bertrand Russell, "A Free Man's Worship" in *The Basic Writings of Bertrand Russell*, eds. Robert E. Egner and Lester E. Denonn (New York: Simon and Schuster, 1961), 67.

Death Without God

1. Lee Strobel, *The Case for Hope* (Grand Rapids, MI: Zondervan, 2015), 144.

How Would Jesus View Islam?

1. Mark Mittelberg, "Would Jesus View Muslims as Enemies?" *The City*, a publication of Houston Baptist University, Houston, Texas, September 7, 2015, viewable at https://www.hbu.edu/News/The-City/Articles/2015/September/Would-Jesus-View -Muslims-as-Enemies.aspx.

How Would Jesus View Muslims?

1. Mark Mittelberg, "Would Jesus View Muslims as Enemies?" *The City*, a publication of Houston Baptist University, Houston, Texas, September 7, 2015, viewable at https://www.hbu.edu/News/The-City/Articles/2015/September/Would-Jesus-View -Muslims-as-Enemies.aspx, emphases mine.
2. For example, see the story of Nabeel Qureshi in his powerful book *Seeking Allah, Finding Jesus* (Grand Rapids, MI: Zondervan, 2014).

Christians Meet a Muslim

1. Adapted from Mark Mittelberg, "Would Jesus View Muslims as Enemies?" *The City*, a publication of Houston Baptist University, Houston, Texas, September 7, 2015, viewable at https://www.hbu.edu/News/The-City/Articles/2015/September /Would-Jesus-View-Muslims-as-Enemies.aspx, emphases mine.

Finding Your Voice, Part 1

1. Bill Hybels and Mark Mittelberg, *Becoming a Contagious Christian* (Grand Rapids, MI: Zondervan, 1994).
2. Mark Mittelberg, Lee Strobel, and Bill Hybels, *Becoming a Contagious Christian Training Course* (Grand Rapids, MI: Zondervan, 1995, 2007).

Taking the Bible Literally

1. R. C. Sproul, *Knowing Scripture*, revised ed. (Downers Grove, IL: InterVarsity Press, 2009), 54 (quoting from Article 15 of the Chicago Statement of Biblical Hermeneutics).
2. Ibid.

Untruths in the Bible?

1. Norman Geisler and William Nix, *A General Introduction to the Bible* (Chicago, IL: Moody Press, 1968, updated ed., 1986), 58, emphases theirs.
2. Ibid., 58, emphases theirs.

True Religion

1. Friedrich Nietzsche, *The Anti-Christ* (New York: SoHo Books, 2013), 18.
2. R. C. Sproul, *The Consequences of Ideas* (Wheaton, IL: Crossway Books, 2000), 159.
3. Quoted in Nick Harrison, *Magnificent Prayer* (Grand Rapids, MI: Zondervan, 2001), 223.

The Inspiration of the Bible

1. From my interview with Daniel Wallace in Lee Strobel, *The Case for the Real Jesus* (Grand Rapids, MI: Zondervan, 2007), 73–74, emphasis mine.

The All-Time Bestseller

1. Mark Mittelberg, *The Reason Why: Faith Makes Sense* (Carol Stream, IL: Tyndale, 2011), 33. (Scripture references are NLT.)
2. A summary of these statistics about the Bible can be viewed at http://www.biblestudy.org /beginner/why-are-there-so-many-bibles-in-the-world.html. Also see "The Battle of the Books," *Economist,* December 19, 2007, http://www.economist.com/node/10311317.

The Bible's Consistency

1. Norman Geisler and William Nix, *From God to Us: How We Got Our Bible* (Chicago: Moody, 1974, 2012), 80–81.
2. Mark Mittelberg, *Confident Faith* (Carol Stream, IL: Tyndale, 2013), 183.

Early Dates

1. Richard Dawkins, *The God Delusion* (New York: Houghton Mifflin, 2006), 118.
2. Lee Strobel, *The Case for Christ* (Grand Rapids, MI: Zondervan, 1998), 33–34.
3. Mark Mittelberg, from his sermon "Isn't the Bible Full of Myths and Mistakes?" in the *Room for Doubt* series (information available at: http://www.roomfordoubt.com).

The Living Line

1. See the rest of my interview with Dr. Licona in Lee Strobel, *The Case for the Real Jesus* (Grand Rapids, MI: Zondervan, 2007), 117–118.
2. My interview with Edwin Yamauchi is published in Lee Strobel, *The Case for Christ* (Grand Rapids, MI: Zondervan, 1998), 89 (the quote from Ignatius is from *Trallians* 9).

"An Embarrassment of Riches"

1. See Justin Taylor, "An Interview with Daniel B. Wallace on the New Testament Manuscripts," *The Gospel Coalition* (blog), March 21, 2012, http://www.thegospelcoalition.org/blogs/justin taylor/2012/03/21/an-interview-with-daniel-b-wallace-on-the-new-testament-manuscripts/.
2. For a detailed discussion of the New Testament manuscripts, see Lee Strobel's interview with Daniel Wallace in *The Case for the Real Jesus* (Grand Rapids, MI: Zondervan, 2007), 65.

3. Mark Mittelberg, *Confident Faith* (Carol Stream, IL: Tyndale, 2013), 187–188, emphases his.

4. See Taylor, "An Interview with Daniel B. Wallace."

Archaeology and the Bible, Part 1

1. This interview with Norman Geisler is in Lee Strobel, *The Case for Faith* (Grand Rapids, MI: Zondervan, 2000), 128–129.

2. See Clifford A. Wilson, *Rocks, Relics and Biblical Reliability* (Grand Rapids, MI: Zondervan, 1977), 42.

3. See William F. Albright, *Archaeology and the Religion of Israel* (Baltimore, MD: Johns Hopkins Press, 1953), 176.

Archaeology and the Bible, Part 2

1. This interview with Norman Geisler is in Lee Strobel, *The Case for Faith* (Grand Rapids, MI: Zondervan, 2000), 129–130.

2. See Colin J. Hemer, *The Book of Acts in the Setting of Hellenistic History* (Winona Lake, IN: Eisenbrauns, 1990).

3. See William M. Ramsay, *St. Paul the Traveler and the Roman Citizen* (Grand Rapids, MI: Baker, 1982), 8.

4. See A. N. Sherwin-White, *Roman Society and Roman Law in the New Testament* (Oxford: Clarendon Press, 1963), 189.

5. You can read archives and current issues of the *Biblical Archaeological Review,* the magazine of the Biblical Archaeology Society, at http://www.biblicalarchaeology .org/magazine/. Accessed December 4, 2015.

Archaeology and the Book of Mormon

1. Lee Strobel, *The Case for Christ* (Grand Rapids, MI: Zondervan, 1998), 134.

2. Joseph Smith, *History of the Church*, 8 vols. (Salt Lake City: Deseret, 1978), 4:461, cited in Donald S. Tingle, *Mormonism* (Downers Grove, IL: InterVarsity Press, 1987), 17.

3. John Ankerberg and John Weldon, *The Facts on the Mormon Church* (Eugene, OR: Harvest House, 1991), 30, emphasis in the original.

4. Bill McKeever and Eric Johnson, *Mormonism 101: Examining the Religion of the Latter-day Saints*, revised and expanded ed. (Grand Rapids, MI: Baker Books, 2015), 132.

A Copycat Religion?

1. Dan Brown, *The Da Vinci Code* (New York: Doubleday, 2003), 232.

2. Among books that promote various aspects of the Mithras theory are: Franz Cumont, *The Mysteries of Mithra* (New York, Dover, 1950); Timothy Freke and Peter Gandy, *The Jesus Mysteries* (New York: Three Rivers Press, 1999); and Dan Brown, *The Da Vinci Code* (New York: Anchor, 2003).

3. Ronald Nash, *The Gospel and the Greeks* (Phillipsburg, NJ: P&R Publishing, 2003), 3.

4. Ronald Nash, "Was the New Testament Influenced by Pagan Religions?" *Christian Research Journal* (1994), 8–15, http://www.equip.org/article/was-the-new-testament -influenced-by-pagan-religions/.

Myths About Mithras

1. Lee Strobel, *The Case for the Real Jesus* (Grand Rapids, MI: Zondervan, 2007), 183. For more detail on these supposed parallels, see the entire chapter, "Challenge 4: Christianity's Beliefs About Jesus Were Copied from Pagan Religions," 157–187.
2. Ibid.

The Bible's Literary Devices

1. Norman Geisler and William Nix, *A General Introduction to the Bible* (Chicago, IL: Moody Press, 1968), 58, emphases theirs.
2. An excellent and accessible book for learning how to better do this is *Knowing Scripture*, revised ed., by R. C. Sproul (Downers Grove, IL: InterVarsity Press, 2009). Also, see other readings in this devotional, including "Taking the Bible Literally," "Untruths in the Bible?," "Distorting the Scriptures," and "Interpreting Scripture."

Interpreting Scripture

1. Adapted from my interview with Paul Copan in Lee Strobel, *The Case for the Real Jesus* (Grand Rapids, MI: Zondervan, 2007), 245–246.

Lost Gospels?

1. Dan Brown, *The Da Vinci Code* (New York: Doubleday, 2003), 303–304, emphasis his.
2. Lee Strobel, *The Case for Christ* (Grand Rapids, MI: Zondervan, 1998), 67.
3. N. T. Wright, *Judas and the Gospel of Jesus* (Grand Rapids, MI: Baker, 2006), 33–34.

Doubting (the Gospel of) Thomas

1. Robert J. Miller, ed., *The Complete Gospels: Annotated Scholars Version* (Santa Rosa, CA: Polebridge Press, 1992), 308.
2. Ibid.
3. Ibid.
4. Lee Strobel, *The Case for the Real Jesus* (Grand Rapids, MI: Zondervan, 2007), 43.

People Who Have Never Heard, Part 1

1. To read the full discussion, see Mark Mittelberg, *The Questions Christians Hope No One Will Ask (With Answers)* (Carol Stream, IL: Tyndale, 2010), 272–274.
2. Ralph D. Winter and Bruce A. Koch, "Finishing the Task: The Unreached Peoples Challenge," *The Joshua Project*, accessed December 5, 2015, https://www.joshuaproject .net/assets/media/articles/finishing-the-task.pdf.
3. Mahendra Singhal shared his testimony in the video "From the Karma of Hinduism to the Cross of Christ: A Spiritual Journey—Mahendra Singhal," posted by Kevin Engle on Vimeo.com, August 5, 2009, http://www.vimeo.com/5964358.

People Who Have Never Heard, Part 2

1. Adapted from Mark Mittelberg, *The Questions Christians Hope No One Will Ask (With Answers)* (Carol Stream, IL: Tyndale, 2010), 274–276.

Are All sins the Same?

1. Adapted from Mark Mittelberg, *The Questions Christians Hope No One Will Ask (With Answers)* (Carol Stream, IL: Tyndale, 2010), 274–276.

Is Judging Always Wrong?

1. Adapted from a conversation with Paul Copan in Lee Strobel, *The Case for the Real Jesus* (Grand Rapids, MI: Zondervan, 2007), 246–247.

Loving Those Who Disagree

1. From my interview with Paul Copan in Lee Strobel, *The Case for the Real Jesus* (Grand Rapids, MI: Zondervan, 2007), 248.

Does Anyone Really Seek God?

1. Adapted from Mark Mittelberg, "Myths About a Movement," *WCA News* (a former newsletter of the Willow Creek Association in South Barrington, IL), September/October 1997, 5.

Responding to Reincarnation, Part 1

1. From my interview with Paul Copan in Lee Strobel, *The Case for the Real Jesus* (Grand Rapids, MI: Zondervan, 2007), 241–242.

Angry Atheists

1. Mark Mittelberg, *The Reason Why: Faith Makes Sense* (Carol Stream, IL: Tyndale, 2010), 30.
2. Ibid. (Bible references NLT), 28.
3. Thomas Nagel, *The Last Word* (New York: Oxford University Press, 2001), 130.
4. Andre Mayer, "Nothing Sacred: Journalist and Provocateur Christopher Hitchens Picks a Fight with God," *CBC News*, May 14, 2007, viewable at https://archive.is /h0nnk.

Biblical Marriage

1. This was a phrase that Lombardi used often and in various forms, usually at the beginning a training season. See David Maraniss, *When Pride Still Mattered: A Life of Vince Lombardi* (New York: Simon & Schuster, 1999), 274.

Alleged Contradictions, Part 1

1. My interview with Norman Geisler is in Lee Strobel, Objection #4 in *The Case for Faith* (Grand Rapids, MI: Zondervan, 2000), 113–142.
2. Norman Geisler and Thomas Howe, *When Critics Ask* (Grand Rapids, MI: Baker, 1992). This has been updated and retitled as *The Big Book of Bible Difficulties* (Grand Rapids, MI: Baker, 2008).

Alleged Contradictions, Part 2

1. My interview with Norman Geisler, Lee Strobel, "Objection #4" in *The Case for Faith* (Grand Rapids, MI: Zondervan, 2000), 113–142.

Alleged Contradictions, Part 3
1. My interview with Norman Geisler, Lee Strobel, "Objection #4" in *The Case for Faith* (Grand Rapids, MI: Zondervan, 2000), 113–142.
2. Norman Geisler and Thomas Howe, *The Big Book of Bible Difficulties* (Grand Rapids, MI: Baker, 2008).

Hopelessly Corrupted?
1. Nabeel Qureshi, *Seeking Allah, Finding Jesus* (Grand Rapids, MI: Zondervan, 2014), 126.
2. From the M. H. Shakir Translation of the Qur'an (Elmhurst, NY: Tahrike Tarsile Qur'an, 1999).
3. Ibid.
4. For help on how to convey this information to Muslim friends, see Fouad Masri, *Is the Injeel Corrupted?* (Colorado Springs, CO: Book Villages, 2006); Fouad Masri, "Building a Bridge to the Bible," in *Ambassadors to Muslims* (Colorado Springs, CO: Book Villages, 2011), 131.
5. Qureshi, *Seeking Allah, Finding Jesus*, 278–279.

A Positive Case for the Bible
1. Adapted from Mark Mittelberg, *The Questions Christians Hope No One Will Ask (With Answers)* (Carol Stream, IL: Tyndale, 2010), 90–93.
2. Lee Strobel, *The Case for the Real Jesus* (Grand Rapids, MI: Zondervan, 2007), 58. Evans is respected by conservatives and liberals alike; has written and/or edited fifty books; and has lectured at Cambridge, Oxford, Yale, and other universities.

A God Projection?
1. Ludwig Feuerbach, "Introduction," in *The Essence of Religion*, trans. Alexander Loos (1873; Amherst, NY: Prometheus Books, 2004).
2. Alister McGrath, "God as Wish Fulfillment?" bethinking, accessed December 5, 2015, http://www.bethinking.org/does-god-exist/god-as-wish-fulfilment.
3. Paul C. Vitz, *Faith of the Fatherless: The Psychology of Atheism* (Dallas: Spence, 1999).
4. For more on my relationship with my father and how it affected my spiritual journey, see Lee Strobel, *The Case for Grace* (Grand Rapids, MI: Zondervan, 2015).

The New Testament Canon
1. Christopher Hitchens, *God Is Not Great: How Religion Poisons Everything* (New York: Twelve, 2007), 113.
2. Lee Strobel, *The Case for Christ* (Grand Rapids, MI: Zondervan, 1988), 66.
3. F. F. Bruce, *The New Testament Documents: Are They Reliable?* (Grand Rapids, MI: Eerdmans, 1978), 21.

The Real Jesus
1. Bart Ehrman, *Did Jesus Exist?* (New York: HarperCollins, 2012), 339.
2. Candace Chellew-Hodge, "Inventing Jesus: An Interview with Bart Ehrman," *Religion Dispatches*, April 25, 2012, http://www.religiondispatches.org/inventing-jesus-an-interview-with-bart-ehrman/.

3. Craig Evans, *Jesus and His World: The Archaeological Evidence* (Louisville, KY: Westminster John Knox Press, 2012), 5.

4. Ibid.

5. James D. G. Dunn, response to "Jesus at the Vanishing Point" by Robert M. Price, in *The Historical Jesus: Five Views*, ed. James K. Beilby and Paul R. Eddy (Downers Grove, IL: InterVarsity Press, 2009), 94–98.

New Testament Forgeries

1. Licona's full response in an interview with Lee Strobel is posted online in "Forged?" BibleGateway.com, accessed December 12, 2015, https://www.biblegateway.com /LeeStrobel/2011/05/forged/.

2. Bart Ehrman, *Forged* (New York: HarperOne, 2011), 134.

3. Ibid.

4. Ibid., 134–136; cf. 77.

5. Ibid., 135–136.

6. Strobel and Licona, "Forged?" BibleGateway.com, https://www.biblegateway.com /LeeStrobel/2011/05/forged/.

Variations in Biblical Manuscripts

1. Bart D. Ehrman, *Misquoting Jesus* (San Francisco, CA: HarperSanFrancisco, 2005), 7.

2. Ibid., 89–90.

3. See my discussion with Daniel Wallace in Lee Strobel, "Challenge #2" in *The Case for the Real Jesus* (Grand Rapids, MI: Zondervan, 2007), 85–87. Also see J. Ed Komoszewski, M. James Sawyer, and Daniel B. Wallace, *Reinventing Jesus* (Grand Rapids, MI: Kregel Publications, 2006).

4. Lee Strobel, *The Case for the Real Jesus*, 99.

Jesus' Impact on the World

1. Adapted from John Ortberg, "Six Surprising Ways Jesus Changed the World," *Huffington Post*, August 13, 2012, updated October 13, 2012, http://www .huffingtonpost.com/john-ortberg/six-surprising-ways-jesus_b_1773225.html.

2. John Dickson, *Humilitas* (Grand Rapids, MI: Zondervan, 2011), 112.

Speculations About a Multiverse

1. This discussion with William Lane Craig is published in Lee Strobel, "Objection #2" in *The Case for Faith* (Grand Rapids, MI: Zondervan, 2000), 78–79.

2. John Polkinghorne, *Serious Talk: Science and Religion in Dialogue* (Harrisburg, PA: Trinity Press International, 1995), 6.

3. Patrick Glynn, *God: The Evidence* (Roseville, CA: Prima Publishing, 1999).

4. Lee Strobel, *The Case for a Creator* (Grand Rapids, MI: Zondervan, 2004), 144, emphasis mine.

The Argument from Morality

1. My full discussion with William Lane Craig appears in Lee Strobel, "Objection #2" in *The Case for Faith* (Grand Rapids, MI: Zondervan, 2000), 79–81.
2. Michael Ruse, "Evolutionary Theory and Christian Ethics," in *The Darwinian Paradigm* (London: Routledge, 1989), 262, 269.

Tale of Two Prodigals

1. Adapted from my full interview with Craig Hazen in Lee Strobel, "The Professor" in *The Case for Grace* (Grand Rapids, MI: Zondervan, 2015), 63–87.
2. The entire parable of the prodigal son is in Luke 15:11–32.

Grace for "Good" People

1. Adapted from my full interview with Craig Hazen in Lee Strobel, "The Professor" in *The Case for Grace* (Grand Rapids, MI: Zondervan, 2015), 63–87.

The Divine Encoder

1. Francis S. Collins, *The Language of God: A Scientist Presents Evidence for Belief* (New York: Free Press, 2006), 1–2.
2. Lee Strobel, *The Case for a Creator* (Grand Rapids, MI: Zondervan, 2004), 237.
3. Ibid., 244. Also, Meyer has since written two books that explore these topics in much greater depth: *Signature in the Cell: DNA and the Evidence for Intelligent Design* (New York: HarperCollins, 2009); and *Darwin's Doubt: The Explosive Origin of Animal Life and the Case for Intelligent Design* (New York: HarperCollins, 2013).

Evidence from Consciousness

1. Teresa of Ávila, *The New Encyclopedia of Christian Quotations*, compiler Mark Water (Grand Rapids, MI: Baker, 2000), 972. Teresa's reference to mansions is an allusion to John 14:2.
2. My full interview with J. P. Moreland can be read in Lee Strobel, "The Evidence of Consciousness" in *The Case for a Creator* (Grand Rapids, MI: Zondervan, 2004), 247–272.
3. Sam Parnia, "Near Death Experiences in Cardiac Arrest and the Mystery of Consciousness," *Scientific and Medical Network*, accessed December 13, 2015, https://www.scimednet.org/near-death-experiences-in-cardiac-arrest-and-the-mystery-of-consciousness.
4. Michael Ruse, *Can a Darwinian Be a Christian?* (Cambridge: Cambridge University Press, 2000), 73.
5. Karl R. Popper and John C. Eccles, *The Self and Its Brain* (New York: Springer-Verlag, 1977), 559–560.

The Evidence of Design

1. Adapted from Lee Strobel and Mark Mittelberg, *The Unexpected Adventure* (Grand Rapids, MI: Zondervan, 2009), 103–108.

The Reality of Heaven

1. These quotes from C. S. Lewis are drawn from several sources, all listed at the website of the C. S. Lewis Society of California. See http://www.lewissociety.org /quotes.php.
2. My friend John Burke has written a fascinating book on this topic called *Imagine Heaven: Near-Death Experiences, God's Promises, and the Exhilarating Future That Awaits You* (Grand Rapids, MI: Baker, 2015).
3. Mark Mittelberg, "Why Should I Think Heaven Really Exists—And That God Sends People to Hell?" in *The Questions Christians Hope No One Will Ask (With Answers)* (Carol Stream, IL: Tyndale, 2010), 249–287.
4. Ibid., 257–258.

Unclaimed Riches

1. See, for example, Unclaimed.org, www.unclaimed.org/what.
2. The material in this reading is adapted from Mark Mittelberg, *The Reason Why: Faith Makes Sense* (Carol Stream, IL: Tyndale, 2011), 101–103.

The Weapons We Fight With, Part 1

1. Charles Spurgeon, in a sermon he delivered at the Metropolitan Tabernacle in Newington, England, on May 11, 1916, titled "The Battle of Life." It is posted online at http://www.spurgeon.org/sermons/3511.htm. Accessed December 4, 2015.

The Weapons We Fight With, Part 3

1. E. M. Bounds, *E. M. Bounds on Prayer* (Peabody, MA: Hendrickson Publishers, 2006), 196.

FOR FURTHER READING

Strobel, Lee. *The Case for Christ* (Grand Rapids, MI: Zondervan, 1998).

Strobel, Lee. *The Case for Faith* (Grand Rapids, MI: Zondervan, 2000).

Strobel, Lee. *The Case for a Creator* (Grand Rapids, MI: Zondervan, 2004).

Strobel, Lee. *The Case for the Real Jesus* (Grand Rapids, MI: Zondervan, 2007).

Strobel, Lee. *The Case for Grace* (Grand Rapids, MI: Zondervan, 2015).

    Note: Student and Kids editions of these Case books are also available.

Strobel, Lee. *The Case for Christianity Answer Book* (Grand Rapids, MI: Zondervan, 2014).

Strobel, Lee. *The Case for Hope* (Grand Rapids, MI: Zondervan, 2015).

Strobel, Lee. *The Case for Christ Study Bible* (Grand Rapids, MI: Zondervan, 2010).

Strobel, Lee, and Mark Mittelberg. *The Unexpected Adventure* (Grand Rapids, MI: Zondervan, 2009).

Hybels, Bill, and Mark Mittelberg. *Becoming a Contagious Christian* (Grand Rapids, MI: Zondervan, 1994).

Mittelberg, Mark. *Becoming a Contagious Church* (Grand Rapids, MI: Zondervan, 2007).

Mittelberg, Mark. *The Questions Christians Hope No One Will Ask (With Answers)* (Carol Stream, IL: Tyndale, 2010).

Mittelberg, Mark. *The Reason Why: Faith Makes Sense* (Carol Stream, IL: Tyndale, 2011).

Mittelberg, Mark. *Confident Faith: Building a Firm Foundation for Your Beliefs* (Carol Stream, IL: Tyndale, 2013).

ABOUT THE AUTHORS

LEE STROBEL

Atheist-turned-Christian Lee Strobel, the award-winning former legal editor of the *Chicago Tribune*, is a *New York Times* bestselling author of more than twenty books. He serves as professor of Christian thought at Houston Baptist University and as a teaching pastor at Woodlands Church in Texas.

Described in the *Washington Post* as "one of the evangelical community's most popular apologists," Lee shared the Christian Book of the Year award in 2005. He won Gold Medallions for *The Case for Christ, The Case for Faith, The Case for a Creator*, and *Inside the Mind of Unchurched Harry and Mary*.

Lee was educated at the University of Missouri (bachelor of journalism degree) and Yale Law School (master of studies in law degree). After investigating the evidence for Jesus, Lee became a Christian in 1981.

Some of Lee's most recent works include *The Case for Grace*; his first novel, *The Ambition*; his first gift books, *The Case for Christianity Answer Book* and *The Case for Hope*; and *The Case for Christ Study Bible*.

He also wrote *The Case for the Real Jesus, God's Outrageous Claims, The Case for Christmas, The Case for Easter, The Unexpected Adventure* (coauthored with Mark Mittelberg), and *Surviving a Spiritual Mismatch in Marriage*, which he wrote with his wife, Leslie.

He and Leslie have been married for forty-four years and have two grown children.

MARK MITTELBERG

Mark Mittelberg is a bestselling author, sought-after speaker, leading outreach strategist, and the executive director of The Center for American Evangelism, in partnership with Houston Baptist University.

Mark is the primary author of the celebrated *Becoming a Contagious Christian* training course (coauthored with Lee Strobel and Bill Hybels). This course has been translated into more than twenty languages and has trained more than 1.5 million people around the world to share Christ in natural and effective ways.

He wrote *Confident Faith*—winner of *Outreach* magazine's 2014 apologetics book of the year—and *The Reason Why: Faith Makes Sense*, an update of a classic that has touched millions of lives. He authored *The Questions Christians Hope No One Will Ask (With Answers)*, and he collaborated with Strobel to write *The Unexpected Adventure*. Mark's other books include *Becoming a Contagious Church* and *Becoming a Contagious Christian*, coauthored with Hybels.

Mark was the original evangelism director at Willow Creek Community Church near Chicago. He later served as executive vice president of the Willow Creek Association. After receiving an undergraduate degree in business management, Mark earned a master's degree in philosophy of religion, graduating magna cum laude from Trinity Evangelical Divinity School. Mark and Heidi have two grown children and live near Denver, Colorado.